Praise for Winning The Paper Chase™

"Today, one problem facing the average person like me is not the availability of technology, but knowing how to effectively sort through and use the enormous amount of technology that exists out there. David Lam's book manual does both. He showed me a numerous amount of "tips and tricks" to integrate my existing system and software (software that I thought I knew how to effectively use). Drawing upon his vast knowledge and experience with technology and business, he recommended software that would help me further streamline my office. This is a must read for anyone who owns or uses a computer."
Angie Vance, Home-Based Business Owner
Livonia, MI

"...Until the setup my office based on your design, I was not filly aware of the great capabilities of my home office, my existing software and hardware. I had become over-run and overwhelmed with paperwork and often wasted time in the simple organization and maintenance of all that paperwork. I am extremely happy now, as I like to keep things streamlined yet accessible. Your system allows fingertip availability of important documents, without keeping every single piece of paper....

Your method of teaching is well worth the system and has given me the confidence to continue to familiarize myself with my system, and learn even more."
Gina Gooden, President, Viable Solution Consulting
Newark, NJ

"David Lam's system provided me with the tools and practical know-how to fully utilize my computer system. It help me reduce my tons of paper into a digital, manageable and content retrievable database. It has also helped me realize the great potential of my home computer as a central storage, information management appliance, and a life organizer for everything else."
John S. Thompson, Full time Administrator, PhD Candidate,
Husband, and Father Of Seven Young Children
Atlanta, GA

Complimentary
From MrSystem.com

Praise for Winning The Paper Chase™

"Anyone interested in getting their life organized must check out David's system. It has taught me how to harness the power of simple computer technology to not only efficiently organize and manage my home office but also to organize, store, and access the voluminous research files I use for my profession. No matter what your individual situation may be, you will find useful and relevant information here. I am confident that David's system will help you establish an efficient work environment that is adapted to your personal desires and needs."
Benjamin Pykles, Archaeologist
La Mesa, California

"Because of my teaching job, I had piles of papers and photocopies lying around. David's expertise was a great help to me to me to get a handle on all of my paperwork. Best of all, when I am doing research now, I do not need to shuffle through endless files anymore. It is because the files are well organized and the computer does all the searching for me!"
Travis Clark, Anthropologist, Temple University
Philadelphia, PA

"I highly recommend to anyone in the Financial Services business that they take a look at this system, keeping in mind that certain files must be retained in hard copy. But the vast majority of their files can be scanned and electronically stored."
Abram Brustein CLU ChFC CLF MSM, Executive Director, MONY
New York, NY

"As the owner of a small business, David Lam's book has given me invaluable insight into a myriad of technological issues. It is like having an in-house computer expert. This book is a must for the small business owner."
Sherri Krensel, Owner Principal, Workplace Environments
Plymouth Meeting, PA

Winning The Paper Chase™

...Maximize Office Productivity And Minimize Cost

Dear Leslie,

By *To Great Life & Wealth!*

Best Wishes,

David Lam

DAVID LAM
CHIEF THINKER
of
www.MrSystem.com

Winning The Paper Chase™
... Maximize Office Productivity And Minimize Cost
Business Essentials Series™ .... Vol. 1
http://www.MrSystem.com

Published by
Joy Life Publishing
© Copyright 2004   David Lam

ISBN 0-9741197-6-8
Printed in the United States of America

About The Author

As a successful financial planner and business consultant, David Lam works with hundreds of home based and small business owners. His own experience with the bombardment of paper and listening to the challenges of his business clients impelled him to create a simple and yet functional Highly Efficient Office™ that anyone can build and use today's technology.

Born in wartime Cambodia, David moved to Hong Kong as young boy and grew up there. He began his formal education in New Zealand, which was completed in Texas. His interests are as diverse as his life experiences. He reads everything from X-men comic books to Chinese Classics, such as Art of War, in the ancient Chinese language. He loves to dance to Rock N' Roll and do the waltz. He has also been a radio show host in Hong Kong.

David has always been passionate about learning and understanding different fields of study. In fact, his close friends call him "Mr System" not only because of his capabilities to build and understand different systems—such as computer systems, tax system, financial and economic systems, but also his ability to explain them in a simple manner.

After many years of working, researching, and studying, he is not only experienced but also certified in the areas of business operation, office computing, and document management technology. He attained the financial industry recognized designations such as CFP™ (Certified Financial Planner), ChFC(Chartered Financial Consultant), and CLU(Certified Life Underwriter). He is also a Certified Document Imaging Architect in the computer industry.

David's financial planning and business consulting clients appreciate his ability to take a complicated process and simplify it—which is what he has done with this book.

He integrates all his knowledge and show you in a simple language how to setup a Highly Efficient Office™. This system will help you maximize your office productivity, minimize costs, eliminate paper, and increase your free time.

Dedication

To my mom, who is a single mom who decided to work from home to raise three of us. The strong tie of our family prevented us to get involved in the bad neighborhood where we lived.

Thank you to my wife who beard with me for so many years. I understand that sometimes one day with me seems like a day that the sun never set.

To my daughter, she makes me work harder on myself every day to become a better person. She is the pride and joy of my life and I will try to be the best father that I could be.

I am also dedicating this book to all the entrepreneurs who dare to make a change in their life and explore their own territory.

If you are reading this book, you are leading a trend that is moving away from using paper as a medium to store information. You are leading a way for a more comfortable and efficient way of managing the overflow of information today. I will show you how you can do it; and let's do it together.

Author's Acknowledgement

Thanks for Joy Life Publishing and so many great people involved in this project. Earni and Stacey have been wonderful in packaging the book ideas into a marketable publication. The art work of Mike, Glen and Ben brighten up the book and lighten up the heavy technical materials. Roman and Michele are the powerful couple in coordinating. Mouy is a great editor to make my writing more understandable. Paul has been very patient in building the website. For everyone whom I missed mention but has made this book a reality, thank you.

Table Of Content Lite

VIII Table Of Content Lite

Table Of Content In Details

✘ *Table Of Content In Details*

Introduction:

One aspect of the American dream is to own and operate your own business. We can exercise our freedom of choice and take more control of our lives. With that freedom also comes increased responsibility; we have to know something about a wide range of topics. The first few years of my career in the financial planning industry, I struggled with using my time and resources effectively. I spent a majority of my time doing administrative tasks rather than growing my business. At the height of my frustration with the inefficient use of my time, I started to find ways to get things done quicker.

In the process of learning how to become more efficient, I realized that technology could not only improve the productivity and bottom line of my business, but also enhance the quality of my life. In addition, I also found I used much less paper than before, I can even contribute to the conservation of the planet. I realize the power of technology and I became a certified technology professional in addition to my role as a business consultant. I started my journey of exploring the power of technology for my clients as an added value service. I am now able to show my clients how to achieve their objectives with the help of technology.

Our life has been changed by technology permanently and pervasively. What we need to do is figure out the purpose of our own life and then, we can use technology as the tool to achieve our goals in a more effective and efficient manner. It is not only helping us do business, but it also helps the earth reserve its valuable resources, the trees.

Within the parameter of technology, going digital, or said paperless, is a movement that comes with the Internet and the technological revolution. It is a process that reduces information on paper and turn it into digital formats and transfer the information freely without the physical medium - paper. That will allow seamless office information management both internally and externally.

Paperless, Seamless Computing, and Paper-less

In the COMDEX Las Vegas 2003 keynote speech, (the largest technology conference in the world, details can be found on www.comdex.com) Bill Gates describe this coming era as Seamless computing. It is the decade that technology finally breaks through the barrier between people, systems and information. The age where we can working in a very natural way with technology; and able to transfer the information without boundary. That mean we can transfer and manipulate information in its digital format and eliminate the need of paper as a medium. It may be the age where we can enjoy another level of productivity and live in a paper-less society.

However, keep in mind that we are only approaching a paperless society; we cannot feasibly eliminate all paper in the current environment, but we are able to eliminate most of the office paper in this decade if we work on that.

Firstly, digital information is not seen as a respected medium when it takes the place of paper. There are a lot of people will prefer the use of paper. For example, many people may appreciate e-card, but probably not to the extent that you would appreciate a card in mail with a real stamp. I surely do not want to receive office documents in paper, but I still love receiving birthday cards and special occasion cards in the mail. In addition, people born before the 70's did not grow up with computer either.

Secondly, not all softwares are able to communicate with one anther. Interoperability of the various software platforms is the final technological barrier. The break though of this barrier will create the Seamless Computing Era that could make a paper-less society practically possible by replacing the office paper documents with various digital formats in a cost feasible manner. That will enable us to enjoy a higher level of productivity. Seamless Computing environment can only be realized if the technology industry come together to create standards and software platforms to enable all of the different softwares to work together to create such a. I hope this can be a reality by the end of this decade.

In the mean time, many technology consultants help their clients integrate various compatible hardwares and softwares into a seamless workable system. The integrated setup can help us better utilize technology to eliminate office paper and create a more productivity working environment.

Thirdly, people should be aware of the potential of technology. Most of the people that I have come across do not realize half of the potential of their computer. If 20/80 is applicable in this case, I will say 80% of them are using 20% of the power of their computers. The other 20% are using 80% of the power.

The more the general population of computer users become aware of the potential of the computer and utilize computer more, the faster we can push the technology industry to come up with the software standards in various platforms to archive Seamless Computing, and hence a paper-less society. That is what I want to see happen and I would like to contribute my effort.

The Challenge and The Solution

From observation, the challenge to consumers is that even if they are aware of the potential benefits of the computer, they will still need help integrating various components and learn how to use the system.

This post challenges to those with limited resources. Firstly, it is difficult to find a consultant who knows software, hardware, connectivity, and business procedure. Secondly, even if the consumer find such a consultant, the consulting fees may not be feasible. It is especially true for home-based businesses and small businesses with a few employees, what I call the micro market. For example, setting up a simple digital imaging system may cost more than $10,000 if you hire a consultant to set it up. How many business in the micro market can afford this budget? It is a very difficult market for many consultant's business models. Many consultants simply abandon this market.

That was the challenge for me when I start my own businesses. I know the technology was there and I could not find help because of the financial constraints. However, I do believe this group of consumers deserve the knowledge and potential benefits of a integrated computing system as much as the larger businesses.

In the last few year, the price of computers, various hardware, softwares and Broad Band Internet access dropped; almost anyone can afford to purchases a computer.

What the micro market needs now is the increase of awareness of the potential of technology and the instruction at feasible price, to integrate various components together.

That is where this book comes into place: increase the readers' awareness of the potential of technology, and help them setup and use the basic computing infrastructure for the Seamless Computing Era.

I want to show the readers the power of the available low cost technology, and how to setup and use the technology to build the basic fundamental blocks of a Hassle Free Office Computing™. The basic structure includes, but not limited to

    i. Basic structure of local wireless networking with broad band Internet Access. I will also mention basic mobile computing units such as Tablet PC and PDA.

    ii. Basic office productivity softwares, such as contact manager, financial managers, and email client software, etc. I will not go over Microsoft® Office package because most people should have experience with the software already.

    iii. Various office procedures, backup, security measures that should be setup for office computing.

This book is the extraction of my three-day seminar: "Hassle Free Office Computing™".

However, I find if I want to raise the awareness of the home-based businesses and small businesses to the potential of Seamless Computing, I need to reach the mass population. If I want to help more people improve their productivity, and conserve our planet, the delivery must be within the reach of the mass population in terms of price.

I decide to deliver my training in a book format, so that it can reach a large number of consumers in a short period of time. I also decided to price this book, so that, everyone can afford it and make an easy buying decision.

I want to see the general population receive the information that they are entitled to. That will enable them to adapt and fully utilize the available technology, which will get them ready to welcome the Seamless Computing era.

When I was taking classes of advanced portfolio management and leadership training at Harvard University, I was thinking how nice it would be if more financial professionals could be able come and learn what I was learning. That will help raise the knowledge level, and hence confidence level of professionals. It is good for the industry after the turmoil, good for the professionals, and the most important, good for the consumers. I am happy that I could be able to raise the awareness in the area of technology.

In this book, I will share with you the strategies that I employed integrating the low cost technology into what I call a Highly Efficient Office™ that will help you to run your office in a extremely effective and efficient manner.

What You Should Have Already

I will help you get into a paper efficient environment, but you should have your equipment and software ready.

- **You have a PC**
  You know how to boot it up, which is as much as turning on the computer. You know how to use the mouse. That is a good place to start.

- **You have Broadband Internet access**
  If you want to have a more smooth digital life, High-Speed Internet Access is not an option. You should use either DSL or cable Internet connection. T1 line is better thatn a DSL or Cable Internet connection, but it is not necessary.

- **Your desire to improve productivity and eliminate 99% of your paperwork**
  You provide the desire to make it in your business and grow. I will provide the technology information to help you. I will talk more about how to handle the day-to-day administration for an office. If you are in the graphic industry and want to know more about graphic manipulation of the scanned images, there are many of those books out there.

The Advanced Readings You May Need Later

Writing such a technical book, I inevitably have to account for a wide range of readers. Some are more computer savvy than others. There are many books in the market that target a single interest. It is not necessary to read every one of them to make the whole system functional. However, they may be helpful when you advance in your journey toward going digital.

About This Book

Anyone can go digital and pursue a paper-less operation if they put up enough money and time. The challenge is to make the process practical and cost feasible. I will suggest a balance approach that recognizes the prevalence of paper in the last thousands of years and the power of modern technology.

The following group of people may find my ideas specially useful for them:
- Home-Based Business Owners
- Small Business Owners
- Professionals With Their Own Practices

I want you to increase your productivity and enhance your business' bottom lines, and still able to keep the initial investment low.

This book is about how to achieve high productivity by using your current computer system and building a practically hassle free operation at a reasonable and affordable price. It is an integration of business workflow and low cost technology.

To help you understand the process, I need to segment the information so that it is easier for you to understand.

The book is separated in 6 parts and each part can stand alone as a learning unit.

Part I : Crystallize Your Vision
Part II : Build Your Private Information Super Highway
Part III: Get Rid Of Cluster For Good
Part IV: Achieve High Efficiency With Low Cost Technology
Part V : Protect Your Investment
Part VI: Never Ending Improvement

You may read the book in sequential order. If you are worried about crashing your computer, read chapter 13 and setup a backup system first.

Icons

These are the graphics that I will use to point out some useful ideas to help you run your business.

This is the bonus idea that will help improve the productivity of your office.

This is the oops sign to pin point those mistakes that users usually make.

This sign is pretty much self-explanatory. I will share with you strategies which will help fix the common problems.

Shall We Dance

I hope that this layout will help you understand the material better. I am very excited to share with you the results of over ten years of trials and errors.

I will not discuss the physical setup of your office, such as lighting, furniture, chairs, etc. There are many books that discusses the physical set up of your office.

What I will discuss is the setup of an integrated computing system, with low cost technology, that can replace paper and improve productivity.

This book is a manual, you need to read it while you are working on your computer. This is the reason it is printed on paper. In the future, I am sure that most people will do their reading with their PDA or Tablet computers. I will consider offering an ebook version. I wish that day will come soon.

With this book, I hope you can grasp the ideas and start to build your Highly Efficient Office™ right away, sparing your valuable time for more important and urgent matters such as marketing, prospecting, self improvements, and family.

I worked very hard to make this book the best value-to-value transaction you can experience.

Of course, I recognize technology changes every second, if you find anything that I should have known of, feel free to contact me or email me at: DavidLam@MrSystem.com.

I greatly appreciate your comments.

©MrSystem.com

With The Right Tools And Strategies, Even The Little Guy Can WIN!

10

LAM Chart™ Of Business Planning
(**L:** Learn **A:** Acquire **M:** Master)

	David: "At the time of starting your own business, your schedule will change from 9 - 5 to 5-9. No one can win this kind of challenge without first searching for the cause of the act. Have you found yours yet?"
Vision	There is no unreasonable dream but only unreasonable time frame: What is your vision of yourself and your business in 1, 3, 5, 10 years and beyond?
Mission	What is your company's mission that direct your daily operation?
Value	What do you value the most? Write it down and don't lose track in your busy schedule.
Beliefs	How do you know that you are complying with your values? What do you know for sure? Write them down and clarify with you spouse and your employees.
Goals And Strategies	Predefine the mile stones of the progress; set the tactic and action plans to achieve that.
Declare Your Plan	Share your plans with your love one and your business associates. You need to know who is in and who is out
Why Would You Like To Be Paper Efficient	You need to clarify the benefits in the future for the time that you are going to invest.
The Perfect Computer	CPU: Intel P4 2GMHz or AMD Athlon XP 2200, and higher 80 GB Hard Drive or bigger 256 RAM and 512 L2 Cache DVD-RW (DVD burner) Window XP Professional 10/100 Mbps Ethernet Card One or Two 56K fax modem Monitor: preferably LCD (Easier on eyes)

CHAPTER 1

Highly Efficient Office™ & Hassle Free Office Computing™

****

In this chapter, you will learn:

➢ **Why Seamless Computing and Paper-less Is Possible and Feasible**
➢ **What Is A Highly Efficient Office ™**
➢ **The Benefits Of Using Less Paper In Business**
➢ **The Significance Of Paper Efficiency To Our Environment**
➢ **The Six Major Steps**
➢ **Do I Need To Upgrade My Computer**
➢ **Purchase The Perfect Computer**
➢ **How Long Will It Take To Set Up The Whole System?**
➢ **Empower Yourself With Technology**

****

As business owners, we have to take risks when starting our own adventures. We start our business with the hard work. We finally build up a client base and have a steady business. What comes along with the clients is the information about them. As our business grows, the office expands; part of the reason our office size continue to grow is that we need more room to store files therefore we purchase more file cabinets. Eventually, we find ourselves surrounded by filing cabinets, and most of the files are idle. However, we still need to pay for the office space every month. We try to use more computer technology and eliminate some of those paper files. However, the files continue to pile up, and we are caught up in other more important things, such as marketing and prospecting.

WE HIT THE PLATAEU OF THE BUSINESS!

Two-thirds of my friends' office spaces are filled with filing cabinets even though most of them are not in the storage business.

Office paper is a barrier to productivity because information is save on a physical medium – paper. It force use not only to manage information itself but also the medium that come along.

We understand a new problem needs a higher level of thinking to solve. Therefore, we go to countless seminars or even hire consulting firms or document imaging firms to give us a feasible solution. They do have good solutions to reduce the information into digital formats. Unfortunately, the total price is easily in five figures. It is not a cost feasible solution for home-based businesses and small offices with a few employees.

So, back to square one: how can you take care of administration work, eliminate office paper that is occupying space in the office and slowing down the workflow? You concluded that the possibility of going paperless is not an option because of the cost. You do not attempt to go paperless because of cost, but instead you continue to do business in the traditional way.

I have a better answer, you can have a Highly Efficient Office™ that maximize your existing equipment with the addition of some affordable technology. The setup can eliminate 80% of your paper.

Why Seamless Computing and Paper-less Is Possible And Feasible

In the introduction, I mentioned that we are still far away from a total paperless society unless our habits change drastically. However, Seamless Computing is feasible and worth of pursuing. It is because that will bring us a paper-less office and bring our productivity to a new level.

In today's modern technological environment; most of the business process could be digitalized and integrated at a very affordable price or even at no additional cost at all. There are a few reasons that such an office is available to everybody.

➤ The Prevalence Of Wireless Connectivity

Increasing penetration of Broad Band Internet access:
The Internet is not going away. The key is how fast we can get information from this awesome channel and how well we can organize the information we collected.

It is feasible for small businesses and home-based businesses to have high speed Internet access, which is an essential element in building a Highly Efficient Office™. DSL and Cable subscription has become affordable.

With the rapid increase of penetration of broad band Internet access, we can now download and upload information instantly. We can use Internet as a huge file cabinet and we only pull out the documents at the time we need them.

The number of Wi-Fi (Wireless-Fidelity, a kind of wireless communicating 802.11 technology) users is rapidly increasing. More hot spots (where you can use Wi-Fi technology to connect to Internet) are setting up including Starbucks Coffee shops and Kinko's. Free Wi-Fi spots are also starting to develop. Mobile computing just getting better and easier everyday.

The information anywhere dream could come true when the first low orbit satellite network is completed. The company that is building the network is Teledesic. (www.Teledesic.com) Guess who is among the major investors? You guessed it, Bill Gate.

Affordability and Simplicity Of Networking
A few years ago, I wanted to set up a peer-to-peer network. I had to hire a technician to do the job. I had to pay for expensive networking equipment and software. These days, the software is a built-in function of the Windows operating system. You can build a peer-to-peer network by yourself without any training. All of the computers in your office can now talk to each other, share files, and share Internet access at a price that your can afford.

Bluetooth is a rapidly growing wireless technology that will replace any wire or cable that you see. Just a few example to illustrate, you can have a wireless cell phone head set, a wireless keyboard, wireless mouse, and even a wireless printer. The low cost and low power consumption of this kind of radio chip create many opportunities to un-clutter your life.

➢ Affordability Of Various Hardware

One important equipment that you need to eliminate paper is a good scanner. Making a high quality black and white scanning is a complex job. The color scanner of course is an even more complex job. It involves the development of a sensitive imaging sensor and components that can translate that digital information into the formats that the computer can interpret, such as PDF, JPEG, TIFF, GIF, etc.

The scanners that we have today produces far better images than those created 15 years ago; today's scanners only cost a fraction of the price. The prices of cell phone, PDA, printer are also lower.

In addition, the computer industry also developed more command standards for hardware communication. For examples, the universal standard of printer and scanner: TWAIN. You can purchase almost any scanner and it will work with any software and hardware.

➢ Affordability Of Powerful Computer With Large Hard Drives

How much is a computer with over 2 GHz speed? It is below one thousand dollars. My first 386 model cost me that much 15 years ago.

Remember the age when there was less than one GB of hard drive memory? This has long gone—as has the price of per Gig memory. We can go to any store to buy an 120 G hard drive for less than one hundred dollars.

When it comes to a digital office, we need large hard drive space to store the information. The price drop of memory does make the Document Management System practical because the price of digital storage becomes affordable to small business owners. It takes a small business at least 40 Gigs to start up the system, and most computers are sold with at least 80 GB of storage. You have plenty of space.

I believe within this decade, we will measure the computer hard drive by TB (Tera Byte or 1000 GB).That is about a trillion memory units!

➢ The Improvement Of Various Software

Even the best hardware needs good software instructions.

For example, there are more and more document management softwares available to the general population. The functions of this kind of generic software have been expanded and improved upon tremendously. You can go to any computer store to purchase this kind of software, off the shelf, for about $100. In most cases, the software can take care of most of your daily business operations, and you do not need to buy or lease the expensive customized software.

There are also a lot of improvement in the productivity software, such as contact manager, financial manager, database, spread sheet, etc.

Unfortunately, there is still a need for standards for the softwares to communicate with each other. The last barrier of a Seamless Computing Era now is the common standards for software communication. The standardization of technology could also offer the consumers peace of mind to spend more money on different hardware and software.

➢ Embrace Of Digital Document By Big Corporations

Today's business is very competitive. That is very difficult to differentiate any products or services. To run a successful business, the big corporation have to keep a very close look on their bottom line. Internet access is one of the cost cutting channel for the big corporations. It is not hard to find a invitation to use their online statement download among your various bills and statements. Because of that, you don't need to take care of a lot of so called "paperwork" while you can download your information from the Internet, pay bill online and even shop online. The use of Internet is unlimited while it is embraced by the big companies.

This is time for us to improve our paper efficiency to save time, save money and save the earth.

What is a Highly Efficient Office™?

Highly Efficient Office™ is a system of low cost technology and procedure that replaces paper with electrons as the medium for transmitting and storing information. I will use "Highly Efficient Office™" and "Highly Efficient Office System™ Interchangeably.

Paperless office is not a new idea. After the invention of the personal computer, there were many attempts to create what we imagined to be a paperless society. Back in 1970's, someone even predicted that computers would wipe out the need of paper.

Unfortunately, the fact is that paper used in the United States alone has almost doubled from 16 million tons to 30 million tons from 1980 to 1995. That is about 400 pounds of paper per adult in this country each year. That means we used over one pound of paper EACH DAY!

The best explanation I see is the shift of mass production of paper to individualized and customized production. More and more people use desktop publishing. Maybe you just used your computer to print a "personalized" card to send to your clients or your friends. We have created a society of massive decentralized printing and file systems. Everybody has his own individual needs to print something unique and impressive. That process in turn poses a bigger challenge to all us: how to manage the massive overload of information in the form of paper documents that comes to us every day.

I have a love and hate relationship with paper. When I started in the financial industry as an insurance agent, no paper meant no applications, no commissions, and no bonuses. In contrast, if I could have more applications, I could have more commissions and more bonuses, and of course, more paperwork.

All I wanted to do was to serve my clients and get my work done. However, the harder I worked the more paperwork I had to handle. It became a vicious cycle. The skills I needed to manage the paper were becoming a means of survival, and the paperwork piled up very quickly. I could never catch up. This kind of pressure propelled me to develop a functional system at an affordable price, and I call the setup a Highly Efficient Office™.

A Highly Efficient Office™ is more than internal communication. It also links you with your parties, such as your vendors or customers. If you communicate with them on paper, you must be able to convert those communications into digital information. Then, your computer can process this information and allow different departments to share and manage the information accordingly.

If you are reading this book, I will assume that you are an entrepreneur and you are running your own business or practice. You may be a financial advisor, a lawyer, an accountant, a direct marketer, a doctor, a dentist, a business owner, or you may work independently or you may have a few key employees.

A Highly Efficient Office™ is an idea that is evolving all the time. As new technology presents themselves everyday, there will be numerous ways that you can improve your system.

The Benefits Of Using Less Paper In Business

You do not need to be a scientist to set up a digitalized imaging system in your office. However, for every new skill in life, there is a learning curve. There will be some behavioral changes in your office either. Your cabinets should not be the primary file storage, though you may want to keep them until you and your staff becomes accustomed to the new system. This means someone has to scan all of the old documents and save them into different folders in the computer. This also means that the office staff will have to go to the computer to pull up the files with the appropriate software to share and manage the files. If there are not any benefits, it is not worth it to do all of these jobs.

The benefits of a Highly Efficient Office™ are:

- Paper is not a very efficient medium for administrative purposes. Sharing of paper documents usually means duplication and the loss of centralization. It is a waste of time especially if you want to share simultaneously. That means someone has to duplicate the paper many times! It only takes a few clicks to multiply digital images and share them with an unlimited number of people.

- We all have experience with misfiling paper. How easy is it to find the paper that you have misfiled? Do you have to go through many files before you determine that it is "lost"? How much valuable time has been lost? Document imaging allows more flexible and multiple indexing, with OCR, or even full–text indexing. It is much easier to locate the files when you do not have to deal with misfiled paper. No more lost files.

- Paper needs storage space and you are not in the storage business. Electronic data is inside your computer, and it does not require paper storage. It saves you all the prime office space you could either eliminate or reallocate according to your office needs. You have to ask yourself how much space can you save if all the filing cabinets are gone. How much rent can you save per year?

- Paper is not a permanent solution because it can easily be destroyed or become deteriorated. Humidity, insect or human error can destroy paper easily. Although we call it "hard copy," how hard is it if you spill coffee on your files? For document imaging, as long as you have a computer and backup, your data is always there.

- Have you ever calculated the time it takes to fill out the paper work, duplicate the paper and file it? Are there piles of paper in your office that you have to file "later"? For digital signal, you scan only once, save and share with everybody in the office.

- Have you ever gotten angry over the paper work? I did. It could be much easier to deal with the information on the computer. I can either copy and paste or simply merge the information.

- The beauty of technology and setting up a system is that you implement the skills and experience into the process that directly improves your bottom line. Let me clarify this issue with the example of a glass factory. If a machine produces glass automatically, the knowledge and skills of making glass is in the process itself. You would have to hire a machine operator. Their job is to simply operate the machine that will do the job that needs to be completed. Machine operating is an easier and simpler job, and it requires a much lower pay. That makes it easier and cheaper to hire a machine operator rather than a skillful glass-smith to make the glass. Can you apply the same concept to hiring employees with less skill more easily and less expensively?

- If most of the paper work could be finished earlier, what could you do with your free time? Could you spend more time with your family and your friends? I would.

The Significance Of Paper Efficiency To Our Environment

The general definition of Efficiency is the ratio of Output and Input. If we can use one page of paper to illustrate 4 pictures, it is more paper efficient than using one paper for each picture. The challenge is if it is effective. For example, are those picture is as clear as we want?

There are a few strategies that we can employ to be more paper efficient in the office:

- **Duplex**: Using both side of the paper.
- **Image Reduction**: print more image on a single sheet
- **Recycle**: Reuse the paper if one side is blank, or use the recycled paper products
- **Selective Purchase:** simply use thinner type of paper
- **Paper Avoidance**: Use paper only if it is necessary

- **Digital Replacement**: Replace paper with digital signals as the media in information transmission and storage, in my case, use computers.

The first five methods are either simply putting more information on paper or use less paper. It cannot change the fact basically we still use paper in this digital age.

In this information age, I found the most practical and effective way to be paper efficient is replace the use of paper in business as much as possible. It is the only way to have 100% of paper efficiency. Let's use computers and transmit information in digital formation.

Unlike the energy efficiency that has a collective effort to conserve usage, paper efficiency is rather overlooked. The reason is probably paper is so cheap that we use it without too much economical concerns.

I could understand in business, the integrity of our earth may not be a major concern all the time. However, remember we are building our economy on the ecology of the earth, not the other way.

As the founder of Earth Day, Mr. Gaylord Nelson, said:
"The economy is a wholly owned subsidiary of the environment, not the other way around."

Unless the technologies can overcome depletion of natural resources forever, we need to stop the unnecessary exploitation of our habitat.

Besides, I believe if we can work on something which is more than ourselves, we could earn a little of self –worthiness.

A typical office worker uses 10,000 sheets each year. Just imagine if we could cut that number in half, how much of the rain forest we could save each year. If we can use more of computer technology to replace the use of paper, we surely can be more productive in getting organized and getting things done, in additional the contributory effort to the environment. The end result is saving time, money and the earth.

The Six Major Steps

Most document management systems will only help you build an infrastructure of computers and a document management system. The fallacy of that is the lack of digital communication with the outside world. Most likely, they will not mention using the automatic sorting tool of your email software and the faxing function of your operating system. Some consultant may neglect to mention the tools in your e-mail softwares or faxing function in your operating system because there is not any money to be made. I try to give you a overview of what is possible with your computer system.

> ➢ **The first step** is define your business and find out what exactly what you would like to accomplish. Value clarification is extremely important because this process can help you to prioritize your activities; and also keep you on track if things go wrong.

> ➢ **The second step** is setting up a network within your computer and Internet access with the outside world. The system could be Client/Server, peer-to-peer and web-based. Increasingly, there are big companies that utilize the latter one. However, in the small business environment, I suggest that you use peer-to-peer network and centralize the storage of information in one computer. This way, your system will act like a client/server system. You can do it yourself and save money here. Until your business outgrows the system, you can then change the system to a true Client/Server system.

> ➢ **The third step** is building a Document Management System (DMS). It will need a scanner to convert the existing and future paper documents into digital format. It also involves a filing system that centralizes the database, indexes the data to search and retrieve, and enables the sharing of information. In a bigger office, we should have an access control procedure for office personnel too. However, in a small business environment, I believe access control to outsiders is far more important than access control to your staff.

The basic functions of a document management system are the following:

1. Build a filing system for the document
2. Capture the information from the paper
3. Save and index the files in your computer for easy retrieval formation
4. Retrieve and manage the data
5. Security measures

➢ **The fourth step** is setting up a what I call a Digital Operation Center (DOC) and communication process so that you can eliminate the need for most of the in-coming paper documents. There are a few kinds of productivity softwares your should purchase. The first one is a Client Relationship Management program (CRM) to centralize the communications. There are so many processes that we can employ to reduce the inflow and outflow of paperwork to a flow of digital data, and I will focus on e-mail, faxing, client data download, accounting, billing, etc…

➢ **The fifth step**— building up a backup system and setting up the standard procedure to operate it. Anything that can go wrong will go wrong someday. It is always good to take preventive measures, such as security setting and regular maintenance in prevention for the worst.

➢ **The sixth step** is actually going back to the recycle the earlier process and fine tuning the whole process. As the world surround us change all the time, we need to continue reexamine ourselves and searching for area for improvement.

After more than 10 years of painful experiences while getting to the root of this problem, I am finally able to reap the fruits of my efforts. Let us celebrate the fact that we can finally eliminate most if not all the paper in our way at a cost that most businesses should be able to afford: less than $500!

- Scanner: $200
- Document Management Software: $100
- Backup disk: $10
- Security software: $ 100
- Some gummy bears: Priceless!

You do not need a state of the art scanner, security system, or backup system to build a Highly Efficient Office™. In fact, you can build a digitalized office with an okay scanner, an okay security software, an okay back up system and some okay software(s). When you integrate the scanner, security software, back up system, and other software, you get a functional and decent digital system that can start to eliminate most of your paper files immediately. The great thing is that the whole system, which I will share with you, can grow with the success of your business.

What I try to offer is the Hassle Free Computing™ experience with the low cost technology. As your business grows, your problems will be more complex. You may need a consultant's assistance. However, the simple setup of a Highly Efficient Office will help you build a body of knowledge and a higher confidence to make an informed decisions.

Do I Need To Upgrade My Computer

There are a few important factors to successfully integrate a scanner and document management software with your current system in order to become a paperless or at least an office that uses less paper.

➢ The Minimum Specification Of Your Computer And How To Upgrade To The Minimum:

- Operating System: Windows 98/ME/2000/XP
- Minimum CPU Speed: Intel Pentium III and equivalent
- Disk Space: 10% of the hard drive must be free, plus another 2 GB of free space on your hard drive. One GB of space can store over 20,000 pages of image.
- RAM: at least 256 MB

Windows 95 is not a valid choice for a digital office. If your computer is using Windows 95 or a model before that, there is not much you can do. Most likely, it will not be very cost effective to upgrade it. This is because the software today occupies a good amount of RAM memory and requires a higher speed computer (CPU). The older computers are not cut out for that. You will need to buy a new one if your operating system is older than Window 98.

➢ RAM Upgrade (256MB And Up)

A few people may have 128MB RAM, which you can actually upgrade to 256 MB for less than $50. If you have a generic computer, you can go to www.google.com and type in the model number of the motherboard. That will bring you to the manufacturing site and you will find out what kind of RAM chip you need. Most likely, it will be PC 100 or PC 133, 128M, 256M or 512 M.

You can then purchase the chip from the local store. Unless you exactly what you are doing, you should not buy online. The reason is that the price of a RAM chip is so low that 128M will cost you about $30. I really do not see any reasons for purchasing a RAM Chip on line because you have to pay the shipping and handling, in addition to the mailing charge and restocking fee if you need a return.

➢ Hard Drive Upgrade (80GB And Up)

As long as you have 1GB of space, I will suggest that you do not get too excited and buy a new hard drive (HD). Try to use the current computer to get used to the Highly Efficient Office™ system, and then you will have a better idea of how big a HD you need. The basic specifications of your new HD should be 80GB or bigger, 100 or 133ATP, and 7200 or 10000 RPM. Hard drive installation should be a half an hour job. You should not have many problems unless you are using a proprietary computer.

Purchase The Perfect Computer

➤ CPU: Intel Pentium 4, 2G MHz and up; or AMD Athlon XP 2200 and up

- Hard drive (HD): 80 GB and Up
- RAM: 256 MB is the minimum. I prefer 512 MB. Unless you use for CAD (if you don't know this term, you don't need to worry about that.) you should not have a need to upgrade to 1GB of RAM.
- DVD-RW: You really should have a DVD burner to burn the back up disk. It can hold 4.7 GB of data.
- Window XP professional: It has more networking and remote access ability than the XP Home version.
- Network Interface Card or Ethernet Card 10/100 Mbps
- Fax./Modem card: For automatic telephone dial. You may want to have an extra Fax modem card if you have a delegated fax line. I will explain more in Chapter 11.

You need to make sure that you have a good onsite warranty when you purchase your desktop. You should buy a three years onsite warranty on your notebook or Tablet computer. An LCD screen normally goes bad after two years, so it is a good idea to purchase a three-year warranty.

How Long It Takes To Set Up the Whole System

Be honest, it does not take long to finish the set up at all. This will only take you a couple of hours to install the scanner and change some of the computer settings.

On the other side, it does take time to convert the existing paper documents into digital formats. It also takes time to get used to the new softwares. However, it is not hard to learn.

I spent most of my time trying different models of hardware and software in the process of setting up my office. It would be a waste of your time to do the same when I can share with you all I know about the Highly Efficient Office™. What you need are:

- Client Relationship Management Software (CRM) such as ACT, Goldmine or your industry's proprietary softwares, etc.
- Financial Manager software, such as Quicken or Money
- Office Productivity Software, such as MS Office®
- A decent scanner (I will help you choose one)
- PaperPort (I suggest PaperPort as the DMS document management software because of it's low price and versatility)
- Security software setup (I will suggest either McAfee and Norton)
- Backup system (use whatever you have now)

Another key to building a successful paperless operation is a well-planned procedure to process the information in your office and then everybody will know how to operate in a such a office.

The Roman Empire was not built in one day, the same as the Great Wall of China, and your Efficient Office.

You know that the technology is available; you know that the price of a decent scanner is affordable and you know that there are so many document imaging softwares out there. The question is:

Can you integrate the concept of Highly Efficient Office™ with your business's goals and operation?

Empower Yourself With Technology

If information is potential power, how can we manage such a valuable asset, and hence, increase our power and income potential? To manage the information well, you must be able to access the specific information you need at the time that you need it.

Let us say your client calls your office for his information, what is the process that you or your staff to go through in order to get that information?

If your staff is able to find what they need on their computer screens, you are on the right track. If your staff needs to go to the paper file, you need to consider a few issues.

- How much time does your office lose every day because they have to go through the paper file to find the information?
- How much time does your office lose because of missing files?
- How much money do you lose by wasting time?
- How many marketing opportunities do you lose because your office does not have enough resources allocated to marketing or client services?

Even after you find the information you need—Let us say your client's date of birth—your question is what do you do with the information. You can send them a birthday card. However, if you have a few hundred clients, that will be costly. How about sending them a standardized e-card? This should not cost you a penny, except the time you or your staff spend designing it. However, you can merge all your clients' data with the e-card and email all the people who have the same birthday or have their birthday in the same week. How much can this enrich your relationship with your client without any additional cost to you?

The importance of a Highly Efficient Office™ is that you can have access to the information you need in a timely fashion. Then through a Highly Efficient Office System™, you can appropriately manage that information in the most cost effective manner. It also helps to manage the information at a much lower cost.

➤ Check The Operation Of Your Business Or Practice:

Could distribution of information be more productive if you go paperless?

Could you monitor the operations and productivity of your office, such as tracking revenue and itemizing expenses, more accurately with a Highly Efficient Office™?

Could a Highly Efficient Office System™ help your record keeping processes? As a financial advisor, I understand compliance in financial service industry is a very important part of the business.

Could you save space and save money if you could convert your paper archive of documents into digital formats? Many of my peers always complain that they seem to be in the storage business after a few years of working in the financial business. How about you?

Would you need less administrative personnel if your office goes paperless?

If you think you could use help, a Highly Efficient Office System™ is definitely worth your consideration. It will put you in line with other businesses, even your competitors.

However, it is always the cost and benefit factors that are involved in the decision making process. In this book, I will not only show you the theory, but also show you what to buy and how to integrate it.

With the proper use of computer technology, you will turn the information into power and you will have a competitive edge over your competitors.

Let's roll.

CHAPTER 2
Crystallize Your Vision

****

In this chapter, you will learn:
- ➢ **Decide Your Company's Direction**
- ➢ **Set Your Company's Goals & Strategies**
- ➢ **Sell To Yourself And Your Staff**

****

Productivity consists of two dimensions, effectiveness and efficiency. The majority of this book shows you how to build a Highly Efficient Office to get thing done. However, this is the linear function of the business. I disservice you if I do not remind you the higher level, the more horizontal functions such as searching for opportunities, define your business and fine tuning the course of business towards the goals, etc. If we do not have a clear target to aim, it is likely to just get busy with no result. This really defeats the purpose of this book, that is helping you to get to where you want to be in a more effective and efficient manner.

Chinese proverb said, "It is the cow that plow the field, but it is the horse that eat the crops." Working hard but going nowhere is no fun. I had been there.

That is the reason that I would like to remind you the basic planning in business.

To make a better decision for your business, it is crucial that you have your business plan. By knowing where you want to go, it will be easier for you to make the daily operational decisions.

Decide Your Company's Direction

I understand that most of you have already read somewhere about all these planning processes. The key is whether you take action. I do not want to repeat too much of what you have learnt, I just would like to pin point the reasons that make it necessary to plan before you implement my system.

No matter what business you are in, you may agree that the market place is very volatile. Entrepreneurs, like you, must stay ahead of the curve. However, new products, new processes and new competitors just keep on showing up and alter the landscape of any industry, just like CDs replace albums in most music stores all over the world in merely fifteen years. The fact is most of the business owners or professionals can barely keep up with the never-ending changes and stay ahead.

➢ Ask Yourself The Following Questions:

When is the last time you took a course to learn about new products?

When is the last time you read the industry journals and magazines to learn about the new trends in your business?

Have you joined any organizations to build a network of your peers or intelligence network?

When is the last time you updated the new technology that can improve the productivity of your business?

When is the last time you researched a better way to market your products or services, to find prospective customers/clients, or to improve your services?

If you think you do not have time to do any of the above, you may have already been left behind. In addition, more competitors are always on the way.

➢ Creating a Vision For Your Business

A vision is where you want your business to go. A crystallized vision of your destiny may help you get there earlier. There is an old saying, "Without knowing where you want to go, how could you know whether you have arrived?"

I suggest that you learn from bigger corporations because they have put a lot of capital and manpower to create visions for their own businesses.

Bill Gates:
One computer on everybody's desk

Federal Express:
The World On Time

Lenscrafters:
Helping people see better one hour at a time

➤ Declare Your Company Mission Statement

Most likely, you are not a soldier. Do not worry; this is not a military type of mission either. However, a business mission statement still needs to be strong and able to fire up both you and your staff.

Microsoft
To enable people and businesses throughout the world to realize their full potential.

Federal Express
"FedEx is committed to our People-Service-Profit Philosophy. We will produce outstanding financial returns by providing totally reliable, competitively superior, global, air-ground transportation of high-priority goods and documents that require rapid, time-certain delivery."

➤ Announce Your Company's Top Values

Values are the answers to the question: "What is important to your company?" This is an ethical check. Your company's value will dictate the your business strategies. This is not only important for you as a person; the clarity of your company's core value is also helping you build the character of your company. Value is the rule that you and your staff should live by everyday. I am going to share a very detailed list of the values of a company that you probably heard of.

Microsoft:
Achieving our mission requires great people who are bright, creative, and energetic, and who share the following values:

Integrity and honesty.

Passion for customers, partners, and technology.

Openness and respect for others and dedication to making them better.

Self critical, questioning, and committed to personal excellence and self-improvement.

Accountable for commitments, results, and quality to customers, shareholders, partners, and employees.

➢ List Your Beliefs

Most companies stop at the stage of listing their values. My question is how could a company know that its values are being fulfilled without a set of its core beliefs. Beliefs are the extensions of your values and the evidence of how valued could be achieve. Beliefs could be some factual statements or some tacky slogans. The important thing is that your beliefs and your values must be congruent with each other. You cannot put integrity as your first priority and believe the bottom line is the most important factor in your operation.

YAHOO is one of forerunners in the Internet revolution. One of its slogans is:

Be crazy but not stupid!

This belief is not bad for a start up Internet portal at it's young age. What are yours?

Set Your Company's Goals & Strategies

After setting up the brains of your office, we need to set up the action plans and time lines.

You should have both long-term goals and short-term goals. The goals should be the corner stones that help you progress towards your vision. The easiest way is to put money towards your company's revenue, expenses and profit. It is also important to put aside a percentage of the growth every month, quarter and year.

It is this amount that measures your progress. Without periodic monitoring, your company may be off track without anyone noticing.

➢ Create Your Strategies To Achieve Your Goals

You should list out the directions of your actions here. If you want to increase your profit by 20% in one year, you will need to break down the progress into 4 quarters.

Your strategies may be look like this:

- Set up the Highly Efficient Office system to streamline the daily operation, cut rental and personnel costs.
- Build stronger client relationships by employing a multiple contact strategy.
- Contact all vendors to communicate with your office through e-mail only
- All outgoing communications should be digital.
- Start quarterly telephone high-touch contact with clients.

After you draft the blue print of your company, you must put it into action. I found the fastest way to draft an action plan is simply put dates and names behind every strategy.

The challenge is whether or not you can get your staff's support.

Sell To Yourself And Your Staff

If you want people, any people, to change their behavior or the way they accomplish their job, you must show them what is in it for them. You need to think win/win.

You need to show your staff that the changes are also beneficial to them in the long haul. However, you may have to prepare to let some people go if they refuse to comply with the new methods of operation. Some people just hate computers and refuse to learn how to use them. This kind of behavior is contagious and will hurt your business.

To make sure your plan will go as smoothly as possible, you must get your staff involved in the drafting process. If you are a one-man company, you should ask for help from your spouse and friends. They can keep you accountable and motivated.

Early in the process, ask your employees to list their most critical tasks and the most annoying work. That will be their priority list and no matter what you say, the list they write will be the list they focus their effort on.

If you want to get the whole office digitalized in three months, you should assign jobs to each of your staff and give them incentive based on the progress they make.

When you have support from your staff, your life will be a lot easier.

One of the application of the 20/80 rule is that take 20% of your time to plan and work hard for the rest of the time. We have done enough mental work and let's get into action now and understand how to build a efficient environment to work.

Have You Ever Said NO Too Soon?

LAM Chart™ Of Building Information Super Highway

(**L:** Learn   **A:** Acquire **M:** Master)

™	*David: "Fear is a very important factor in getting into business yourself, because it keeps your adrenaline flow and keeps you on the edge. That will help you to give your best, face the challenge and go for it at full speed. "*
1. High Speed Internet Access	Call the local phone company like Verizon and ask about either DSL or Cable modem service. Most company will provide one CAT 5 cable to connect the modem to your main computer.
2. Design You LAN	**The best network for home office and small business is a Peer To Peer Wireless Network based on the Wi-Fi 802.11G technology**
3.a Purchase Router	Router: buy a WIFI compatible router i.e. 802.11 G. For example: **Linksys Wireless-G Broadband Router WRT54G (Approx.$80)**
3.b Purchase Wireless Adapter	For desktop computer, I will suggest 802.11 G USB 2.0 wireless Example of this is **Linksys WUSB54G Wireless-G USB Adapter (Approx. $70)** For notebook computer, get a 802.11G notebook adapter like: **Linksys WPC54G Wireless-G Notebook Adapter ($60)** If you may need to access a corporate wireless network, you should get: **Linksys WPC55AG Dual-Band Wireless-G Notebook Adapter ($80)**
4. Installation Of Hardware	• Connect the Cable/DSL modem to the router (WAN plug) with a CAT 5 cable that usually supplied by the Cable company • Connect your router to the main computer with the CAT 5 cable included with your router. There should be a Ethernet connection in your computer. If not, you need to install a 10/100 Mbps Ethernet Adapter. • If it is a wireless network, you need a wireless adapter for each computer you want to share Internet access without wire. Just simply hook up the adapter to the computer with a USB cable.
5. Installation Of Network Software	Follow the instruction manual or my instruction in this book.
6. Setup The Network Access Control	Set up MAC address filter for each wireless adapter connections. In addition, setup user password for each of the computer.
7. Share The Files And Equipments	Right click on each resource and check the sharing selection.

CHAPTER 3

Build A Wireless Network In 30 Minutes

****

In this chapter, you will learn:

- ➢ **Internet Access and Networking**
- ➢ **What Network To Setup**
- ➢ **What Hardware You Will Need**
- ➢ **Installation of The Hardware**
- ➢ **Installation of The Network Software**
- ➢ **Configure Your Broad Band Router**
- ➢ **Set Up User Accounts For The Computer**
- ➢ **Share Printer And Folders**
- ➢ **The Mobile Elements of the GNS: PDA Phone**
- ➢ **The Mobile Elements of the GNS: Tablet PC**
- ➢ **Remote Access To Your Computer**
- ➢ **Set Up Internet Explorer Home Page**
- ➢ **Organize Your Favorite Web Pages**

****

To replace paper as the medium to store and manage information, we must make sure we can transfer and manage the information seamlessly in the business process.

We must have an internal information sharing infrastructure inside a company to reduce the need of paper. In a small office environment, a simple network and the sharing of files and peripherals should be able to accomplish this purpose.

We must also have access to the vast amount of information and document outside of the office. This can be done with a sharing of high speed Internet access.

If you step out of your office, you should be able to carry the information with you and have the access to the information you need. You need mobile computing and remote access to your data in your office.

I refer the whole setup of infrastructure inside and outside of your office as the Information Highway. In this highway, you can drive as fast as you want and you will not get a ticket.

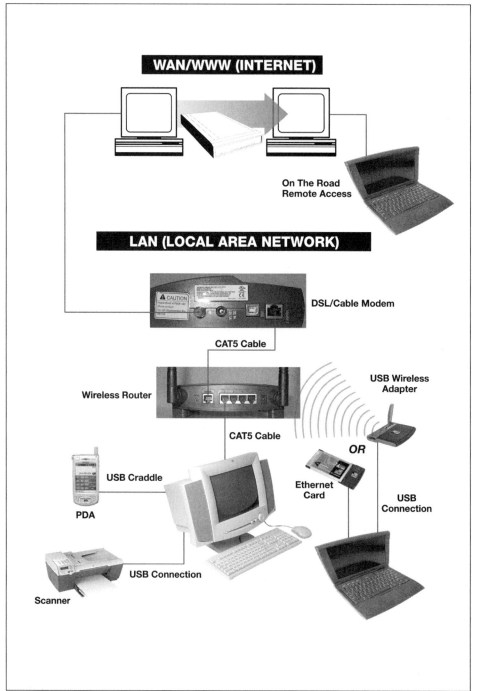

Figure 3.1 Information Super Highway

Internet Access And Networking

The whole idea of a Highly Efficient Office System™ is to save, share and manage information in digital formats rather than information on paper. Therefore, the prerequisite is to have a digital infrastructure to enable the flow of information in digital formats instead of on paper.

There are five basic elements in the this digital infrastructure :
1. High Speed Internet Access
2. LAN (Local Area Network) You will need it if you have more than one computer at home or in office
3. PDA phone (Personal Digital Assistant with a phone)
4. Notebook computer or Tablet computer (if the power of PDA is not enough)
5. Remote access (if your need to have remote access to your "main" computer)

That is these the backbone of digital information infrastructure that allows us to fulfill the promise of a paper-less Office.

Depend on your situation, you may not need all five components. The first three are considered to be necessities and the other two are really optional.

We want to be able to communicate with the outside world without paper fast. Therefore, you must have access to digital information that is inside or outside of your office, and you can tremendously diminish the need of information on paper.

Luckily, most of the big corporations also strive towards paperless communication with their customers for the sake of cutting costs. For you to align yourself with this paperless global trend and benefit from it, you must have Internet access in your office. Internet, WWW, world wide web actually is a port of a Wide Area Network (WAN). However, it is almost interchangeable nowadays. The access to Internet should preferably be done with the setup of high speed Internet access. I emphasize using high speed, which can be DSL, cable or even a T1 line. If the outside parties keep on sending you papers, you still need to allocate resources to take care of that paperwork.

I emphasize the high speed Internet access because the dial up 56K modem is not cut out for business. It is just too slow. However, it is a good idea to have some free dial up service set up in case of an emergency, you can set up some free dial-up services with companies like www.netzero.net and www.access-4-free.com.

If you have more than one computer at home or in the office, a local area network (LAN) enable to share Internet access, information and equipments, such as Internet printer.
I will show you how to build a peer-to-peer LAN.

In addition, you will also need a mobile unit such as Personal Digital Assistant (PDA), notebook computer or tablet computer to extend the network when you are out of the office.

What Kind Of Network To Setup

If you are a one-man band and do everything yourself, it may be that networking is not important issue. However, if you have two or more computers to work with, such as a desktop in the office and a notebook computer for working on the road, you will need to network these two computers and let them share information. You may also want to share the Internet access and printer. Networking then becomes a necessity rather than an option.

Benefits of a network:
- Communication between the users of the network via email, net-meeting, audio or video
- Sharing digital information between the users
- Sharing a single high speed Internet Access
- Sharing computer resources, such as drives and folders
- Sharing printers and saving money

➤ Peer-to-Peer, Client/Server And My Suggestions

There are two types of LAN setting: peer-to-peer and client/server. You may use either one of these for your business.

The client/server network provides better security because the central computer maintains a list of passwords for every user. The administrator also has better control of access to company information. Client/Server network centralizes all the information in one central computer, so it is easier to perform administrative duties. However, a Client/Server network also requires more expertise to set up.

In a peer-to-peer network, every computer maintains it is own set of passwords and user information.

Most of the smaller offices will have fewer personnel and those personnel also have to handle different tasks and share different information. Just like you and your assistants, your assistants are likely to do most of the administrative work, if not all, so you would have more time to prospect of see the existing clients.

For a small office with fewer than ten computers, I suggest that you set up a peer-to-peer network and save all the documents in one folder in one computer, such as "My Documents" under your user files. This could help to centralize the documents and information to share. In our case, we will create a Office Data Folder in My Documents Folder. I will discuss more about that in Chapter 5.

I will show you how to setup a peer-to-peer network with a router and connect to the Internet through high speed Internet access.

➢ Wired Or Wireless

With the tremendous price drop in wireless routers and access point devices, a wireless network becomes a feasible solution. However, you also need to know your information is in the air surrounding your office. Although hackers cannot smell the information, they can get your information rather easily if you do not protect it. If your office is in a business building, you would rather have a wired network. If yours is a home office, a wireless network would not be a bad choice; I don't think you like the wires running through your home.

What Hardware You Will Need

This is my final suggestion: build a wireless peer-to-peer network, if you have more than one computer, with a high speed Internet access.

You need both hardware and software to set up a peer-to-peer network. Let us talk about the hardware installation first.

➢ NIC (Network Interface Adapters)

It is called a "NICK card." It is a circuit board that you plug into the expansion slot (PCI) in the computer. Actually, most computers, either desktop or notebook, will come with one NIC inside. Most likely, you do not even need to buy one.

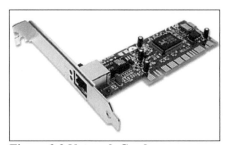

Figure 3.2 Network Card

There are a few different features that you need to know if you need to buy it.

- **Bus (Slot) type:** For a desktop computer, you can buy a PCI card. There are a variety of brands that can by found at an affordable price. The alternative is a USB network card that you can plug into the USB port of your computer. I will say, at this stage, that a PCI card is better because it cost less. For a notebook computer, there is an Ethernet card.

- **Speed:** There are three different kinds of speed. The more you pay, the faster you get. However, faster does not mean better if the other components do not support it. These speeds are 10Mbps, 100 Mbps and 1000Mbps. Most of the cards sold today are 10/100 Mbps dual speed. That is the one you should have because most of the routers today only offer up to 100 Mbps in speed. Most of the cards sold today are 10/100 dual speed.

➢ Network Cables

When you look at network cables, you may think you can use telephone lines and save a few bucks. If you really do it, you are going to go insane trying to get the network connected because it will never connect correctly.

The technical term for a network cable is a Cat 5 cable and they have a flatter and bigger clip at each end called RJ45 connector.

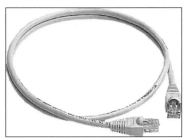

Figure 3.3 CAT 5 Cable

Since you are not going to make the wire yourself like most professionals, you may just walk into any computer store and ask for a Cat 5 cable.

First, measure the distance between the router and each computer in your office because Cat 5 cables come in different lengths. (To make yourself sound like a professional, you may want to know Cat 5 stands for: Category 5E cables.) If you buy a router, it usually include a rather short CAT 5 cable for your connect the router to your main computer

You also need one cable to connect the router and the cable modem or DST modem but it is usually provide from you Internet Service Provider.

Hub and Router

In ancient Internet age (about five year ago), some people used a hub to set up a peer-to-peer because of the high cost of a router. Today, a hub is about $40 while a wireless router is $80. There is not much price difference. I suggest that you use a router instead of a hub. The exception is when there is only dial up Internet connection available in your office. That makes a hub the only choice because a router does not work with dial up Internet access.

Let me explain the differences between a hub and a router by examining what we want to accomplish. We want a device that can help us connect to the Internet and share that connection with the other computers in the office. At the same time, we want to connect all the computers in the office together.

If you use a hub, you need to set up the main computer as an Internet Access point with a NIC. Then you need to install another NIC that connects to the hub and shares the connection with other computers. That means that computer needs to be on all the time while you use the Internet. First, you need to install two NICs in the main computer. Second, you run into the risk of disruption if this main computer is down. Third, there are more settings and you need more knowledge to set it up. Fourth, using software to setup Internet sharing has more error that using the hardware.

Are you confused yet? Just go to buy a router.

➢ Network Router

There are two kinds of 'connector" that you can use to link the computers together and share the high speed Internet access: a hub or a router. I urge you to use a router.

Figure 3.4 Linksys Wireless-G Broadband Router WRT54G

A router has two circuits and a firewall built inside already. You can plug the Internet Modem cable into its WAN port and the router becomes the access point of the Internet. It can automatically share the Internet access with any computer that connects to the router automatically.

The second circuit in the router will connect all the computers together so they can talk to each other. You kill two birds with one stone. There is no setting required, such as naming your computer, assigning different IP addresses for each computers, etc. The router gets it all done for you!

Most routers also have built in firewalls that stop hackers getting into your computer.

Even if you have just one computer, it is not a bad idea to get a router for its built in firewall.

If you have Window 98/ME/2000/XP operating system, setting up a peer-to-peer network should be a breeze; it is built in the operating system.

My router choice is **Linksys Wireless-G Broadband Router WRT54G. It cost approximate $90.**

Installation Of Hardware

1. **Install NIC**

   Most likely, there should be a NIC card in each computer already and you don't need to do anything. Even if you need to install, the process is very simple anyway. You need to turn off the computer first. If you geek around computers long enough, you know that installation simply include opening up the computer case and inserting the NIC into the expansion slot of the computer.

   It is even easier if it is a notebook computer. Just insert the Ethernet card into the Card slot.

   Most of the hardware installation is plug and play ready. When you turn on the computer, the Windows operating system will detect the NIC and install the software to run the NIC for you automatically.

2. **Install the router**

   Carefully examine the box to see if all of the parts are included. Then, find a convenient place to put down the router. I prefer somewhere you can see the lights on the router. Sometimes, the DSL and Cable Internet access may disconnect or slow down for no reason. You do not want to try to fix everything else before you find out that it is just the Internet connection itself. The lights on the router can let you know if it is "live" with the Internet. After you find a good location to put the router, connect the power supply of the router. You can also follow the instructions of the router to set it up; it may require you to install the software first. Most routers take 5 minutes to install.

   For those computer/s that you want to connect through wire, connect every one of those with the CAT 5 cable. Just simply insert one end of the CAT 5 cable to the NIC of each computer and connect the other end to the port of the router. The sequence is not important because the router will route the Internet signal to each computer and allows each computer to talk to each other automatically. With a wireless setup, the only wired computer is your main computer.

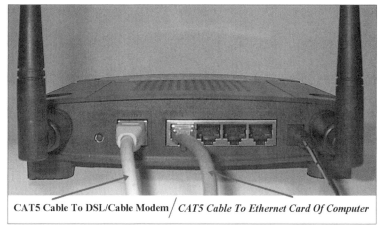

CAT5 Cable To DSL/Cable Modem / *CAT5 Cable To Ethernet Card Of Computer*

Figure 3.5 Connect the router to Modem and PC

3. **Connecting the Modem to the router**
   I assume you have a cable modem or DSL connection
   already. Make sure your DSL/Cable modem is hook up.
   Use the Cat 5 cable to connect the modem to the
   WAN/Internet port of the router.

Installation Of The Network Software

Windows 98/ME/2000/XP has the network software
preinstalled already. You do not need to go out and buy any
software. The router should also come with software and an
installation manual.

There are a maximum of four different types of software you
need to install.
- NIC driver
- Clients Software
- Services
- Protocols

➢ NIC Driver

This is the software that connects your computer's CPU and
the NIC card. It enables your computer to communicate with
the NIC. If your computer comes with a NIC, the software is
installed already. Windows 98/ME/2000/XP includes most of
the drivers for the NIC also. Even you need to install a NIC; it
is usually a plug and play device. That means once you start

the computer, Windows will detect the NIC and install it for you. If this is not happening, your NIC should come with an installation disk too. Just follow the Windows instructions to install the driver.

➢ Install Client's Program

This is the software that enables your request for resources from another computer in the network. Let us say, from your own computer, you may open up a file in your assistant's computer. The Client's software redirects your request to the network.

1. **Click Start/ Setting/ Control Panel and double click on the Network & Dial Up Connections icon** (For Windows XP, Click Start/ Control Panel/ Network and Internet Connections/ Network Connections).

2. **Right click on the Local Area Connection icon.** This brings up the Local Area Connection Properties dialogue box. Make sure the NIC in the Connect Using box is the NIC that you have. If there are more that one connection, highlight the one that connect to the router through the cable.

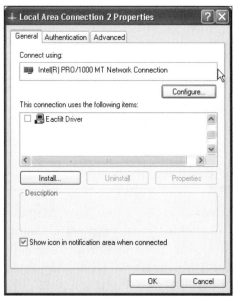

Figure 3.6 Local Area Connection Properties

3. **Click on Install Button.**
    This brings up the Select Network Component Type
    dialogue box.

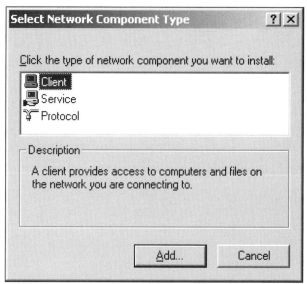

Figure 3.7 Select Network Component Type

4. **Highlight Client and click on the Add Button.**
    This brings up the Select Network Client dialogue box.

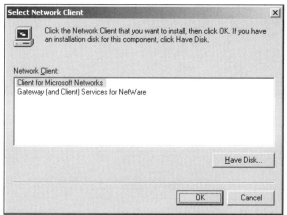

Figure 3.8 Select Network Client

5. **Highlight Client for Microsoft Networks and click OK.**
    Wait a few minutes and the Local Area Connection
    Properties box will reappear. You should see the 'Client for
    Microsoft Network' listed in the box.

➤ Install Services

It is the software that loads up resources needed for the
Windows operation system to work in a network environment.

1. **Click Start/ Setting/ Control Panel and double click on
   the Network & Dial Up Connections icon** (For Windows
   XP, Click Start/ Control Panel/ Network and Internet
   Connections/ Network Connections).
   If you are still in the Local Area Connection Properties box,
   you can go directly to step three to install the Service
   program.

2. **Right click the Local Area Connection icon.**
   This brings up the Local Area Connection Properties
   dialogue box. Make sure the NIC in the Connect Using box
   is the NIC you have.

3. **Click on the Install Button.**
   This brings up the Select Network Component Type
   dialogue box again

4. **Highlight Service and click the Add Button.**
   This brings up the Select Network Service dialogue box.

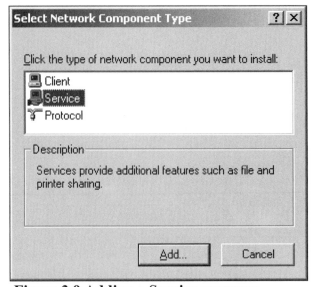

Figure 3.9 Adding a Service program

5. **Highlight File and Printer Sharing for Microsoft Networks and click OK.**

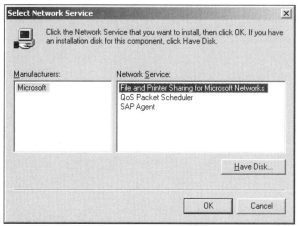

Figure 3.10 Select Files And Printers Sharing

6. Wait for a few minutes and this will bring you back to the Local Area Connection Properties box. You should see that the File and Printer Sharing For Microsoft Networks is added. Check the box and you can click the Close button to get out or you can continue to add the other components.

Now, the computer users in your company can share files, drives and Internet access. You may need to change the sharing properties of the drives or the folders.

7. Install Client's program
All you need to do is highlight the resource that you want to share and right click the mouse. Then, click properties and go to the Sharing tab. Check your choices and you are done.

Figure 3.11 Sharing or not share

➢ Protocols

If you follow the router setup manual, most likely you have
setup this software already. Protocol is a language that is used
to communicate between the computers in your network. You
must choose a common language between the computers.
Windows 98/Me/2000/XP has three languages for you to
choose from. The most popular one is the TCP/IP. My choice
is also TCP/IP because it works well with the router and
Internet. For your business, which should be the primary
reason you bought this book, you can add another router or hub
to the router and you can still using the same setup. A lot of
routers nowadays support over 200 computers! In addition, it is
also the most common language for those big LANs the big
companies use. Most important of all, it is the language used
by the mother of every network – The Internet. It is the
computer language that allows infinite growth in your company.

1. **Click Start/ Setting/ Control Panel and double click on
   the Network & Dial Up Connections icon** (For Windows
   XP, Click Start/ Control Panel/ Network and Internet
   Connections/ Network Connections).

2. **Right click on the Local Area Connection icon.**
    This brings up the Local Area Connection Properties
    dialogue box.

3. **Click on the Install Button.**
    This brings up the Select Network Component Type
    dialogue box.

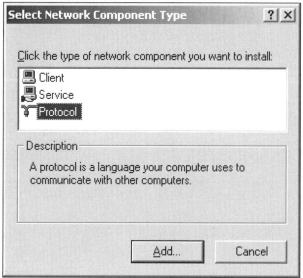

Figure 3.12 Select Protocol in Select Network Component Type

4. **Highlight Protocol and click on the Add Button.**
    This brings up the Select Network Protocol dialogue box.

5. **Highlight the Internet Protocol (TCP/IP) and click OK.**
    Wait for a few minutes and the Local Area Connection
    Properties box will reappear. You should see that the
    Internet Protocol (TCP/IP) is added. Check the box beside
    it.
    Now you need to set the properties for the Protocol.

6. **Highlight Internet Protocol (TCP/IP), and then click the
    Properties button.**
    This brings up Internet Protocol (TCP/IP) Properties.

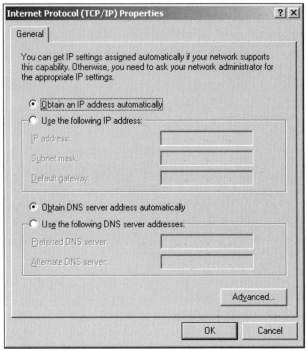

Figure 3.13 TCP/IP Properties setup

7. **Check Obtain an IP address automatically and Obtain DNS server address automatically.**

8. **Click OK and return to the Local Area Connection Properties box, you can click on Close to exit.**

Configure Your Broad Band Router

All you need to do now is configure the router. It is a simple and yet important step.

1. **Open Internet Explorer and type in the address**: 192.168.1.1. This address is for Linksys router. If you use other brand, just the installation manual. This will bring up the log in window

Figure 3.14 Type the IP address of router

Figure 3.15 Enter Password

2. **Type in the default password and leave the user name empty**
   This will bring up the setup page of the router. In the setup page, select your time zone, leave every thing intact and click Save Settings button. Then click Continue button.

Figure 3.16 Router Setup Page

3. **Go to the administration tab and enter the new password twice**
   Click the Save Settings button at the bottom and then click the Continue button in the next pop up

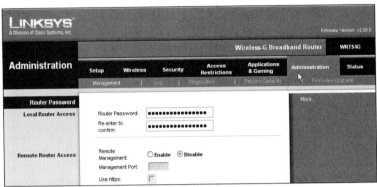

Figure 3.17 Change The Password

4. **Go to the Access Restrictions Tab.**
   This is the step to filter the wireless access to your router and hence your important data.

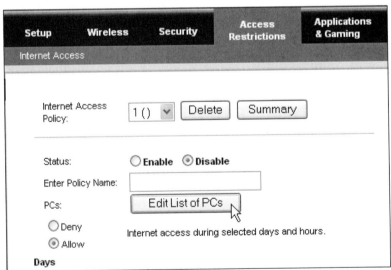

Figure 3.18 Access Restriction Control

5. **Click on the Edit List of PCs**
   This bring up the List of PCs table. You can allow only the computers that you want them to access your network by entering their IP address or MAC addresses. The best way for you is using the MAC address. MAC address is the unique

code of each adapter in the world. This is the DNA of the adapter. Let say if you use the Linksys Wireless-G USB Network Adapter, you will find the address on the box or under the adapter. Simply copy all the wires adapter MAC addresses into the list. You don't need to type in the MAC address of the adapters what you wire thru the CAT 5 cable directly into the router.

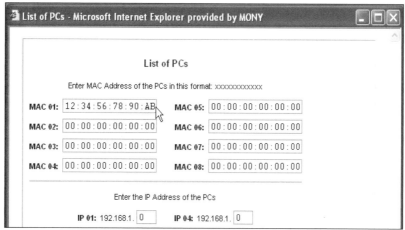

Figure 3.19 List of PC MAC addresses

6. Save the Settings and then click the Continue button

7. **For your own convenience, drag and drop the IP address into the Link bar**

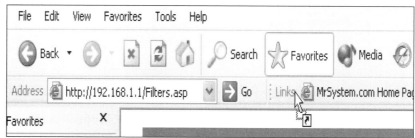

Figure 3.20 Drag And Drop The IP Address Of The Router

8. **Click the Save Setting in the Access Restriction page and close the Internet Explorer**

9. **I suggest you to test you new password immediately by click the on the IP address link and enter the new password.** It is because most router manufacturer use the similar default

IP address and password. If you do not change the password immediately, it is a great security risk.

For those who still use a hub and dial up network:
Please use a router instead of a hub. You will save a lot of time by avoiding potential problems. Unless you only have dial up Internet access or use client/server network that I do not instruct in this book, you should not use a hub.

If dial up Internet access is your only option, then you need to install a fax modem and a NIC. You need to work on the fax modem and find out the IP address that is assigned by your ISP. Highlight Internet Protocol (TCP/IP) and click the Properties button. You need to fill in the IP address and Subnet mask.

You also need to go to the Share Tab and enable the sharing of dial up access. You may also need extra software, such as Sygate, to enable the computer to share the dial up Internet access.

After setup the one with dial up network, you need to highlight the NIC in the Local Area Network Properties box and do the work all over again.

If you have a DSL or a cable modem and you insist on using a hub, you need two NICs in your computer that is connect to the DSL or cable modem. You need to go back to the Local Area Connection Properties dialogue box. Highlight the second NIC that is used to connect to the hub and set up the whole thing again. You MUST assign an IP address different than the one provided by your ISP to the second NIC. If you do not do it correctly, you will have an IP conflict. You then need to share the connection and assign IP address to each computer. My suggestion is: do not waste your time on using a hub to setup a peer-to-peer network. It just does not worth it. Good Luck.

Refresh IP address

If this is not the first time you connect to Internet with your computer, you may find you cannot go online. It is because your computer register a IP address that is different from the one assigned by the new router. It is a usually problem in setting up a new router.

The solution is extremely simple either. Go to Start / Run and type in winipcfg (short for Window IP Configuration).

In the pop up window, click Release All button and then Renew All button. That will allow the router to assign your computer a new IP and share the Internet access.

If you purchase Linksys Router, they have 7 day/ 24 hours support service.

Find the MAC address of your wireless network adapter or NIC

You can find it on the NIC Card or on the bottom of your adapter. If it is not there, you can easier find the MAC address with the window operating system. Let us assume the NIC or adapters are connect to the computer.

1. Go to Start/Program/ Accessories/ System Tools/ System Information
   This brings up the System Information dialogue box.

2. Go to Components/ Network/ Adapter.
   This brings up a list of adapters. Find the adapter and copy the MAC address once you find your wireless adapter.

Set Up User Accounts For The Computer

If you use Windows 2000, it may prompt you for a user name and password when you try to link to another computer. For example, if you use your computer as the main computer, your staff must link to your hard drive. You then need to add a user account for each staff. Follow these instructions to create user accounts for each of your staff members:

1. Click Start/ Setting / Control Panel / Administrative Tools/ Computer Management

The Computer Management dialog box will appear.

2. Go to Computer Management (local)/System Tools/ Local Users and Groups/ User

A list of users will appear on the right pane

Figure 3.21 Computer Management dialog box

3. Right click user and select New User

Fill in the blank for user name, full name. User name and full name could be the same as your staff's log on id in another computer. I do not think discretion is that necessary in a small business. I will leave the password blank and all the box following box blank because you usually want your staff to connect to the data anyway.

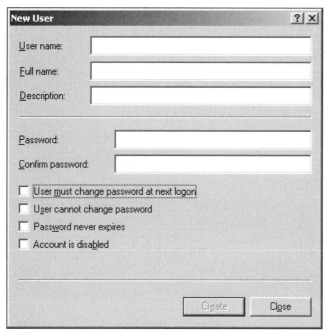

Figure 3.22 New User Dialog Box

Share The Printer And Folders

A laser printer is an expensive equipment and it is also a paper generator. I suggest you not to use it as much. However, it is still an necessary equipment in a office and it is better be shared in the office.

There are two major way to share a printer:

- You purchase a hardware call Print Server. You hook up the printer to the print server that in turn connected to the router. In this setup, every computer in the office can access the printer independently. The only bad thing about that is a print server cost about $70-$150
- Connect the printer to one of the computer and share that printer. It could save you money by eliminate the need of the print server. However, the computer that the printer is connected MUST be turned on to enable the sharing.

If you bought a Print Server, it will come with manual to show to how to set it up. I will show you how to share without the Printer Server. Both processes are rather simple. It is a two steps process.

- You allow sharing of the printer from the computer to which the printer is connect to.
- You go to the computer that you would like to share the printer with, and add that printer through a Wizard software.

Step I: Allow sharing of the printer

1. From the computer to which the printer is connect to, go to Start / Printers and Faxes /

2. Right click on the printer you want share
This brings up the pop up menu

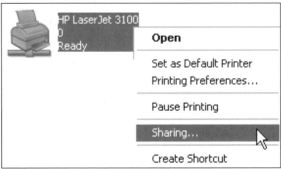

Figure 3.23 Allow sharing of the printer

3. Click Sharing ….

This brings up the Printer's Properties Window. Check Share
This Printer and click OK

Figure 3.24 Allow sharing of the printer

Step II: Add and link the printer to the other computer. From the computer that you want to use this printer, follow the procedure.

1. **Go to Start/ Printers and Fax**
   This brings up the Printer and Faxed Window

2. **Pick Add Printer in the Printer Task**
   This Bring up the Add Printer Wizard Warning

Figure 3.25 Add Printer

3. Don't worry about the warning, click next

This will brings up the Add Printer Wizard

Figure 3.26 Add Printer Warning

4. Don't worry about the warning, click next

This will brings up the Add Printer Wizard. Check the network printer and click OK button

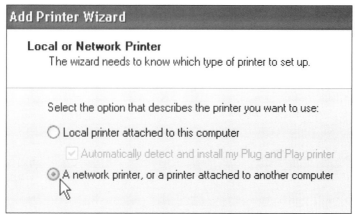

Figure 3.27 Identify the type of printer

5. Just click Browse for a printer and click Next button.
Your computer will automatically browse for all the printers in your local network.

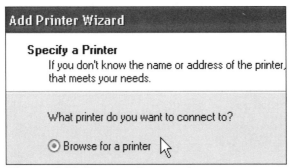

Figure 3.28 Browse for a printer

6. Highlight the printer you want to use and click Next button.

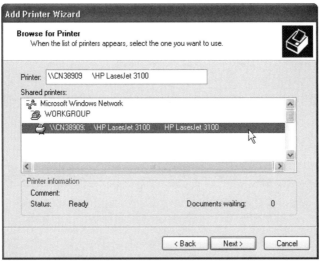

Figure 3.29 Link To the printer

7. **Most likely, this will be your Default Printer, so just check Yes and finish the adding printer process in the next window.**

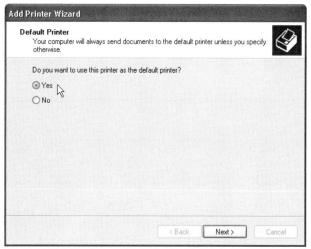

Figure 3.30 Select if your want it to be the default printer

The network printer now will be your default printer and you can use it just like it is connected to your computer directly. Just one reminder, you must turn on the computer to which the printer is directly connected to.

➤ Share The Folders

You can share the other resources like folders and resources with the similar procedure.

Right click the Start button and select Explore. Use the folder hierarchy tree to find the folders or files that you want to share. Right click the folders and select Properties. Go to the Sharing tap and select Share this folder on the network.

The good news is that you don't need to do it on every single files. I will show you in Chapter 3, how to create a Office Data folder. Then you can simply centralize your data in this folder and share the access of this folder.

To share the folders or files, all you need to do is:
- Find the folder or file
- Right click on the folder/file
- Select Properties/ Sharing/ Share this folder in network and type in the share name.
- You will share the Office Data folder that you are going to create.

Use a Router or Install A Firewall

You may ask the reasons that people hack into other people's computers. Hackers are usually motivated by two factors. Some hackers would like to get into people's computers just for fun. Some others would like to find your credit card information and steal your money. It is especially dangerous if you use high speed Internet access and keep the connection on all the time.

You can stop the intrusion with a firewall. A firewall is a software or hardware that prevent unauthorized entry into your computers through the Internet.

A router will have a built-in firewall and you do not need to worry about hacking. It is better than using a software firewall because software may cause conflict of your Internet connection.

For further security, you may change the administrator's password to prevent unauthorized access to the router setting in your company. Your staff has very easy access to the router because all the router manufacturers use similar IP addresses for their routers. You may simply follow the manual, type in the IP address of your router in the Internet Explorer address bar and change the password as directed.

You should find setting up the network is not that complicated at all and you can do it.

The Mobile Elements Of The Information Highway: PDA Phone

Unless you always stay in your work place, you need an extension of the network on the road. This is where a PDA phone comes into play.

I do emphasize the idea of a PDA phone. You may have a cell phone and a PDA now. There is no rush to go out and buy a PDA phone, as the new models come out very rapidly. However, it would not be very convenient if I needed to call someone and their phone number is in my PDA, because then I need to carry both devices.

Since most of us either have a Palm Pilot or a Pocket PC, I do not think I need to further explain what a PDA is.

As the power of the chip doubles every 18 months, the PDA is getting more powerful rapidly. We see there is a lot of merging of functions within a PDA. Most of the PDA phone has email and web browser already. It is really working as a portable computer without **boost up**. For business needs, your next PDA should have at least have the following capacities:

- It must also be a cell phone.
- It must be compatible with the Contact Manager software of your CRM software.
- It should have a digital voice recording capacity.

Depending on you personal needs, I would suggest an optional camera to capture the memorable moments in life and a Global Positioning System (GPS) to go traveling.

➢ How To Select a Good PDA Phone

First , you need to select a wireless provider. You should ensure good reception first. There is no point to having a great phone if there is not good reception. After finding out which are the better providers, you need to find the best calling plan for yourself.

After finding a carrier, you may select the best PDA phone available for you. There are a lot of different functions of the PDA phone. However, there are only three I will pay attention to:

PDA Phone	Kyocera 7135	Palmone® Treo 600	Samsungs SPH-i600	Samsungs SPH-i700
OS	Palm OS® 4.1	Palm OS® 5.2.1H	MS Pocket PC 2000	MS Pocket PC 2000
RAM / MB	16	32	32	64
Price w/sign up	$529	$499	$499	$599
Carrier	Verizon	PCS Sprint AT&T	Verizon	Verizon
Voice Memo	Yes 2min limit 5 msg.	N/A	N/A	Unlimited
Camera	N/A	YES 0.3 M	N/A	YES
GPS	Optional	N/A	N/A	N/A
Vibration mode	YES	YES	YES	YES
Weight/ ounces	6.6	5.9	6.4 oz	6.9 oz

Table 2.1 Comparison of PDA Phone

- Must be compatible and able to synchronize with your CRM software (ACT! can work with both Palm and pocket PC)

- Voice Recording (Palm based PDA has very limited recording ability)
    1. Record your thoughts before you forget them
    2. Record something you need to do, such as a letter you need to send or some other instructions. You can then pass this information along or download directly to a computer for your assistant to finish the work.

- Camera: It is a very important function if you would like to develop a closer relationship with your clients. Simply take some pictures and email them with a few words after you have done some business. Your can download the picture to your computer and link it to your CRM easily. It is helpful to keep pictures of your clients or associates when you start to have a lot of contacts. One thing you need know is that the resolution of the picture is very low and you could not print a clear picture. It is only for screen view.

Most likely, these three functions should to help you organize and save more time. Unfortunately, there is a dilemma in today's PDA phone design. Samsungs SPH-i700 has all three additional function and work well with ACT!. Treo 600 is smaller than the Samsungs but it does not offer the voice recording function. Use the chart to find the best option in your particular situation.

The Mobile Elements Of Your Information Highway: Tablet PC

If you need to buy a notebook computer, I will suggest you consider a Tablet PC.

My dream comes true when I heard about the development of Tablet PC a few years ago. I thought, finally, I could hand write into a computer and use the notebook computer like its name implied.

Tablet PCs arrived in the market place in the beginning of 2003. There are only a handful of vendors producing the Tablet PC, such as Acer, Fujitsu, HP, Gateway and ViewSonic. The list of manufacturers grows rapidly.

There are mainly two different models: the Slate Models and the Convertible model.

I have tried a few models and I like the relatively high accuracy of hand writing input of the Window Journal program.

Tablet PC also comes with speech recognition system. You can even command the computer with voice rather than mouse or keyboard. It could be useful if you don't like typing not much.

I do agree Tablet is a very promising technology that will help cut down the need for paper for the road warriors in the long run. Especially with the newly developed Pentium M chip and wireless Wi-Fi (a wireless network standard) technology, it definitely offer a good solution for mobile computing. However, manufacturers still need to work on the two hours long battery of a Tablet PC to make it more useful in a long meeting.

Remote Access To Your Computer

Personally, I like to download my database into my notebook computer and go out to work. I will synchronize the database when I get home.

If you really need to get access to your data outside of your office, remote access is the process that connects you to your main computer/server at home or office.

There are two simple methods to do it:

- Use the Remote Desktop Connection of Window XP Professional
- Use some connectivity software, such as PC Anywhere.

I will show you the FREE way. I will illustrate the remote access by using the Window XP. There are a few thing I need to point out.

- The host computer (The computer you want to access to from outside) must be running the Window XP Professional, not Window XP Home version.
- You host computer will not be available to use for the people in the office when you are connecting to it from outside.
- You must use the User name that it registered in the host computer as a user already. It is mentioned earlier in this chapter.
- You must know the IP address of the host computer at the time you try to connect to it.
- If you have a firewall setup, you must open the TCP port 3389 to allow the remote access.

- The Client Computer (the one you use outside of the office) can be running other Window operating systems. However, you need to install the connection software into the client computer. Simply put the Window XP professional disc into the cd-rom of the client computer and click "Perform Additional Tasks" when a window pop up.

➢ Set Up The Host Computer

1. Right click on My Computer icon
This brings up the pop up menu.

2. Click Properties
This brings up the System Properties window

3. Go to the Remote Tab
You will see the following window. Check the box of Allow users to connect remotely to this computers.

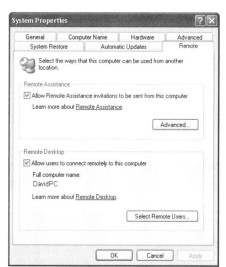

Figure 3.31 System Properties

4. Click the button of "Select Remote Users"

This brings up the Remote Desktop User Window. Remember you add User Account to your computer earlier in this chapter. That step add a LOCAL user to your computer. Now, you actually add the remote access privilege to the local user. Therefore, you can only add those people who has the User Account setup already.

Figure 3.32 Add Remote Desktop User

5. Click Add button

This brings up the Select Users window. Type in the user who need to access this computer in remote. Make sure all the names should had a Use Account in this computer already. You MUST add their name to the User Account first. If not, there will be a error message after you click the OK button.

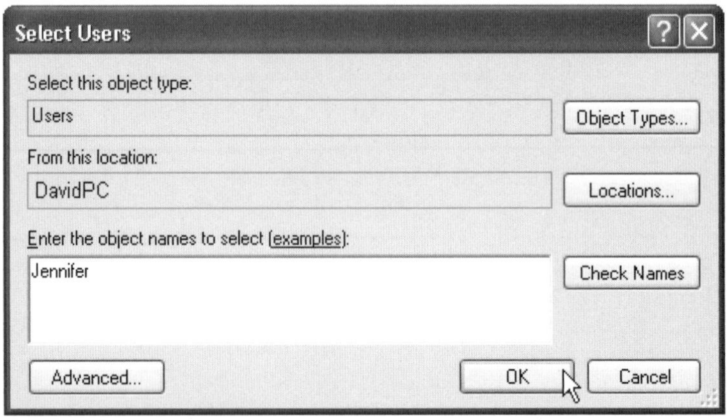

Figure 3.33 Fill in the name of remote user

➢ Find Out The IP Address Of The Host Computer

When you try to connect to the office computer from outside via the Internet, you must tell the client computer (the one you use remotely) where is the host computer. In the Internet world, every computer is assigned a IP address when it is on line.

There are two kinds of IP address, Static and Dynamic. You need to pay a good sum of monthly fee to your ISP to get a static IP address, usually it cost more than $100 just to have a static IP address. Otherwise, your ISP will assigned you a IP address in random, that is what we called dynamic address. Even if your use cable or DSL connection, your ISP will assign you a new IP address every once awhile.

I do not suggest you to spend extra money if remote access is the only reason that you need a static IP address. There are two way you have remote access without one, you can check out the IP address before you go and hope that you ISP does not assign you a new one between you leave the office and remotely access the host computer. You may also have someone check the IP address of the host computer when you try to connect to it. Not the best and convenient way but can save you some money.

Here is how to check out the IP address of a computer if you don't have a router.

1. Go to Start / Run
   Type in CMD

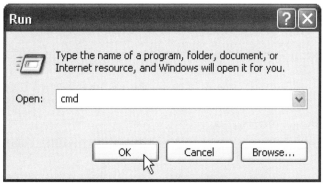

Figure 3.34 Type in the old fashion DOS command

2. Type ipconfig after the cursor and click enter

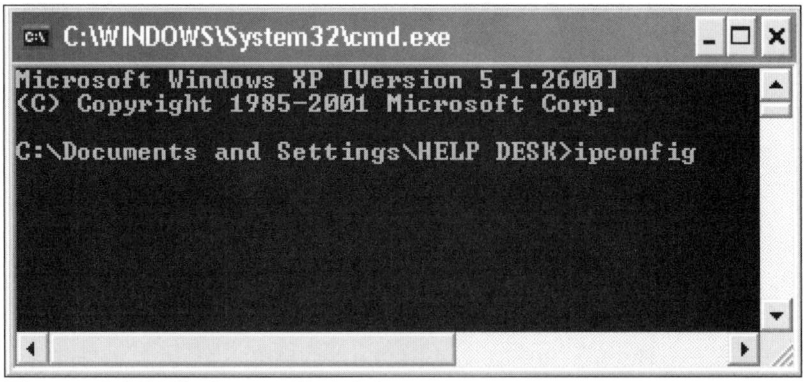

Figure 3.35 Find you IP Address

Figure 3.36 List the IP Address

You may notice that my IP address is not my ISP's assigned IP address. It is the router's IP address. Therefore, this method will not work if you install a router.

The easy way is find a website that will check your IP address. I can give you the best way: go to my website, www.MrSystem.com, and book mark my business resource page. Once you visit my web site, there will be a pop up window asking for your permission to book mark the page. Simply click OK a couple of time and you have all the tool in your browser.

1. **Simply click the link in of Find Out Your IP Address and the address will be shown in your web browser.**

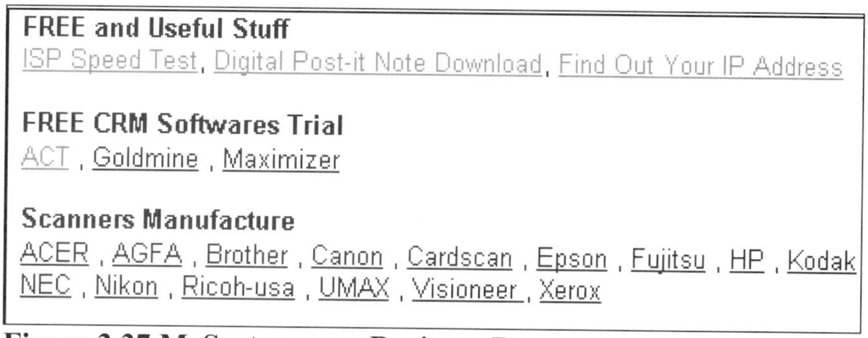

FREE and Useful Stuff
ISP Speed Test, Digital Post-it Note Download, Find Out Your IP Address

FREE CRM Softwares Trial
ACT , Goldmine , Maximizer

Scanners Manufacture
ACER , AGFA , Brother , Canon , Cardscan , Epson , Fujitsu , HP , Kodak
NEC , Nikon , Ricoh-usa , UMAX , Visioneer , Xerox

Figure 3.37 MrSystem.com Business Resource page

➤ Set Up The Client Computer

Now, Imagine you are in a hotel and would like to link to your office computer (the host computer) with your note book computer. The host computer must be turned on, you added the user name to your host computer remote desktop user list, and you must know the host computer's IP address. If you are using Window XP home edition and any version before that, you need to install the Remote Desktop Connection from the Window XP Professional disc. Pop in the XP Professional disc and click Perform Additional Tasks. The following are the step to get connected.

1. **Go to Start/ All Programs/ Accessories/ Communication/ Remote Desktop Connection**
   This will brings up Remote Desktop Connection window.

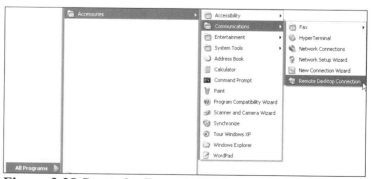

Figure 3.38 Start the Remote Desktop Connection function

2. **Type in the IP address of your host computer and click connect**

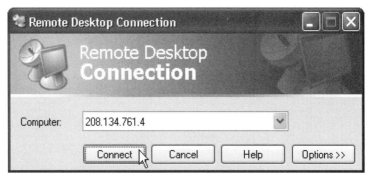

Figure 3.39 Remote Desktop Connection

You can see the process is not that complicated but it does require a very important software: Remote Desktop Connection from Window XP Professional. If you have the Window XP Home Edition already, you may purchase PC Anywhere and install in both the host and client computer.

If you and your staff need to access the host computer so often, you should consider subscribe your own static IP address. Just call up your ISP (Internet Service Provider), and they will be more willing to tell you.

This finishes our discussion of building a information infrastructure for you to access information inside and outside of your office.

To make the set up easier for you, I would suggest you to go to our company's web site, www.MrSystem.com, and download the Business Resources Page. All the equipment and software vendors will be listed there.

This conclude the setup of the infrastructure that enable the flow of information in digital formats instead of paper.

The following is a couple of important steps if you use Internet frequently.

Set Up Internet Explorer Home Page

When you have both networks installed, you can start to do the paperless business. You now have a basic infrastructure of the information flow. You can use Internet as the connection to the outside world and share the information inside your office. This is just like you have built the highways and the local streets. The next step is how to drive around and get to where you want. That is the workflow design. In the following sections, I will show you the basic workflow and the softwares that you need. In the mean time, let's talk about how to store the information that you collect from the Internet.

Most of us may need to research information in the Internet from time to time. Since you only need to pay for Internet access per month, there is no variable cost of information except your own time. You can get as much as information for free now. The challenge of this is how to save and category the raw information into a systematic arrangement, and allow you to locate the information you need at the time you want.

It is a extremely important step and Internet Explorer does make it very easy to do. All you need to do is using the Favorite tool to create hierarchy of folders. Let me show you.

If there is any website that you like to go immediately when the Internet Explorer pop up, you can set it as the home page.

1. Open Internet Explorer (IE)

2. Type in the web address in the address bar and click go.
This bring you to the page you type in, surf to the page that you want to be the home page.

3. Click Tools/ Internet Options
This bring up the Internet Options Window

4. Go to the General Tab
Click Use Current button in the Home Page section. You will see the address bar change to your current page URL.

5. Click OK to confirm.
After you set your home page, you need to save and organize the pages.

Organize Your Favorite Web Pages

This is a very simple function but I found a lot of my clients did not utilize. In research or any other business processes, I strongly suggest you to keep record of your work. Let's do it once and be able to save your experience and result for later use. That is important in time management. Let say you are search for the topic of Management Skill. Let's create a folder hierarchy of Business > management > your page.

1. Start Internet Explorer and go to the page you want to save
Let say it is MrSystem.com :)

2. Click the Favorites button in the tool menu
This will bring up the Favorite Tool Bar

Figure 3.40 Using the Favorites Tool

Figure 3.41 Favorites Tool Bar

3. Click the Add icon in the Favorite Tool Bar

This will bring up the Add Favorite Window. You can save this page into certain folder, or in our case, create a folder system to save the pages.

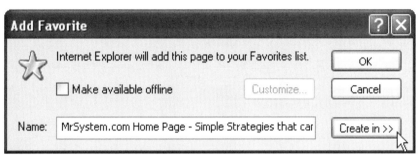

Figure 3.42 Add Favorite Window

4. Click Create In button

This expands the Add Favorite Window and show the New Folder button

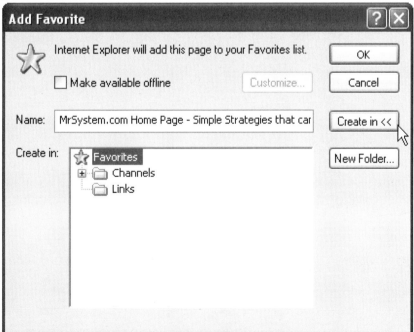

Figure 3.43 Expand the Add Favorite folder

5. **Click the New Folder button**

   This bring up the Create New Folder pop up window, type in the new older that your would like to create, in our case, the Business Folder.

Figure 3.44 Type in the name of the new folder

6. **Click OK**

   Now you create a Business folder. If you would like to add the Mrsystem.com page in this folder, you can click OK in the Add Favorite folder. However, let's go one step further and create a sub-folder in the Business Folder.

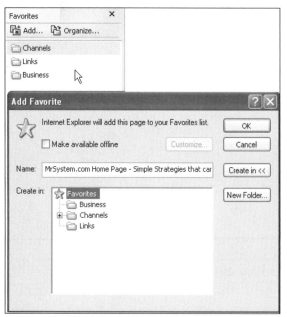

Figure 3.45 Created a new folder – Business

7. **Highlight the Business folder and click the New Folder button**

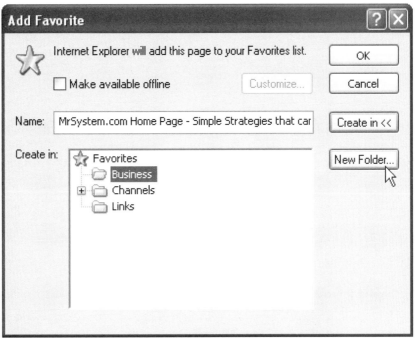

Figure 3.46 Create sub folder inside Business folder

8 **Click the New Folder button in the Add Favorite window**
This bring up the Create New Folder window. Type in the name of the sub folder, in this case, Management

Figure 3.47 Create sub folder

9. **Click OK**

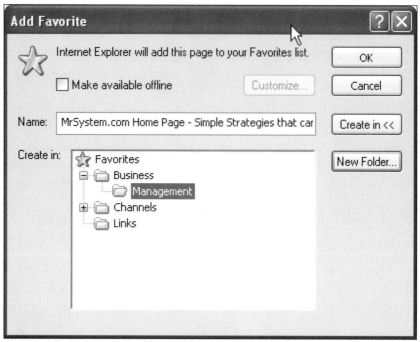

Figure 3.48 A sub folder is created

10 **To save the page in the sub folder**
You can high light the management folder and click OK.
MrSystem.com will be save in this folder. If you want to look
up the MrSystem.com page when you are not online, you can
check the box of Make available offline.

You can use this process to create any level of folder system
you need to remember the web page. I will suggest you to
create a folder similar to the paper folders that you are using
now. That will help you to remember where the web pages are.

In additional, I will show you how to take a snap shot of the
web page and save it your computer in Chapter 6.

Simple strategy that will help you to reconnect you Internet connection 80% of the time.

Of course, everything works fine until the problems show up. The most frequent problem I have is the breakage of Internet connection. Most of the time, all it takes is reboot the modem.

Make sure the data light of the cable modem is on and stable; if the data light is off and you cannot get online, then you should unplug the power supply for both the cable modem and the router from the wall sockets for at least a minute. Plug the cable modem back in first and wait until the lights are all stable. Then you can plug back in the power supply for the router. It should have the problem resolved. You may call you Internet Service Provider (ISP).

Any system can only be as reliable as its' weakest link.

It is very difficult to justify hurting your business by partnering with a unreliable ISP. If you find the problem persists because of the ISP, you will be better off change your ISP.

Now, let's look at the how to eliminate the paper cluster in your office by building a digital filing system.

Part III: Get Rid Of Paper Clutter

Are You Techno-Empowered Yet?

88

LAM Chart™ Of Document Management System

(**L:** Learn **A:** Acquire **M:** Master)

TM	*David: "If you want to dream, better dream big. There is no limit, no ending, and best of all it is totally FREE. But big dream does not carry a lot of value if you don't work hard at it."*
Purchase a Scanner With Paper Feeder	HP Officejet 5510 is a excellent beginner's choice. You may also purchase HP LJ 1012 LaserJet Printer ($199)
Purchase Of PaperPort Deluxe 9.0	It is a great choice of a sophisticated document management software with a price tag less than $100. The flaws falls are there are no version control or access control.
Installation	It is a very simple and straight forward process to install a scanner and PaperPort
Build a File "Office Data" In My Document Folder	It will become your folder of all the image, document, folders and files. Link it to PaperPort program in your computer. Then link it to the other computers in your office. Create a hierarchy of folders within this folder
Start a Standard Work Procedure And Build a Hierarchy Of Folders	**For every document and files:** 1. Discard 2. Delegate (Discard , Manage, File, Scan) 3. Do It Now 4. Do It Later **Folder:** 1 WIP 2 Do It Now 3 Do It Later
Centralize The Information	Either scan the paper document or move the electronic files under the hierarchy of Office Data folder. Use PDF to save text images and use Jpeg to save pictures.
Digitally 'Read' All The Document Once	Use the update Simple search to process OCR (Optical Character Recognition) once of all the folders and files inside 'Office Data". PaperPort 'READ' all the files and build a table that allows you to search based on the content of the image.
Use The Tools In PaperPort	You can use the document tools and image editing tools to do a lot of administration work. These are a couple of good examples: 1. You can drag and drop the file into the program icons in Send To Bar. This is the conduit allow you to email, fax, fill in the form, OCR, etc. 2. You can put a digital note on a file to remind yourself or instruct others what to do.

CHAPTER 4

Select And Install
A Good Scanner

****

In this chapter, you will learn:
- ➢ **Basic Functions Of A Document Management System (DMS)**
- ➢ **Document Management System Goes to Main Street**
- ➢ **Different Types of Scanners**
- ➢ **How A Scanner Works**
- ➢ **Four Kinds Of Interface/Connections**
- ➢ **Other Features Of A Scanner**
- ➢ **Make An Informed Buying Decision**
- ➢ **Where To Find A Scanner For Less**
- ➢ **Some Words Of Caution**
- ➢ **Before Installation**
- ➢ **Hardware Installation**
- ➢ **Scanner Software Installation**

****

Do you want to eliminate the paper cluster without breaking your bank?

It is easier to get productive if we all have unlimited resources. Since that is not the case for most of us, we do need to do our home work to get the biggest bang for the buck.

Most of my clients do not realize the possibilities of some of the following:
- Purchase a great scanner below $200
- They are able to use a great document management software that can
    - o Scan the documents into PDF files directly
    - o Index the image by file name, subject, key word, etc. and retrieve the file by all these fields

- o Digitally "read" every image into text without changing the images themselves; and retrieve the image by the CONTENT!
- o All these can be done by a software that cost less than $100!

Eliminating the paper cluster just got easier and cheaper! You can eliminate most of the existing idle document and build a digital cabinet for the future inflow of information with less than $300.

There are three major components of a DMS

1. A scanner with Automatic Document Feeder (ADF)
2. A document management software
3. A set of procedure of handling the existing paper folders and the incoming paper document

I will explain each of the components.

A scanner is nothing more than the visual sensor of the computer and it can move the information on the paper as images into your computer hard drive.

A document management must be able to help you index, retrieve and manage the document images.

Office procedure, filing system must be installed to have a set of rules for the office personnel or yourself to follow.

When you put these three component together, the whole system should able to eliminate 90% of your paper files and 50% of your paperwork.

I offer a lot of technical information about scanner and document management system in this chapter. If you just want me to help you to buy a scanner, you can just read the chart of the comparison of scanner, and the section about buying decision.

Basic Functions of A Document Management System (DMS)

There are so many different small businesses but the basic functions of a good DMS should have include:

1. Scan & capture the information from other media
2. Centralize the data and save the documents disregard the formats
3. Index and retrieve the documents by different fields and content
4. Intuitive managing and manipulating of the documents
5. Control the access to data and share it with the staff

➤ Scan & Capture The Information From Other Media

You need a decent scanner to capture information from paper documents and convert it into digital image. The major advantages are saving labor and saving time in the long run while dealing in a non-perishable electronic media. However, DMS should also provide other ways like print to and web capture for today's Internet use. You should be able to file documents easily. For that reason, most of the digital management software will allow you to file visually.

➤ Centralize The Data And Store The Information In Different Formats

DMS should replace most of the file cabinets in your office. However, there will not be much benefit to you and your staff if you do not centralize your files in your computer. That means you should be able to drag and drop the files into a folder.

The format in which you save the data is also very important. You want to store your image in a universal format that will not change with time like those of proprietary formats.

By this, I mean the format of all the popular image formats such as GIF, TIFF, JPEG, PDF … Imaging you could not open different formats of file and you have to go in and out of a system to search for another program. This is not quite as nice and not much better than a paper file.

➤ Index The Files By Different Fields And Content For Easy Retrieval

You may have built a very organized filing system. However, it is always a good idea to be able to retrieve the image with different search criteria.

Beside title of the files, a good document management program must be able to index the document by more fields, such as subject, comment, keyword, author, etc. That will make things a lot easier if you forget which folder you put the file in.

The program must be able to "read" (ORC: optical recognition Character) the image and save the content of the image, without change the image itself. It make a big difference when you forget anything about the document but a few key words in the content of the document

➤ Intuitive Managing And Manipulating The Documents

After you capture the information, the system must be able to manage the document as needed. Add notes, remarks, and signatures, touch ups …

DMS must able to work on the images in the same way you work on paper documents. That means you should be able put notes and other annotations onto the images. The only difference is that we use a mouse or digital pan to do it.

With the OCR function; the software should be able to directly link the editable digital document to different programs in order to process them as needed. The DMS is a conduit from the paper document into the processing software like MS Word, Excel, and Access.

Besides, DMS should have a form filling function that works with OCR to create a fillable form from a paper document.

If you need to fax or email the images, it should be a matter of a click in a good DMS.

Even in the majority of office environments, most of the documents are text based. It would be a good idea to have image editing software in case of some family or personal image project.

➤ Control The access To Data And Share It With The Staff

Since you centralize all the data in one big folder in one computer, you also run the risk of losing them altogether. Computer crashes are not a fun experience. Hackers and your competitors may be interested in your data. Accidents could happen sometime as well. One of my friends got both of his notebook computer and back up disks burnt in a car fire.

If knowledge is the power, it takes special care to protect it.

Document Management System Comes To Main Street

Actually in the old days, a DMS was a privilege of sizable corporations because of the compatibility challenge of integrating the scanned image into different processing software. Luckily, with the advancement of the scanning technology, the needs of a Document Management System drive the development of the scanners and softwares and now it has become available and affordable to everybody.

The office system that we are going to build together will not be as sophisticated as the enterprise solutions. However, the enterprise solutions are not going to fit your needs either because of the extensive changes, involvements and costs.

We are going to use the available technology at the best price we can get and build a efficient office. This may mean buying an OK scanner, an OK paper management system, and an OK access control. However, the end result is a functional system that will adjust to the growth of your business along the way. In the meantime, you can acquire the knowledge and experience of a Efficient Office, more than that; you are reaping the benefits of saving time and money for your higher priority goals such as health, creativity, and family ...etc.

All of these could be possible with a scanner, the document management company and a thorough procedure.

Different Types Of Scanners

To build a DMS, you need a scanner. Scanners gives the computer the visual power to take a snap shot. Basically, a scanner is a machine that takes the image from an object and reproduces the image in a certain digital format to process or display.

Before you go on further, let me explain two very important terms in DMS, bit and Bytes. It is not a typo when I use Bytes.

bit: the smallest unit in computer signal. Every meaning information is composed of 8 bits of information. For example, letter a in computer is composed of 8 bits, every 8 bits make up of 1 Byte of information. Because of the potential confusion of these two units, the b in bit is always a small letter while the B in Bytes is always a capital letter B.

In the last 15 years, there have been many different types of scanners that have evolved and developed to adapt to the market needs. Compared to 15 years ago, most scanner models produce better quality images and are smaller in size. Scanner are also a lot cheaper than they were a few years ago.

You can go into any office equipment store and look at all the different scanner.

➢ 1. Flatbed: $50 - $700

Figure 4.1 Flatbed Scanner

This is the most common type of scanner. It works like a copier. It is popular because it fits into a lot of people's needs and budgets. To scan a page, magazine or book is usually a matter of a click. It is great for a few pages of text or graphic documents.

However, to build a Highly Efficient Office, you need to scan your entire clients' files. It is going to take you a long time to finish one clients' record with the flatbed scanner because you have to scan them one by one.

➢ 2. Flatbed With an ADF (Automatic Document Feeder): $250 - $900

Figure 4.2 Flatbed with ADF

It is a dream machine for a Highly Efficient Office. It can scan multiple copies of documents at one click. It also has a flatbed, which can be used for some non-standard size paper, like photos, memos, or note pads. The advancement of this type of machine and the tremendous drop in its price are important to propelling the paperless idea. If you want to have a simple machine to solve your paper problems, this is the first type of scanner that you should consider. Besides, there are a few varieties of this type of scanner too.

The challenge is if you want you staff to share the scan function from the staff's desktop. There are only a couple of models under one thousand dollars to be able to work in a networking environment. They are HP 7450C and HP 7490C. You can go up to the digital print workstation and the price tag begins at $3000.

➤ 3. Multi-Function Scanners: $250 - $700

Figure 4.3 Multi-function scanner

This is a great machine if you want to attach it to a single computer and share the printing function with other computers in your office. Warning: many this type of multi-function machine will not work well in a network environment. You can try to use a print server to share printing in the office but you could not share scanning.

My technician and I have tried five different models and brands and we have none of the scanner works in a network environment. The scanning function of all models, that we tested, only work with the computer to which the scanner is directly attach to. You may share the printing function but not the scanner function of this kind of machine. Some of multi-function digital document center is able to work in network environment but the price tag starts at about $3000.

There are two different variations of this type of scanner: sheet-fed only or flatbed with automatic document feeder. Even if you have to pay a premium price for the latter one, get it. You will find it much more convenient to have a flatbed scanner for scanning non-standard size paper and a ADF for a stack of documents. Sheet feed alone is not a good choice if this is your only scanner. You do not want to scanner a inch of documents page by page.

This kind of scanner always has a printer function, either inkjet or laser. That is another crucial decision you have to make when you purchase this type of scanner. You are better off purchasing a scanner with a laser printer function, if this is the only printer that you will have.

➤ 4. Sheet-Fed: $50- $250

This is for the road warriors who need scanners on the road or any body who does not have enough space in his office. You can scan multiple pages at one time and store them into a single image file. This is not a good choice in the office because of the low resolution and slow speed it offers.

➤ 5. Business Card Scanner: $250

Figure 4.4 Card Scanner

This is very good for those people who need to meet a lot of people and contact them afterwards. You can scan the business cards that you collect with this type of scanner and the data will input into a variety of Client Relationship Management software, such as ACT, Goldmine, Maximizer etc. That could save you a lot of time. It should be an additional scanner rather than your primary scanner because of its limited usage.

➤ 6. Photo Scanner: $300

This technology has come a long way. Usually an internal scanner can scan photos one by one. With the improvement of scanning, storage and display technology, it becomes an automatic photo feed scanner. If you have a lot of pictures of your past, this is a great machine to digitalize all the pictures, store them and then manipulate them with photo editing softwares. It is just like buying a video converter and using it to convert all the VHS tapes into digital images and then store in your hard drive. This saves space and prevents the deterioration of the picture.

➢ 7. Pen Scanner: $130 - $180

Figure 4.5 Pen Scanner

This is the fun type. If you do a lot of reading and research, this kind of scanner is very useful. When you try to remember information from magazines, books, and newspapers, you can just simply scan the information with this pen scanner. If you need to scan more than a few lines, it will become inadequate because the scanner can only scan one line at a time.

➢ 8. Negative Scanners:

From the name, you should know what this scanner is used for. It was a standalone scanner that is used to scan photo negatives. Nowadays, it is usually a removable attachment of a Flatbed scanner. In a regular office environment, I cannot find the much use for this machine unless you are in a photo-related business. However, if you really need to scan the negative and require a high resolution, then, it is the only option that you have.

➢ 9. Handheld Scanner: $100 – $600

Fig. 4.6 Hand Held Scanner

Instead of feeding the document through the scanner, you roll the scanner over the documents. This type of scanner cannot offer you a high resolution especially for pictures. However, it is still good for road warriors who scan mostly text. Besides, many of this kind of scanner are used to scan bar codes in supermarkets and libraries.

How A Scanner Works

The basic function of the scanner is to look at an image and send the image to the computer. As a user, you do not really need to know the mechanical details of the scanner. What you need to know is its basic function and simple mechanism; that knowledge will help you select a suitable scanner for yourself.

➤ The Sensor

It is an important part of the scanner for obvious reasons. The quality of the sensor determines how good the reprint image on the screen or paper will be! The sensor actually is a set of individual photosensitive cells. It reads the image of the reflection of a light and then sends this signal to the chip (microprocessor) in the scanner, which sends the signal to the computer.

There are three signals in the sensor.
- First: the reflection of the light to the sensor
- Second" the signal between the sensor and the micro processor
- Third: is the signal from the microprocessor to the computer through the interface/connection

When you turn on the scanner; the light is also on to get ready to create the first signal.

➤ The Light

A light is a light; even if we put it in a scanner, it is still just a light.

The light shines on the subject that you need to scan and the reflection of the light is sensed by the sensor. Usually, the light and the sensor are mounted together. Since we, most likely, need to scan full pages of documents rather than just one line, the light and the sensor must "read" the whole page. Therefore, either the sensor or the paper must move along each other or stay together.

➤ The Motor

The motor is the mechanism that moves the paper across the sensor in the sheet-fed scanner. In a flatbed scanner, it moves the sensor across the paper. In a multifunctional scanner, the motor moves either way automatically, depending on where you put the paper.

➤ The Chip (Micro Process)

When the photocells sense the reflective light form, they transfer the signal to the microprocessor. The microprocessor then interprets the signal and sends the data to the computer through a connector /interface. As Gordon Law states: the power of microprocessor is double 18 months, the power of the processor has increased so much in the last few years that it allows you to buy a great scanner for a few hundred dollars.

➤ Interface/Connection

In the technological world, just like any other profession, unfamiliar terms can scare off regular people like you and me. However, if you really take the time to understand those terms, they are not that difficult to understand.

"Interface" is no more than the connection between your scanner and your computer. It is the path by which the signal from the microchip is transferred to the computer's microprocessor or Central Processing Unit (CPU).

What you need to know is the different between these interfaces and how these differences affect your system and hence your buying decision. There are four kinds of connections, sorry, I should say interface.

Four Kinds Of Interface/Connections

➢ Parallel Port:

Your computer will certainly have a parallel port. It is used with the printer, but there are many devices that can be connected to your computer by using this port/connector.

- Pros: Since almost all computers, including notebook computers, have a parallel port, this kind of interface should guarantee that your scanner can work with almost any computer.
- Cons: Parallel ports are the slowest out of all of the available interfaces. Worst of all is that it occupies the printer port and you are unable to use it unless you do the following:
  i. Plug and unplug the connection whenever you need to use it. Not a very convenient choice.
  ii. Most of the scanners allow you to "daisy-chain," or connect the scanner to whatever devices that you use with that port, such as a printer or a Zip Drive. Of course, this leaves you open to more errors and, needless to say, it is going to slow the transfer of signals.

➢ Universal Serial Bus (USB and USB 2.0)

In the last few years, USB has become more and more popular. You can hardly find a computer without USB ports. My new desktop computer comes with 6 USB 2.0 ports! We even have the USB 2.0 that is 4 times faster than its processors. In reality, USB 2.0 is valuable for it is fast speed and simplicity in installation. These are some of the many advantages but very few disadvantages of USB ports.

- **Pros**
  i. It can support up to 127 different devices per USB port. How many devices do you have?
  ii. It is fast. It can transfer 480 megabits or 480,000,000 bits per second. To give you an

idea of how faster this is, I will compare it to a 56K modem. Your 56K dial up modem transfers 56,000 bits per second at maximum speed. That means a USB port is about 8,500 times faster than your dial up modem. USB 2.0 is about 30,000 faster!

iii. It is compatible with all kinds of operating system like Windows 98, ME, 2000, XP, and Mac OS.

iv. It is a very inexpensive port option if you want to add more to your computer.

v. It do not have to reboot the computer. That means you can plug and unplug your scanner from the computer.

- **Cons**
    i. For the older computers like PII and Mac, USB ports cannot be found for those machines. Of course, you may find a converter, but I recommend that you buy a new computer. Today's operating systems and softwares require a large memory and CPU speed that will make your old computer obsolete. Do not fight it; buy a new one.

I suggest that you purchase the USB connections for your office because it is both efficient and inexpensive.

➢ Firewire

This is the wire that can catch on fire very easily... OK, no. It is just another very unique term in the computer field. Of course, you can remember it by the correct technical name: IEEE-1394 High Performance Series Bus, but I will call it Firewire. It can handle 63 devices and the speed is fast. If you need very high quality color image scanning, Firewire connection is what you need.

- **Pros:**
    The computer does not have to be rebooted and it transfers data at a faster speed.

- **Cons:**
    This is not a popular interface and usually only used in high-end scanners.

Unless you are pursuing very high speed of transmission or very high quality of scan image, you don't usually deal with Firewire.

➤ SCSI (Small Computer Systems Interface, Pronounced as Gut-Si)

Hackers have used this technology for sometime now. As technology advances, we now have the privilege that once belonged to hackers and big corporations. The interface supports up to 15 devices in one port and is used for both internal and external devices.

- **Pros**

  It is fast. However, with the new USB 2.0, this advantage of SCSI is diminishing.

- **Cons**

  You need more time and knowledge to install a SCSI card into your computer. It is also more expensive compared to a UBS card.

After reading the interface section, you will probably agree that the USB is the best option available. Lucky for us, the majority of the middle and lower end scanners use USB connections. It helps to keep the cost down while still maintaining a high-speed data transfer speed.

Other Features Of A Scanner

➤ TWAIN And WIA

I will be honest—I do not know what these acronyms stand for. They are the standard software protocol and Application Programming Interface (API) that most of the normal scanners use to communicate with the computer. The other standard is called ISIS but you will rarely encounter that. As long as your scanner is TWAIN OR WIA compatible, you are pretty much guaranteed to be able to use any computer and any software to control that. For additional information on TWAIN, go to www.twain.org.

➤ Resolution And Interpolation

Just like some people have good eyes and some people have great eyes, some scanners also have good or great vision. A computer's resolution indicates how small of an image the scanners can read.

I have two reminders for your concerning resolution. First, do not mix this up with the print resolution. That is a measure of the printing resolution if you buy a multifunctional printer.

Second, the resolution of a scanner is usually expressed by the optic resolution and interpolated value. Optic resolution is the one I will use here.

Interpolated resolution is how software cheats your eyes by filling in the blank spots of the scanned image. It is always an inflated number compared to the optic/raw resolution. I would not care too much about that number.

The resolution of a scanner is usually measured in dpi--the number of dots scanned per inch of the original image. Sometimes, this is expressed in two numbers, such as 600*600. The first number is the number of photo horizontal sensor cells and the second is the number of vertical cells. What matters the most is the first number, not the second. The higher the numbers are, the higher the resolution and better quality of images.

Beware: I did not say the better the results. The higher the resolution, the slower the scanning process and the bigger the file. It will take you longer if you scanner at a higher resolution. Those are not necessary requirements in most offices.

If you are in the imaging, photo, or graphic business, it will make sense for your to scan with a higher resolution. However, for most office work, people deal mainly with text only, and so a higher resolution will not help you do your job any better. A machine with a higher resolution capability will cost you more money.

Sometimes, you will see only one number such as 4800 dpi. This is still correct and, actually, it is the way that high-end scanner are labeled. This number is the measure of the pixels that the scanner scans horizontally. Most professionals will use this number as a measure.

Fortunately, most scanners today will satisfy have resolution up to 4800 dip. The good news for you is that, for text documents, 200 dpi is good enough for most scan jobs! If you want a software to read and translate the image into editable text, OCR function, all you need is 300 dpi! This should be the bottom line when you choose a scanner for your office or home. I just purchased my new scanner, which has a maximum resolution of 4800 dpi and cost me less than three hundred dollars.

➢ One Button Scan:

Most scanners will include this feature. A couple of years ago, you would have had to pay more for a couple of buttons that allow you to scan images without going to the computer panel. Today, a single button is a standard feature on a scanner no matter how inexpensive it is.

➢ Paper Size Handling:

Most of the scanners are made for A4 size paper. As long as your scanner has ADF (Automatic Document Feeder), you do not have to worry about paper size. Even if the flatbed scanner is for A4 size, you can still scan the legal-sized paper with the ADF.

Make A Informed Buying Decision

Now, you are equipped with the functional knowledge necessary to purchase a suitable scanner for your office.

➢ For a Document Management System, You Need a Scanner With The Following Features:

- Flatbed with a ADF
- TWAIN standard compliance
- Minimum optic resolution 200 * 300 dpi
- Preferred Interface: USB 2.0

In the market place, you can find a lot of flatbed scanners for less than a hundred dollars. I strongly discourage you from purchasing that type of scanner. You should purchase only if every one of your clients' folders only has one page. If this is not the case, you will run into a lot of trouble scanning the folders and organizing them. It is going to take you hours and hours and it will not be worth it. Trust me.

To buy a scanner, there are a few decisions you need to make.

Now Let us compare a few models in the market, and let me show you how to make a buying decision.

We will compare four different models and I will share my opinions about them.

I assume you want to buy a scanner to build a Highly Efficient Office. The next question is whether or not you also need a printer. I will discuss four scenarios to illustrate the buying decision and to help you to get the best bang for your buck.

Comparison Of Scanners

	HP 5510	HP 6110	HP 3330mfp	HP 7450c/ Hp 7490C
Price	$199	$299.99	$699	$699
Network Ready	No	No	No	YES
Flatbed With ADF	Yes 20 sheets	Yes 35 sheets	Yes 50 sheets	Yes 50 sheets
Resolution /dpi	1200*1200	1200*1200	2400*1200	2400*2400
Interface	USB	USB	USB/ Parallel	USB SCSI
TWAIN	Yes	Yes	Yes	Yes
Other functions	Inkjet printer Fax Copy	Inkjet printer Fax Copy	Laser Printer Fax Copy	None
Color depth	36 bit	48 bit	24 bit	48 bit

Table3.1   Table of Four Scanner Models

If you need to scan both sides of the documents or you need share the scanner with other computers, you will need the new HP 9100C series. There are three different models that can share scan function and perform duplex scanning. However, this series is a high end one and you will need to pay about $3000 for these scanners.

➢ Either Your Need a Inkjet Printer Or Not

HP Officejet 5510 is a great basic machine for home business and small business. It can scanner with a ADF, fax and print out decent color inkjet picture. For scan function, you mostly need up to 300dpi resolution. It can offer 1200dpi. Unless you work primarily with color graphics, you may need get a scanner with 48-bit color. You may appear to you slow in the beginning when you try to scan all your paper documents into your computer. After that, the automatic scanning capacity of 20 pages at a time is plenty for most of the home based business I know.

Some people argue that if you use a multifunction machine, a problem with one function will affect the whole operation. My thought is that the machines today are very reliable, and the multifunctional machine is justified by the price and the simplicity.

For a price under $200 with all these functions, you can hardly go wrong.

➢ If You Need a Laser Printer:

You can get a decent laser printer for $250. However, you can also select HP 3330mfp for $699, which would be more convenient because it also includes a scanner, a copier and a fax machine. This will save you some time; you could make copies directly from the machine rather than scanning the documents first and then printing it out from a separate printer. Besides, you may also have extra fax machine as a spare. Some people may become concerned when part of the machine breaks down, thinking that they cannot use the other parts. First of all, I do not think today's machine breaks down as easily. Secondly, you may buy a two year extra warranty on the scanner if you are really concerned about the breakdown. However, I would not buy a 3320n MFP, which has a internal print server (for share within the office). The difference in price is about two hundred dollars, which enables me to buy a good external three port print server and a nice dinner. Please remember that this machine will only share the print function, not share the scan function. The computer that is directly connected to the scanner is the one that can scan document.

Another option is buying a HP 5510 as a multi-function scanner and also buy a start up laser printer. It is a great choice to start with a low end but functional HP LJ1012 LaserJet printer

One reminder is that most of the scanners are not network ready. For multifunctional scanners, you can share the printing function, but not the scanner. You cannot share the

scan function of a multifunctional printer! I have tried so
many models but I have not had any success yet. If you
have any success with that, please share your discovery
with me.

➤ If you have a lot of paper or you need to share the scanner

If you need to scan 100 pages a day in the long run, I would
say that is quite a bit. In that case, speed is a necessity for
you. You need to buy the fastest scanner available at this
price range and you want to use an SCSI connection that
will give you the fastest transmission. I would not even buy
the HP 7450c listed here because I would not want to
install the SCSI myself. In that case, you should consider
HP 7490c with an installed SCSI connection for about $899.
HP 7490c also have sharing capacity. What I need to warn
you of is, after reading this book, you may find ways to
eliminate the majority of your incoming paper documents
already.

I do not think a few scenarios that I describe here can cover
all the unique situations you might have. I just want to help
you get an idea of how the cost and benefit technology
could be evaluated in the purchasing process.

Today's entrepreneurs can start up with a shoestring budget
as long as you have some good ideas and guts. When your
business grows and you know more about your exact needs,
you can then buy a different machine for different needs
but always look at the dollar sign when making your
buying decision.

Do not let the WANT part of your brain affect the NEED
part of your business decision. Fugal is a good virtue not
only in daily life but also in business.

Where To Find A Scanner For Less

You can do your research download the business resources page in my website, www.MrSystem.com, or by going to the manufacturers' web sites listed below: www.HP.com, www.lexmark.com, www.canon.com, www.brother.com, etc. After you find a few models you are interested in, try going to a shopping site such as www.shopping.yahoo.com or www.pricewatch.com for a better price. You will find lists of web sites in Appendix A.

After finding out how much you would pay for a machine on the Internet, I suggest that you then go shopping in a store for comparative purposes. Whether you ultimately buy from the store is a topic we will discuss later.

However, it is important to go to a few stores to find out more about the scanners that you want to buy. You can look at the machines or even have a demo printout. Most of the time, you can get a second opinion from the store salesman, who can help you make an informed decision about which scanner to buy.

Now, there are two schools of thought on shopping online versus buying from the retail store.

➤ The Advantages Of Buying On Line Are:

Price is lower:
This is the first reason why I shop on line. I think most online buyers have this reason in mind too, do not you?

Save my tax dollars:
Unless the online company has an office in your state, you will save the sales tax.

Online saving is a time saver:
I am trying very hard to build a Highly Efficient Office, and online shopping will create less paper: you will receive your receipt by email, and tracking of your purchase and contact with the company are also mostly sent via email. However, you need to know exactly what you are looking for.

You can always find the merchandise:

If what you want to buy is a rare or brand new item, you may not get it from the store or even the manufacturer. However, you may find it in the online store. When the HP 2500 color printer just came out in November 2002, I could not find it anywhere in the retail stores. Finally, I bought it from an online company and had it four days later.

In China, there is a proverb: you cannot find a noodle with both ends pointed. This means that nothing is perfect. This applies to online shopping as well.

➢ The Disadvantages To shopping Online Are:

You can get mugged:

For any kind of transaction, you may get ripped off. The store may not send you your purchase on schedule or may not even send it to you at all. The worst is that your personal information may be stolen. I will only shop online if they use a SSL (Secure Sockets Layer), which is an encryption technology that protects your personal and credit card information from hackers. It is the industry's standard for online transaction.

Not much personal help:

When you buy online, you have to make your buying decision on your own. Online stores usually provide you with a lower price because you receive fewer services. The service you might miss the most is consultation with a salesperson that can help you compare different scanner models.

Difficult to exchange:

Unless the company sends you the wrong merchandise, you will be responsible for the cost of shipping, even if you change your mind. Most of the online stores charge restocking fees for returned merchandise. Beware of that.

Shipping may be costly:

Although you may save money on taxes, most online sellers will make you pay for shipping and handling. The bottom line is whether you can save money and still get what you need.

Even though you may pay a higher price, shopping at the local retail store does provide a few important advantages:

➤ The Advantages Of Buying In a Store Are:

Personal assistance in shopping:
Personally, I have learned so much from the sales people at the local computer stores. This is what online stores do not usually provide. You can search for information, but you need to know what you are searching for online. At a store, a salesman can help you compare and filter through information.

Demonstration:
Even if you are just window-shopping, you can try the merchandise out. This is very important when buying equipment.

Simple return:
This applies to most of the big chain stores. Usually, for electronics, a customer usually has a 2-week, 100% satisfaction guaranteed policy. Although some may claim to have a 15% stocking fee, you usually can get away without paying that charge unless the merchandise is a computer system.

➤ Where I Purchase My Equipment

Most of the time, I will surf the Internet, as I mentioned, to find what might be suitable for me. I will find those models and then I will shop in the local stores. For the hardware, if the price is not much different, I will purchase it in the local store for the learning experience I get when talking with their sales people and the convenience I have in making a return.

As an investor and a "Pseudo-techno guy," I will look to my pocket in technology spending too. Once, I paid $650 on line for a flat panel monitor that has a store price of $899. To get those savings, I purchased it on line and used the extra money to buy a few bags of gummy bears that is my favorite candy. For something like $20, I will forgo the saving but the convenience of shopping in the local stores. There is no definite rules in bargaining shopping. The more you do, the better you become. The good news, every body can become better by more practice .

Some Words Of Caution

➤ Avoid Refurbished Machines Unless It Has a Warranty

I think you can get a lot of bargains by shopping around rather than buying a used machine. Refurnished machines are used machines. Most of these machines had defects in them. By law, the store cannot sell it as brand new and they have to cut the price. Most of the time, the price cut is not that much. If you buy one with a " sell as is" condition, the package may not even have all the accessories that come with the merchandise.

➤ Do I Need The Extra Warranty?

With the competitive retail environment, most stores try to generate revenue by financing and selling insurance (warranty). Whether or not you need this really depends on the value of what you buy. The more expensive and complex the merchandise is, the more it makes sense to get a longer warranty. For my notebook computer, I do not mind spending a few hundred dollars for my investment. An LCD monitor will cause me a thousand dollars already.

For a scanner that cost less than $200, in addition to the simple design and short cycle of new products, extra warranty is not really necessary.

However, please do register your machine for the usual one-year warranty. Don't let anything that benefit you and is available for FREE get away.

Shopping with automatic discount

I understand you probably are thinking about how to get the digital office done with even less money. Most office equipments are not like grocery that you can buy in bulk and save money, especially in home based or small business. You can save money, without spend too much time in search for bargains and coupons, by building store credits and credit card reward points.

Build point with credit card purchase:

You should check if your credit has reward points from your purchases. e.g. American Express has the OPEN small business credit card. You can accumulate point with your purchases. Second, you can have extra saving if you purchase from it's partners, such as Staples. You can apply through 1 (800) Now-Open or visit their website at www.americanexpress.com.

Accumulate store credits:

You can apply to be store member from company like Staples. You will earn store credit from your purchases.

Build a chain of discounts and rewards:

If you shop in the Staples as its membership with American Express credit card,

- you will earn credit card credit for each dollars
- 2% saving of the purchase
- earn one store point for each dollar of purchase

Sign up email coupons from the stores:

As the competition in retail is very fierce, there are many office supply and electronic stores will lure you into their stores by sending you advertising and email coupons. Build a email coupon folder (The instruction is in Chapter 9) and sort the coupon into this folder. You may find more savings.

Find out more about your credit card and the stores that you shop, you may find there are some discounts that you miss. It may sound trivial but it all adds up in a year.

Before Installation

Since USB is very common nowadays and most of the scanners use USB connections, installing scanners are a simple and straightforward job. However, there are a few tips I would like to share with you.

➤ Keep The Box!

It could be as simple as tearing off the box and plugging in the power cord and connection wire. We get excited to set up our new toy. I encourage you to keep the original boxes for the scanner or any other machines that you bought. As I mentioned before, I like to buy from retail stores, and if you have to return merchandise, you will have to return it in the original box.

If you need to send any machine for repair, the original package will save you a lot of agony, as well.

Since I am an ebay-er, I have found that merchandise is worth much more if it is in the original package. However, if your space is so limited that you have to throw it away, try to keep it at least for the period of warranty.

Hardware Installation

The installation of a scanner is usually a matter of connecting a cable between the scanner and your computer. It is very simple and easy.

➤ Parallel Port

If you are using a scanner with a parallel port, then you need to do a daisy-chaining process. This is quite a fancy name for unplugging the parallel cable of the printer and plugging it into the printer port of the scanner. Then plugging the parallel cable of the scanner to the computer's parallel port. Now your computer, scanner and printer are daisy-chained!

For the parallel interface, you need to reboot your computer to make it work.

➢ USB And Firewire Installation

If you are using a USB interface scanner, you will find that all you need to do is use the USB wire to connect the computer and the scanner. USB and Firewire, which are plug and play connections. "Plug and Play" means the operating system in your compute will recognize the hardware or scanner and it will be installed automatically. Just "plug" the scanner into the computer's connection and it will be installed and you can "play" with your new toy right away. You do not even need to reboot your computer.

Today, I probably should not have to explain what hardware or software is. However, I once heard that a writer's job should include explaining terms in order to make the book more useful. I am to share with you what they are. Hardware is the hard part of the machine, the device itself. Software is the program that instructs the device what to do. The software is the program and it is installed on the disks that comes with the scanner.

You connect the device, turn it on and plug it into an operating computer. The operating system will search for the installation disk or Windows installation software. Just follow the steps and you should not have too many problems.

If you buy a multifunctional scanner, it is very important to read the installation guide to save you time, whether it uses either a USB or a Firewire.

➢ More About USB Connections

- Since USB is getting popular, most computers with Windows98 and the later models, Mac OS 8, will have USB connection.
- If you do not have enough USB ports, you will need to buy a USB hub. It is just like the electric extension cord with a few more outlets. A four ports USB 2.0 costs about $20.
- I suggest that you buy those with electric supply. Sometimes, some devices may need a boost of electricity.

- It is better to plug the scanner and printer directly into the computer's USB port and plug the other devices into the USB hub. The reason is: printers and scanners will draw more power than most of the other devices and even a powered USB hub may not be able to support them.
- If you have only two USB ports and you have more than two USB devices, then plug the printer into the computer's USB and let the scanner share USB port, by plug into a hub, with the other devices. A printer draws more electricity than other devices. Unless your USB hub has a power supply, it cannot support a printer.
- If it is still not working, then plug the scanner into the computer's USB hub and buy a converter for all the other devices.

Scanner Software Installation

The scanner will most likely come with a scanner driver and bundle softwares. The scanner driver is the program that instructs the scanner what to do. Bundle softwares usually include a document management program, a photo editing software and an OCR software.

If someday, somehow, you lose the driver software for the scanner or need to update the driver, go to the software download section of the manufacturer's website.

It is very important to update the driver software especially if you upgrade your operating system, such as from Windows 2000 to Windows XP. If you do not update, you can get those annoying error messages.

Be honest, if you have an older scanner for which you cannot find the driver, I will suggest that purchase another one. The improvement in scanned images and the increased scanning speed will make this purchase pay for itself. Your machine may be just too old.

Unless you really want to keep the older scanner, you can go to the following sites and try to find your drivers:

http://www.windrivers.com
http://www.drivershq.com
http://www.driverzone.com
http://www.driverguide.com
http://www.mrdriver.com

Visit www.MrSystem.com and you will have all these website available to you at your finger tip. In addition, I update the page regularly. You will always have the latest technology updates.

Installation of the driver and the bundle software is very straightforward and you can follow the directions of the scanner software.

However, if your bundle software does not include PaperPort, then you will have to buy it. This is the brain of the Document Management System for your Highly Efficient Office.

Let's talk about the document management program.

CHAPTER 5

Select And Setup Your Document Management Software

****

In this chapter, you will learn:
  - ➢ **My Choice Of Document Management Software: PaperPort**
  - ➢ **Disadvantages of PaperPort**
  - ➢ **Advantages of PaperPort**
  - ➢ **Install PaperPort**
  - ➢ **Basic Desktop Structure Of PaperPort**
  - ➢ **Page View Window Of PaperPort**

****

To build a DMS (Document Management System), you need two major components. You need a scanner with document feeder, and a document management software.

There are not many paper management software options for the general public or small business solution without spending thousands of dollars in consultation fees and a tremendous upgrade in your computer system.. There are only a handful of paper management software, such as PaperPort, Caere PageKeeper, and Acrobat Filler, etc. The one I will use to illustrate is a widely used document system: PaperPort.

My Choice Of Document Management Software: PaperPort

I use it because it is a simple and easy way to manage documents. With the help of its intuitive desktop design, it is very easy for anyone to learn and shorten the training time for your office personnel. Another reason is the compatibility of this software with other commonly used softwares like MS Word, Excel, Access, Outlook, Lotus note, and WinFax Pro.

You should buy Deluxe 9.0 or Pro Office versions. It is because these two versions allow you scan documents directly into PDF files. PDF is the most widely used format to share files around the world. This is because PDF is relatively small, keep the image unchanged, and everybody can use a PDF viewer, which is widely distributed without fees, to view the files.

The list price of their version 9.0 is only $99.95 and the pro office version is $199.99. The major different is that the Pro version can convert some major business documents, such as MS Word, Excel into PDF image. If you are going to buy a new scanner, the package may include PaperPort LE version. You can use it for a while until you know which full version will suit you better. You then can easily get the upgraded version cheaper by surfing the Internet.

Disadvantages Of PaperPort

With the low price and versatility of PaperPort, you also get limitations.

- **No access control.** PaperPort does not come with an access control function. In addition, there is no trail record of access. Therefore, the software is better suited for home or small workgroups rather than a large office that may need more security and access control. However, in a small business environment, you cannot limit your administrative assistants' access for her to help you effectively. Therefore, this limitation should not be a major concern. In addition, to help you to build a DMS system, I will show you how to set up access privileges for different users in your computer with the built-in administrative tools from Windows. That will be the access control for your DMS.

- **ScanSoft, the manufacturer of PaperPort, only provide installation help for free.** Calling the company with questions will cost you money. However, Scansoft does have knowledge database online for you to do your own searches.

- **PaperPort only works with PC.** Sorry Mac users. There is not much I can do.

The importance of DMS is the potential for a seamless transformation from paper documents into digital formats. Digital format, so far, is the most effective and efficient way to manage most information.

Advantages of PaperPort

➤ Intuitive Desktop Pane To Keep You Organized

PaperPort is an excellent solution for archiving because it offers flexibility in a storage and viewing system.

Once you like a folder to PaperPort, you can view almost every formats of documents in thumbnails. It is easy to retrieve. PaperPort is network ready and you can share the folder with other users in the office.

➤ Easy Scan And Capture

PaperPort works with a large range of scanners. You can scan your documents with any TWAIN or WIA scanners. PaperPort also has it is own printer drivers to convert the format of the document images. In addition, there is a web capturing function that will help you store web pages.

➤ Save In Versatile Formats

It is a very important to decide in what kind of format you are going to save your result images. Of course, you can save the scanned image in PaperPort's proprietary MAX format. However, you can also save it in other popular and universal formats, such as PDF and Jpeg.

Personally, I avoid propriety formats like MAX or FXR for archive. It is an especially important issue when your business is developing. You do not want your software to dictate what kind of system you are going to use in the future. You also need to consider the size of the image that your are going to save, should you convert the original images. For all your text images, I prefer PDF. If you have graphic documents, JPEG should be a good choice.

➤ Easy Indexing And Easy Retrieval

After all the hard work you put into scanning your paper documents into computer, you probably would like to retrieve your documents. PaperPort has a very intuitive desktop view to help you organize and manage your documents.

- **Colored folders.** You can simply use different colored digital folders to classify the kind of information you store.

- **Adding search criteria.** Besides the title, you can add other search criteria retrieval, such as keyword, author, etc.

- **Context search.** PaperPort calls it a simple search. Actually, PaperPort will use its OCR technology to recognize every document. When you use a simple search, you can call up the database and find the keywords that you are looking for INSIDE a document.

➤ Intuitive Managing And Editing Document

You can use the folder option on your desktop and see all the colored folders. On the other hand, its intuitive approach also creates thumbnails of each of your documents. You can retrieve the document just by double clicking on the thumbnails and individual windows will open. There are documents and graphic editing tool bars for you to add annotation or edit of the images.

There are a few different versions of PaperPort on the market. The prices are quite different also.

Unless you prefer to save your MS Word document, Excel spreadsheet directly in PDF, you probably would not spend $100 for that feature in PaperPort Pro 9. Even if you want to save them to PDF, you can use Deluxe 9.0 to print the file into PDF files.

If this is your first document management software, I will suggest you to buy the PaperPort Deluxe 9.

If your scanner comes with PaperPort LE or your have an older version, you get PaperPort Deluxe 9 upgrade that will save you $30.

	PaperPort Deluxe 9	**PaperPort Pro 9 Office**
Street Price	$99.99	$199.99
Upgrade version	$69.99	$149.99
Scan directly to PDF	YES	YES
Edit PaperPort Created PDF	YES	YES
Annotation on JPEP, TIFF,	YES	YES
Create PDF from MS Office Directly	NO	Directly

Table 5.1 Comparison of Versions of PaperPort

Install PaperPort

➤ Where To Buy Your Software

You can order from ScanSoft directly by going to its website or other shopping sites like www.pricewatch.com.

Of course, you can also support your local stores, but software is a universal product. For the same product, let price be the determinate factor.

➤ Avoid The Traps Of Installation

Now, the time has come. Installation of PaperPort is a simple and straightforward process and I will assume that you can take care of that yourself. However, here are a few remarks about installation.

If you are using Windows NT, 2000, XP, you need to log in with the administrative privileges.

You should close all the other programs running, especially the anti-virus program, to ensure a smooth installation.

Now, you can start the installation process and put the CD-ROM into the drive. Mostly, the installation should start automatically, if it does not, then click Start > Run> d: Setup.exe (or whatever is the name of your CD-ROM drive). When you first start PaperPort, it will populate its Send To Bar with the software compatible to itself.

The Basic Desktop Structure Of PaperPort

The desktop is divided into two windows: the Desktop Window and the Page Window. Inside the Desktop Window are two panels and four bars; the Page Window has two sidebars. Let us talk about the Desktop Window.

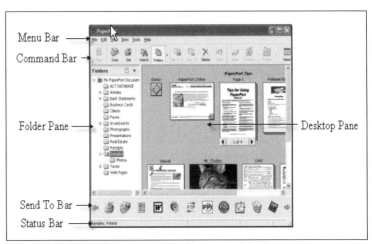

Figure 5.1 Desktop Window PaperPort

➢ Desktop Window

It is the default window when PaperPort starts.

- **Menu bar.**
  Just like the menu bar for any window program, this lists all the functions in the pull down menu.

- **Command Bar.**
  This is divided in the Desktop/page window view; from the scan to the folder button are the controls for the Left pane, the further button controls the items in the right pane.

- **Send to bar.**
  PaperPort is a basic paper document management program and sometimes it is necessary to use other programs to work on the image. In that case, you can use PaperPort as a conduit between the image and the other programs. PaperPort will link to all these programs and populate this bar automatically when you first use it.

  PaperPort works with a wide range of programs that includes spreadsheet, word-processing, graphic, Online services, e-mail, fax, etc. This is the linkage between PaperPort and other common Windows software like Word, Excel, Quicken, Act, etc. All you need to do is pull the icon from the right pane (desktop pane) to the icon in the "Send To Bar"..

- **The Status bar.**
  You can have a quick look at the information of the selected folder, items, or button in both panes.

- **Left Panel/Folder Pane, Scan, Get, or Search Pane, depending on what you pick**
  Here you can choose the scanner to scan, get the digital image from the digital camera, search the files by different criteria and list the folder visually.

- **Right Panel/Desktop Pane**
  You can choose how to look at you files. The thumbnail view is a very powerful tool.

You can choose how to look at you files. The thumbnail view is a very powerful tool.

Page View Window Of PaperPort

If you click any item (a document or graphic image), this will bring up the page window for the file manipulation. The item will be in the middle of the window for enlargement or reduction.

Figure 5.2 Page View Window

> **Left Toolbar/ Annotation Toolbar.**
> There are two tool bars on the side of the Page Window. The left one is the Annotation Toolbar, mainly for text documents, and you can use high lighting, text, posted notes, handwriting, arrows and stamps on the image just as if you would with your paper document. All of these are visuals too.

> **Right Toolbar/ Image Editing Toolbar.**
> This tool bar is on the right hand side of the Page Window. You can rotate, crop, sharpen, erase, etc. You can perform basic touch ups on the graphic image.

Now you have the scanner and software of the Document Management System (DMS) The rest of this part is going to discuss how to setup the system and the procedure operate your scanner.

CHAPTER 6

Build A Digital Cabinet

****

In this chapter, you will learn:

- ➤ **Get The Documents Ready**
- ➤ **Create a Mother of All Business Folders**
- ➤ **4D Workflow System**
- ➤ **Basic Indexing System I: Folders & Files**
- ➤ **Build Your Assistants' Digital Trays**
- ➤ **Move The Existing Files And Folder Into The Office Data Folder**
- ➤ **Basic Indexing System II: Content Indexing**
- ➤ **Basic Indexing System III: More Indexing**
- ➤ **Organize Your Filing System In The Simple Ways**
- ➤ **Retrieve Files If You Know Where It Is**
- ➤ **Search Of My Beloved, But Lost Files In PaperPort Folder**
- ➤ **Search Of My Beloved But Lost Files In ???**
- ➤ **Organize The Paper Documents**

****

Have you ever get frustrated because you were not able to find a piece of document. It may be the document that you saw somewhere in the office but you just not able to find it.

With the DMS, you may index them in different criteria such as file name, author, keyword, etc. You can also keep the original image of the document and ask the software to 'read' the image. Later, you can search the file by it's content! However, the first one you need to do is organize and categorize all you existing documents.

You can also imagine: you are moving from one office to another one. You will spare the space and put the cabinets into the new office, then, you move your files, box by box, into the cabinets. The same ideas apply when you move from the paper to digital filings system. The difference is that your files are moved from a physical cabinet into a digital folder. You need to arrange and file your digital documents as you would your paper files. Even with the DMS, you still need to organize the files to make your office run smooth.

Get The Documents Ready

I like to suggest my client to have some boxes ready. The paper should be divided into four categories:

- **Original document is required**
  I don't think any body would like to throw away their Birth Certificate, Diploma or Deed, etc. You may need to file these documents again but it should not be the bulk of your cabinets

- **To be scanned**
  Well, it will takes some time to scan these document. My suggestion is put the boxes at some where irritate yourselves and forces yourself to get it done.

- **To be shredded**
  The documents with personal information and shredding is required for security purpose

- **Discard**
  These are the box usually make my clients very hesitate if they should throw that away. If you do hesitate, just keep them in the To Be Scanned boxes.

  A question usually come up in the process is how long should keep the documents?

  This question originated from the paper file concept. This question does matter for you to setup the digital image because your need to know which documents you can throw away without scan.

  However, after you setup the digital imaging system, you should not worry about when you should delete the image files. It is because image usually occupy a small portion of your hard drive space, you really don't need to worry about when to delete them.

The following is a simple chart of how long you should keep various document to help you decide which your documents needed to be thrown away. However, you better check with your accountants and attorney to decide your own unique needs.

Documents	Length of require storage
Tax return	Forever
Tax Return Supporting document	Examples are: Receipts, home improvement documents, 6 years after the file date
Contract	7 years after the contract has expired
Insurance Record	4 years after expiration
Mortgage records	3 years after the home is paid off

Actually in a digital imaging system, how long to keep a digital document is not quite important as it there any reasons that you HAVE TO keep the paper document. It really depends on the regulation in your industry.

Create The Mother of All Business Folders

The first steps in building your DMS is to decide where you would like to file your document images and give office personnel access to the digital files in a more productive manner.

The filing system should provide different methods of searching. The key is, those who retrieve and manage the files must easily understand the filing system. If every one is very used to and comfortable with the filing system that is used in the office currently, then the easiest transition will be to keep the current filing system and use it when converting to the DMS.

It is human nature for people to resist change. If the DMS resembles the current filing system, your staff will not resist this new method of filing because it is similar to the old way of filing paper. Filing your DMS in the same manner as you would your old paper files will cause less problems and confusion among workers; it also requires less training. This will increase the likelihood that your staff will use the DMS on a regular and consistent basis; the new system will be a success

I will use the terms file/ image/ item interchangeable throughout the book. To avoid confusion, file is usually any existing item in a folder. An image is the scanned document or pictures. An item is any files, or images that are put into the document management software.

Before you file any document, you need a cabinet. The computer system is just like the filing you have with your cabinet. You need to find a place to put the files in first.

One of the key concepts in Highly Efficient Office is centralization of data. You do not want everyone to have their own filing systems; you want to have a centralized system so that you can avoid a potential disaster.

You will be better off if you had a computer that would act like a server in a client/server system; you should store all your data in this computer. The computer with the stored data could be yours or someone who acts as the administrator in the office. I understand that could be you, owner always works harder. You need to create a folder titled, or something similar to, "Office Data".

If you already have a centralized filing system in your computer, you do not need to create one. If you do not have one yet, it will be better for you to build a centralize data folder for your office. It will be easier to retrieve, manage, and backup data.

You can create the "Office Data" folder anywhere you want to as long as it is in the hard drive and every body in the office know about that. "My Documents" is a good choice. A lot of people would like to put their documents in "My document". The Window operating system also assumes that you will put your important information into this folder. This is where Windows has built in default folders like My ebook, My movie, etc. It is pretty convenient to put all your company's folders in here. When you back up the data, you should back up My Document, My favorite, Cookies. However, the location of My Document folder is different in Window 98/ME and Window 2000/ XP.

In Window 98/ME, there is no user log in and "My Documents" folder is located in the C drive. The path is:

- C:\"My Documents"\

In Window 2000/ XP, the path will be different. It is because the Window is ready for a network and the folders are prearranged according to each user. Your My Document folder is under your user folders. The folder path should looks like this:

- C:\Setting and Documents\Your user name\My document

There are three stages to create this master folder; in our case, we name it Office Data. All other folders can be stored in this master folder.

I. Create an "Office Data" folder in the My Document folder.

II. Link the "Office Data" folder to PaperPort and it will become a PaperPort folder.

III. Link the Office Data folder to your staff 's PaperPort programs in their computers for the purpose of centralization.

(You can really choose wherever you like to create this Office Data file in the computer, you may even use the My Document folder as your master folder. You just need to keep that in mind I create an Office Data folder inside My Document folder in this book.)

➢ **I. Create an Office Data folder in My Document folder**
  1. Double click on "My Computer" in Window's desktop.
  This will open up a window, which shows the C drive and other   equipments that you have.

  2. Double click C: (name of your hard drive)
  This brings up all the folders in the C: drive

3. **If you use Window 98, click on the "My Documents" folder icon. If you use Window 2000/XP, click Documents and Settings/ your user name/ "My Documents".**
This will bring up the "My Documents" folder.

Figure 6.1 User's Folder in Window

4.**Click on the "My Documents" folder icon**
This will bring you into the "My Documents" folder.

Figure 6.2   My Document folder

5. Click menu bar File/ New and name the new folder "Office Data"

Figure 6.3 Create A New Folder in My Document

Figure 6.4 Creating "Offices Data" folder in My Document folder

6. Share the "Office Data folder" with other people in the office. Right click the Office Data folder and select

Figure 6.5 Share the Office Data folder

7. Go to the Sharing Tab and check both box of "Share this folder on the network" and "Allow network users to change my files"

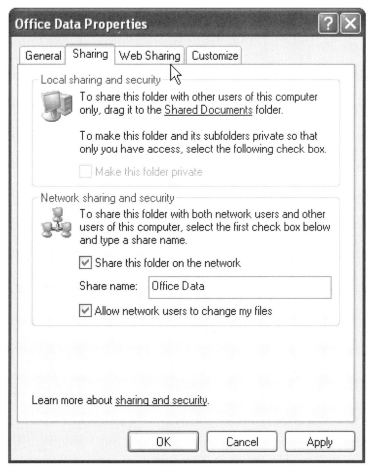

Figure 6.6 Share the Office Data folder and allow changes made

After you create a master folder, "Office Data", you then need to link that to PaperPort and "Office Data" becomes a PaperPort Folders. PaperPort Folders are the folders listed in the folder pane. All of these folders are linked to the PaperPort for document management only. We did not move its physical location in the drive when we "add" it to PaperPort.

➤ II. Link the Office Data Folder To PaperPort And Become a PaperPort Folder

1. **Click the PaperPort icon in the desktop to start PaperPort or click Start/Programs/Scansoft PaperPort/ PaperPort.**
   (If the right panel is not the Folder Panel, click the Folder icon in the menu bar.)
   This brings up the PaperPort Folder pane.

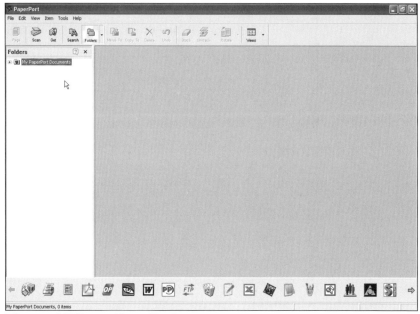

Figure 6.7 PaperPort Desktop

2. Click Tools>PaperPort Folders
This bring up the PaperPort Folders dialog box

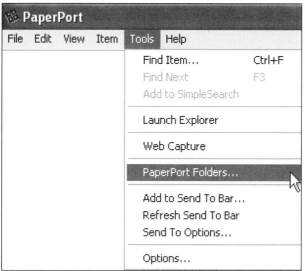

Figure 6.8 Go to PaperPort Folders Window

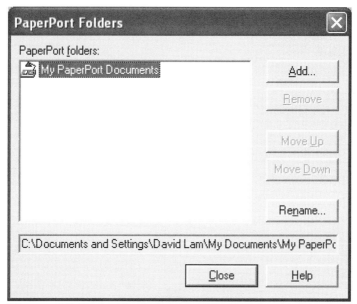

Figure 6.9 PaperPort Folder Window

3. Click on the Add button

This bring up the Browse for Folder window. Go to Your user names document/ Office Data folder

Figure 6.10 Browse to the Office Data folder

4. Click OK.

You should see that the Folder Panel has added the "Office's Data" folder.

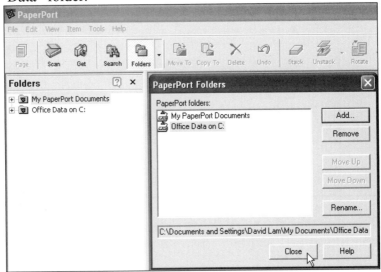

Figure 6.11 Link Office Data folder into PaperPort Folder

➤ **III. Link the Office Data folder to your staff 's PaperPort programs in their computers**

1. Install PaperPort in each computer you want it to have access of "Office Data" folder and then following the instruction.

2. Start/Programs/Scansoft PaperPort/ PaperPort
   This brings up the PaperPort Folder pane.

2. Click Tools>PaperPort Folders
   This bring up the PaperPort Folders dialog box

3. Click on the Add button, double click on the "My Network Neighborhood" or "My Network Places" to find the "Office Data" folder in the main computer. If you get an error message that states that you cannot access the folder, you need to go back to the main computer. You then find the "Office Data" folder, right click on it and this will allow the folder to be shared.

You need to repeat the process until each computer has an "Office Data" folder in their PaperPort Folder pane. You only need to complete the process once on each computer. If you add any subfolders into this folder, they will be automatically detected.

When you finish adding an "Office Data" folder onto PaperPort of all the computers, you need to move all of the data folders into this master folder. You can create new folders in the "Office Data" folder or you can simply drag the existing folders into the "Office Data" folder. I explain how to do this in the next section.

Workflow System

With the traditional document management system, we usually have In Tray, Out Tray and WIP (Work In Process). You can still use the same concept and do it with the computer. However, first of all, you must decide what you need to do with the incoming documents. There is a simple way to prioritize the administration work by divide them into four categories.

Prioritize your documents:
1. Discard
   Throw these documents away

2. **Delegate** (if you have assistant)
   After you scan or convert this type of documents into digital formats, drag and drop them into your assistant's 'Do It Now' or 'Do It Later' folders according to the urgency. Use the note pad function of PaperPort to instruct your assistant to file or scan, etc. One very important task for your assistant or yourself is sending request to all the outside companies to send you eStatements instead of paper statements. If you are by yourself, these documents should be put into your **Do It Later** folder.

3. **Do It Later**
   Important work but not quite urgent and you can do it later. After you reduce these document into digital formats, save them in the Do It Later folder in PaperPort

4. **Do It Now**
   Those works that you need to it yourself and you better do it quick. Put it into the Do It Now Folder in PaperPort.

Folder to be created in PaperPort:
1 **WIP**
2 **Do It Now**
3 **Do It Later**

I put number before the name of the files, so that, they will be arranged in the order of number, or the urgency I assigned. With PaperPort, you can easily check the status of the files into your own folders or your assistants' folders.

Basic Indexing System I: Folders & Files

There is a saying in Chinese, "Prevention measures will be better than the remedy."

If you could organize the files and folders better, you may not even need to use the search functions of PaperPort. A well thought out designed DMS and procedure should be able to prevent your office from losing documents again.

Basic and simple usually work the best, especially in the small business area. In business, files are usually kept in a certain folder, in a certain drawer, and in a certain cabinet. To make the digital transition as smooth as possible, the DMS should be able to duplicate the paper filing system with multiple levels of grouped folders.

The easiest way to build a file system that your staff will not reject is to get them involved in the building process. Here's how you can go about building a system together: Ask your staff to meet you at the main computer in a peer-to-peer network; or your sever in a client/server network. You should get input from each staff member, and create a system that works well for you and your staff. Remember to get every staff input so they feel that this filing system is theirs also; this will help them embrace the new system instead of rejecting it.

➢ **Add a sub folder to the "Office Data" folder.**
  1. **Start PaperPort and go to the Folder pane in the computer where the "Office Data" resides.**

  2. **Right click on the "Office Data" folder and select New Folder**
     This bring up the New Folder dialog box.

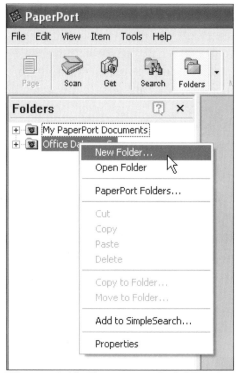

Figure 6.12 Create a sub folder in Office Data folder

3. Type in the name of your sub folder

You can name the new folder accordingly and choose the color of the folders.

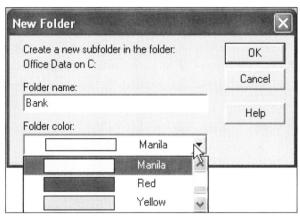

Figure 6.13 New Folder dialog box

To create a subfolder of the sub folder, all you have to do is right click on the folder you want the subfolder to be under, and select New Folder. You can now design a folder system so that you can categorize your folders and files, such as tax, bank, finance, etc.

Figure 6.14 Create a sub folder in a sub folder

Build Your Assistants' Digital Trays

If you have a few assistants and each of them has their own traditional In Tray, Out Tray and Work In Process Tray, I will suggest you to build the same tray system in Office Data folder. You first create each person's folder under the Office Data folder and put a number in front of each person's folder. The reason of putting a number in front of the name is that you always has the person's folders at the top the folder hierarchy and easier to find and supervise.

After that, you create the tray folder for each person. You can use color coding for different folder. Work In Process probably deserve a bright red color. Your filing system may look like this:

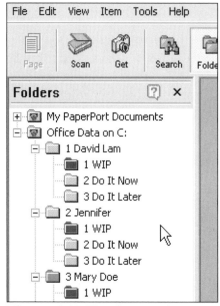

Figure 6.15 The folder hierarchy

Move The Existing File Or Folders To "Office Data" Folder

It is a very important step to centralize your files and it will make the back up steps much easily. The most intuitive way of doing it is to split the computer screen and do the drag and drop.

1. Click on the My Computer icon in the Windows desktop Locate and open Office Data folder, then resize the window to half of the screen.

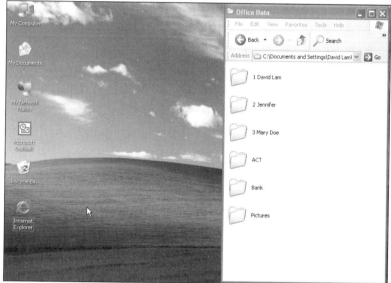

Figure 6.16 Resize PaperPort to occupy half of the screen.

2. Right click Start button

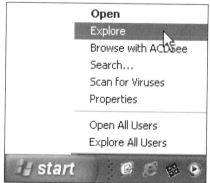

Figure 6.17 Right click the Start button

3. Select Explore and open the Window Explorer
Resize the Window Explorer window to half of the computer screen

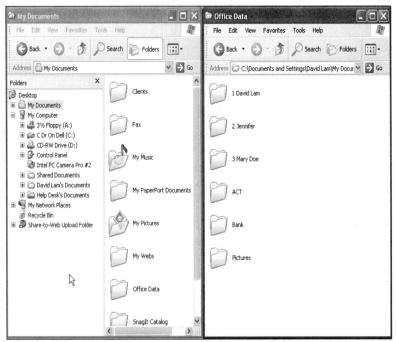

Figure 6.18 Split the computer screen

4. You can use the Window Explorer window to search for all your office files, folder and database into the Office Data folder.

It is a very important to the paperless operation because we can centralize all the data into one single location, in this case, the Office Data folder.

After you complete this step, you can go back and use color coding to differentiate between the folders.

Some of my clients asked me why I did not simply put all the office folders and files into My PaperPort Documents folder that is created automatically during installation. Why should I create anther folder call "Office Data" folder.

There are a couple of reasons for this step.

1. I am not obligate to use PaperPort folder. I don't need to move my folders if I change the document management software. I will not risk the mistake to erase my database if I need to uninstalled PaperPort.

2. It could be confusing for the office personnel if I use My PaperPort folder. It is because every computer has its own My PaperPort Document Folder. I want the main computer or the server has the only Office Data folder. (or any name of the folder of your choice)

Basic Indexing System II: Content Indexing

"Simple Search Indexing" is a very useful powerful tool in PaperPort. What it does is that PaperPort will "read", OCR (Optical Character Recognition) function, all the index fields and contents of files that could be either texts or graphic images. It will not change the image files, such as PDF, but build a meta data table that you will not see. Then, we can search the files by the different index fields and the contents of the files. It will pull up a list of result and

Simple search actually will put the text into its metadata and will match your search criteria.

The warning is: In the beginning, this is going to take a long time for the computer to "read" all your documents if you have a few years of paper files scanned into your computer. Fortunately, you can do the simple search update automatically.

After you install PaperPort and move the entire business files, folder and database into the "Office's Data" folder, you could execute the simple search update on the whole folder and let it run for the whole night. The benefit is that the entire document will be 'read' and recognized. We can then search for the files by the content and the name of the file. You do need to do the Simple Search for every computer in the office. Fortunately, the whole process is automatic but just take time.

➤ Start Manual Update

This is what you need to do in the very first beginning. After you move all your files and folders into the Office Data folder, you need to OCR the whole folder once. That will allow you to search your file by content.

1. Highlight the folder you want to perform Simple Search Update, OCR (in the very first beginning, that is the Office Data folder).

Figure 6.19 Select the folder to perform SimpleSearch Update

2. Go to the Command Bar and click the "Search" icon
This brings up the Search Panel

3. Check the box of Use SimpleSearch index. If you do not see the Update Index box, expand the select by clicking the double allow sign. (The Search functions above are not relevant when you perform a update)
This will bring up the Update Index box

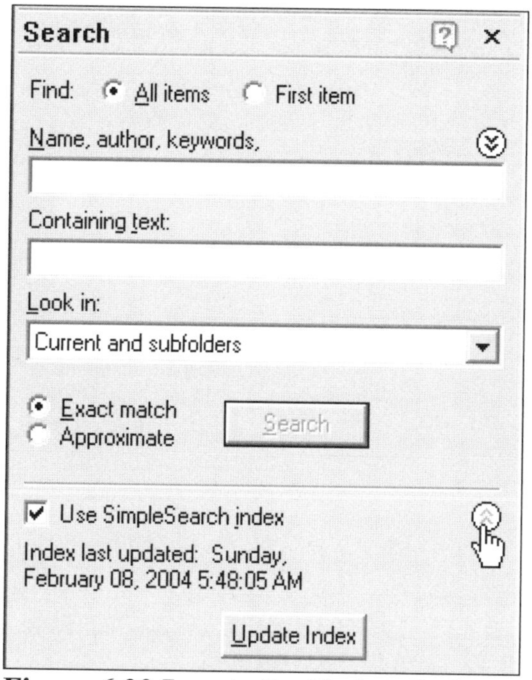

Figure 6.20 Locate the Update Index box

4. Click the Update Index box.
This will start the SimpleSearch update and that will take a long while for the first time. I would suggest that you do it in the evening and leave the computer run for the whole night.

➤ Set Up an Automatic Update Of Simple Search Index

It is the most convenient way to update your PaperPort content search database after you finished update the whole Office Data folder

1.Go to the menu bar and click Tools / Options
This bring up the PaperPort Options window

2. Go to the Search tab and check the box of "Automatically Add Any New or Modified Item".
You can change the default period form 15 minutes to any interval that you need. It will be able to update the thumbnails of the item too. Check the box of "Refresh item thumbnails while updating"

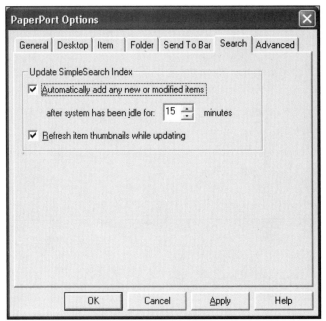

Figure 6.21 PaperPort Options

➢ Add a Folder Of Simple Search Database

When you add a new folder of document and you want PaperPort to 'read' the folder right away and add to SimpleSearch database. There is a very simple way.

1. Right click on the Folder in the Folder Panel and choose "Add to Simple Search".

You may want to add a file Simple Search database. You can execute the following:

➢ Add Files To SimpleSearch Database

Simply right click on the files in the Folder Panel and choose "Add To Simple Search" and PaperPort will add it automatically.

Basic Indexing System III: More Indexing

Depending on your business and your purpose of setting DMS, your file should have a few options of indexing for easy access and retrieval later. In PaperPort Deluxe 9, you have more than just the file name to index the images and documents.

You can assign different properties to the items in PaperPort and then use those properties as search criteria to retrieve the item in PaperPort. The item properties included

1. Page name
2. Author
3. Keywords
4. Comments

If you want to check out the properties of Mr. Chubs, just right click the thumbnails and click Properties.

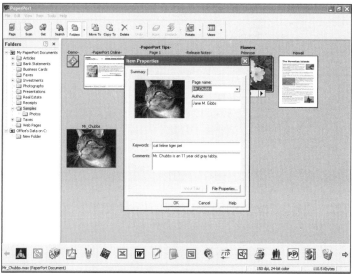

Figure 6.22 Setup file Properties

We will discuss indexing images later.

KISS

Although there are many ways that you can index the folder and files in PaperPort, my suggestion is KEEP IT SIMPLE and I won't explain the last S.

I found the most effective and efficient way is transferring the paper filing system into the digital format. Grouping the folders and files together is still the easier and the most sensible. For example, you can use a folder called Clients and save all the clients' information into this folder. You can create a sub folder for each client and name each client folder in the format of Last name, First name. It just works like the paper folders.

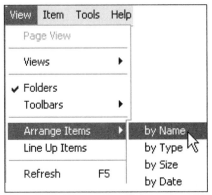

Fig. 5.23 View the folder by different criteria

After all the work in installing the scanner and building a digital filing system, you need to work on the new system for a while to get used to it. I promise you that in the long run, you will save time, save money and you will have more free time and still make great money. It is because you increase productivity in your office by many folds with low cost technology.

I will show you how to work with the digital image in the later chapters.

Organize You Filing System In The Simple Ways

PaperPort is great in organizing documents because of its intuitive approach. You do what your do before but just on the screen now. With the thumbnails in the Desktop Pane and the Folder pane, you can move the files easily between folders.

Let say your assistant just finished a file and she want you to confirm some changes, she can simply drag and drop move the file into your folder. She can even help your to prioritize by dropping either into '2 Do It Now' or '3 Do It Later' folders.

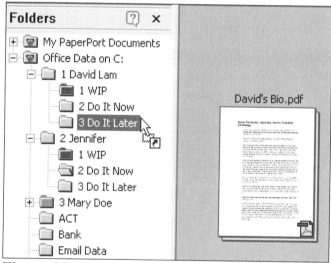

Figure 6.24 Drag and drop document

Beside that, you can also use color to make organizing a little bit easier. Let say you want to make WIP folder red. To do this, you need to do the followings.

1. Right Click on the folder that you want to change color

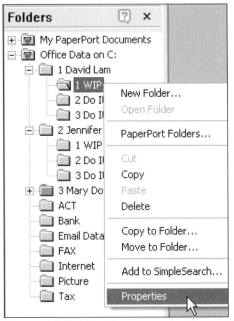

Figure 6.25 Folder pane in PaperPort

2. Select Properties

This brings up the Folder properties dialog box. You can also change the name of the folder. Then, pull down the menu to select a color check OK.

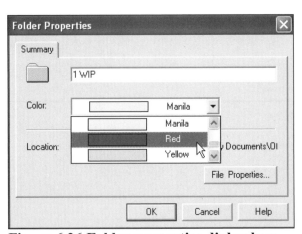

Figure 6.26 Folder properties dialog box

You can also arrange the folders in the PaperPort Desktop with a few keystrokes.

1. Right click anywhere on the PaperPort desktop
This will bring up the mini menu

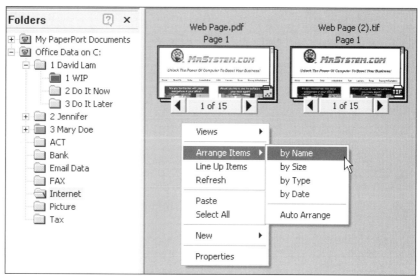

Figure 6.27 PaperPort Desktop

2. Click on the Arrange Item and select the way you would like the thumbnails to be arranged.
You can arrange the thumbnails By Name, By Size, By Type or By Date. PaperPort will rearrange the thumbnails in a neat order; from top to the bottom and from left to right. Personally, I like the thumbnails to be arranged by Name and I name my clients' folder by their last name first, i.e. Lam David.

How to arrange file by date:

When I scan documents and arrange them by date, I will put the year first, then the month and the date. The file names look like this: 2004 01 01. Therefore, even if I arrange the desktop by name; the thumbnail will be arranged in the order of time.

Don't have time to do all the scan?

There are mega office supply like Staples or Office Depot could do that for you. That will cost you about five cents a page to scan. They can scan the whole stack of paper into a single PDF file. Then, you can convert the file into PaperPort PDF file and sort the files into different folders.

1. Create the folders that you need in PaperPort to categorize the files.

2. Save the PDF files into the new folder in one of the PaperPort folder

3. Use Acrobat Reader to open PDF file by right click the file and select Open.

4. Print it to PaperPort Black & White (This will create a PaperPort PDF file that can sort very easily on the screen)

5. Right click the big PDF file and select Unstack. You then can sort the file page by page into different files.

Retrieve Files If You Know Where It Is

Have you or your staff ever lost paper documents and tried to locate it for hours? If you build a good DMS, you will find it rather easy to look for any digital documents and you do not need to sweat and suffer from the agony of searching for misplaced documents. Highly Efficient Office system could be your lifesaver in that sense.

Retrieve files should be a matter of clicks if you have a good filing system. Let say I want to read my bio in my In Tray folder:

Retrieve Files If You Know Where It Is

Have you or your staff ever lost paper documents and tried to locate it for hours? If you build a good DMS, you will find it rather easy to look for any digital documents and you do not need to sweat and suffer from the agony of searching for misplaced documents. Highly Efficient Office system could be your lifesaver in that sense.

Retrieve files should be a matter of clicks if you have a good filing system. Let say I want to read my bio in my In Tray folder:

1. Start up PaperPort by clicking Start/ Programs/ Scansoft PaperPort/ PaperPort

2. Click Folder in the Command Bar

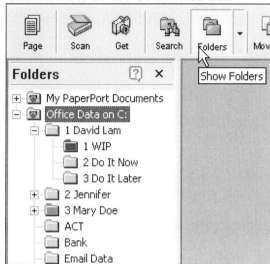

Figure 6.28 Click the Folder button

3. Click the +sign and expand Office Data folder if it is not expand, or simple the folder that store your files

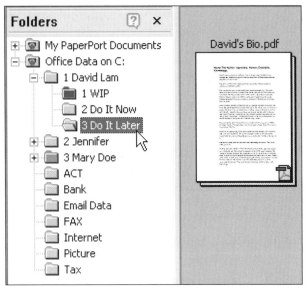

Figure 6.29 Click the folder that you saved your files

OK. So much for the easy and obvious. How about if you forget where you put your files? The worst scenario is that you do not even put it in the My Document Folder! That means it is out of the PaperPort. The files that you want to find now is somewhere in the hard drive. Let us start to search the file in the PaperPort first.

Search Of My Beloved, But Lost Files In PaperPort Folder

Life is beautiful until problems show up at the door. Unfortunately, problems never come alone. Most of the time, you or your staff misfile because the business is too busy. You filed the documents in a rush and then you forgot where you put it. That mistake will take you more time to correct than if you could do it right the first time. My first advice is, no matter how busy you are, stay cool and you will get things done more efficiently. If you don't have time to do it right, you will have even less time to correct it either. Luckily, with the Highly Efficient Office system and the Window operating system, you can locate your missing files with much less effort when comparing the process to the paper filing system.

How to search really depends on how bad the situation is and what kind of format you saved the document in. If it is a image file and you did fill in the property box, you can use name, authors, keywords, or comments search to find it. If this is a text document and you have already used Simple Search once on the PaperPort Folders, you can even use Content text search. You can also choose all or a specific folder to look into. Since you lost the files and you probably forgot the name and format of the file, I will suggest that you search with names, authors, keywords and comments first. If there is no match, then fill some keywords in the Containing Text. You will better off to search all the PaperPort Folder and use Approximate index searching.

Since I suggest that you save every file under Office Data in My Document and put it under the PaperPort's Simple Search function in the earlier chapters, that is the place we should start the search.

1. Start PaperPort program

2. Click the Folder button in the Command Bar
High light the Office Data Folder

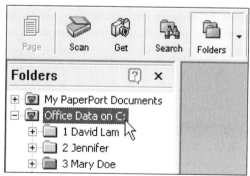

Figure 6.30 High light the Office Data folder

3. Click the Search icon in Command Bar
This brings up the Search Pane

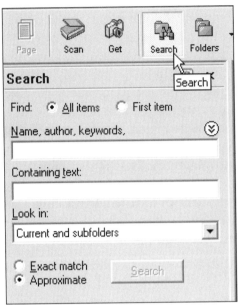

Figure 6.31 Search Pane

4. Type in the search criteria and select Current folder and subfolder, if you are not sure the name of the file, use Approximate search

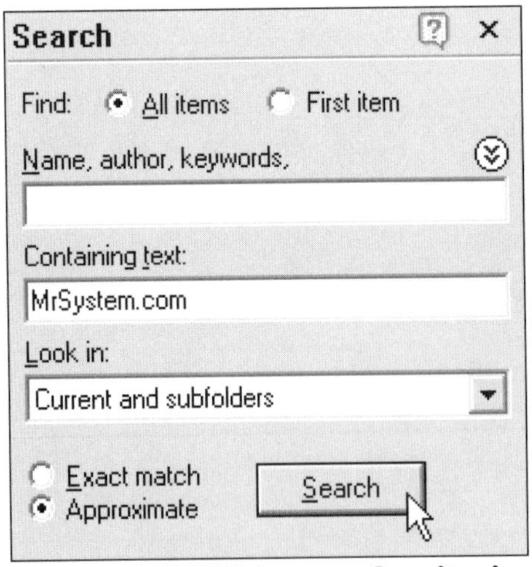

Figure 6.32 Fill in search criteria

5. Click on the Search Box

>   The search research result will be on the PaperPort desktop.
>   Click the file you want and that brings you to the file

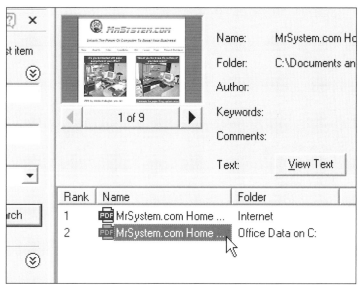

Figure 6.33 Click the file to want

Search Of My Beloved But Lost Files In ???

Have you ever lost a document and the whole office has to stop everything to locate that important document? It could be quite painful, couldn't it? However, with the Highly Efficient Office system, you will not need to stop the normal operation of your business again. It is because you save the document digitally in your hard drive and you can get great help in locating files right in your computer. After you search for the file in Office Data but in vain, you can search the file in the whole hard drive. There is a built in search engine in the Window operating system. However, this function is limited to file names; and content search for basic word, spreadsheet and database files. It does not include the content search of image files.

1. Click Start/ Search/ All files and folders

Depending on your version of Window, there will be some slight difference. This brings up the Search Companion.

Figure 6.34 Search function in Window OS

2. Type in the file name and Look In the C drive

You may have to do this a few times and use different key words to search. You need to check all drives. In the Look In box, you can change the drives to search for the files and you can go to the other hard drives to search. It may still take some time, but it will be so much better than the lost paper documents.

In the past, it may take you a few hours to locate a lost document. It only takes a few click in a Highly Efficient Office. Life just got a little bit better with Highly Efficient Office System.

Organize The Paper Documents

After you scan most of the paper document, there should not be many paper document you need to keep. However, there are always exception, like your birth certificate.

One way to keep a record of the paper is creating a electronic Paper folder in the Office Data folder to keep track your real paper.

Let say you have some applications or contracts that you need to keep for legal purpose. Simple create a folder under Office Data, name it whatever you like. You may call it Paper Document and further create subfolders to imitate the way that you have in paper files.

You can simply scan the document into this folder and file it accordingly. You can also create a empty time for keep track only.

1. **Start PaperPort by Start/All Programs/ScanSoft PaperPort 9.0/PaperPort**
   Right click on Office Data and select New Folder.

Figure 6.34 Create a new folder

2. Type in the name of the new folder, e.g.4 Paper Documents

Click OK. You just create a new folder

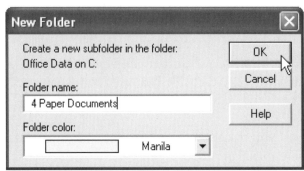

Figure 6.35 Type in the name of new folder

3. Go File/ New/ PaperPort Image Item

If you need to keep a scan the image, just use the scan function. It you just need to keep track the documents, you can create an empty item in the folder by using New/PaperPort Image Item. Type in the name of the document and click OK.

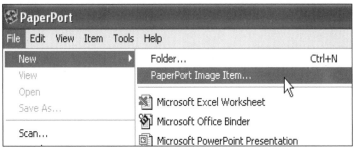

Figure 6.36 Create a empty image time

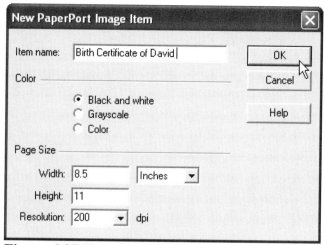

Figure 6.37 Type in the name of the document

4. Keep Track on paper document

After you build your record of the paper files, you can track the documents very easy by setting View/ Details and choose the properties of the file to view.

Figure 6.38 Select the way to view the folder

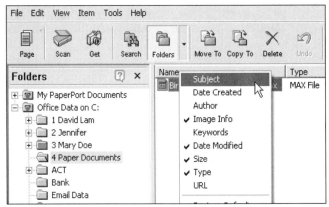

Figure 6.39 Select the properties to view the files

You can then perform a SimpleSearch Update. That will include the document in the paper files if you scan them. Now, even if you forget which paper to look for, you can use the Containing Text search to locate the paper documents.

There are more tools to explore in the PaperPort and you should a good start by now. Let us look at the further manipulation of the files just like what you usually do to the paper documents.

CHAPTER 7

Scan, Capture And Retrieve Documents

****

In this chapter, you will learn:
- ➢ **Image Formats**
- ➢ **Different Capture Methods**
- ➢ **Scan The Documents Into PaperPort**
- ➢ **Advanced Scanning**
- ➢ **The Overview Of The Scan Process**
- ➢ **Create PDF Files Without Using Acrobat**
- ➢ **Download From Digital Camera**
- ➢ **Capture And Archive Web Pages**
- ➢ **Convert File Formats**
- ➢ **Capture Images By Direct Import**

****

You, now have the scanner set up, you know what a DMS (Document Management System) is, and you know where the files should go into your computer. It is time to scan and capture whatever documents, files, magazines, and articles you need into the computer.

I will discuss the basic scan and capture function and that will solve 90% of your needs in your office. Before we start, let's discuss about what kind of format should we capture the image into.

Image Formats

I assume that you are a businessman who wants to integrate a Highly Efficient Office system into your business so that you can streamline your work; or you are a homemaker who tries to eliminate some papers. However, you still need to learn more about different formats of images. This knowledge will help you make an informed decision later on.

➤ PDF (Portable Digital Format)

It becomes the most widely used format for business to transfer and download documents. PDF is a open standard for both graphic and text. PDF is also small in size. The best feature of PDF is that it will look exactly like the original image when you convert any images to PDF. It is the best format to use when share with out side parties because most of the people will have Acrobat Reader to read this format. This is the format that I will suggest you to use for archive for text documents. PaperPort also offer Searchable PDF file. It takes a little bit longer to scan the documents but it worth the time. It is because your scanned image becomes content searchable right away. You don't need to depend on SimpleSearch update function to 'READ' the document later.

➤ PDF Searchable Image

In PaperPort, you will find a selection of PDF Searchable Image. It will have a better accuracy to recognize (ORC) the text in the document. It is especially useful if you have a lot of legal document and other content-essential documents to save and retrieve. However, it needs OmniPage Version 11 or higher as a OCR engine. In addition, it also has a larger file size compared to regular PDF.

The regular PDF format works just fine for regular user. You can update the Simple Search that in turn will perform OCR on your files.

➤ JPEG

JPEG is also a very popular format or pictures. It is the best format to use with color images, such as pictures, photo, … etc. The reason: the images are compressed and the files are small enough that they can be sent through email.

➤ MAX

MAX is a proprietary format. One important feature of PaperPort is that it is a very good conduit format to work with those format that PaperPort do not support. Second, it is the format that you can use to make type in form if you don't have OminPage.

➢ TIFF (Tagged Format)

TIFF is almost as popular as PDF; both formats are universally used. TIFF is developed by Microsoft and Aldus. With the power of Microsoft, TIFF becomes a very portable format that almost every program can accept. For text documents, it is a very good format to save for archiving. This format should not go out of style anytime soon. In addition, it is the format that some of the big document management systems use. That will help you, as your company grows, transfer your images into the higher-level document management system.

You can scan images directly into PaperPort as TIFF. However, Tiff files are not compressed and the files are very big. It could be 500MB for a page of document! There are different compression of TIFF format. The rule of thumb is: Use Group 4 for single page. Use Multi-page group 4 for multiple pages.

For archive purpose, Tiff Group 4 is good enough and it saves a lot of space in your hard drive.

➢ GIF (The Graphic Interchange Format)

This is the most popular format for Internet Graphic. It's small size offers fast transmission. It can also support animation. Since the compression only eliminate redundant data in Gif, also known as lossless compression Scheme, the finished image still has a good quality. However, it is not a regular format to save for a Highly Efficient Office. GIF is the format for building a web site.

➢ BMP (Bitmap)

Huge is the first impression of this kind of format. It is developed by Microsoft and therefore, every window base program will support this format. However, there is no compression of this format and you cannot save more than 256 colors. In regular office environment, I do not find a lot of use for this format.

➢ Suggestion

A good DMS must give you the ability to save your document for a long time. However, there are so many different formats. You should choose a format that is not endangered of extinction.

My suggestion is: that for archive purpose, you should

- Save Word , Excel, Access file in their original formats. These softwares will not go away for a long time.
- Scan text document image into PDF, or Searchable PDF formats if you have OmniPage 11 and up.
- Scan picture into JPEG format.

PDF and JPEG are choices of image formats. They are small in size and they universal standards.

Most of the corporate Document Management System use either PDF or TIFF as archive formats. In addition, more and more larger document management systems use PDF as the archive standard.

One of my very successful businessman clients once told me, business is a process of progress. To progress to the next level, we need to build an infrastructure to support the potential increase of business. To apply his principle, you help your business grow to the next level; you will alliance your system with the big boy. When you company grows, you do not need to convert all the document images. The transfer to a corporate paperless solution will be much smoother.

For color picture images, you would be better off to save them into JPEG. JPEG is the most popular and compact format for the picture files. You can save, send and even use it to print your own photo. It is also universally accepted by most of the graphic editing programs.

Now, let's discuss different methods to capture the image.

Different Capture Methods

With most other programs, you create a new file and then save the file to the folder that you choose to. In PaperPort, the logic is reverse. You have to choose which folder that you want to save the file into before you capture the image. Therefore, you will find in the instruction that I always need to decide at first which folder I want the image goes into.

The conclusion is that your are better off building an organized folder system and saving the document images into the different folders.

There are many ways to capture the documents or images into PaperPort for you to further manipulate. Then, you can view, edit, annotate, index or render, OCR and/or export into other programs to process what you want to manage.

You can capture images with or without scanning:
   I.   Scanning documents, photo, images … into the PaperPort Folder (those folders that link to PaperPort by putting them into PaperPort Folder Panel)
   II. Printing to PaperPort from other source programs
   III. Capturing directly from web page
   IV. Downloading form digital camera
   V.   Direct Importing

Scanning, downloading, direct importing, printing, and capturing are conversion processes; you are converting from one format to another.

If you can create and link your folders to the PaperPort Folders Panel, scan your documents then you will solve 80% of your problems. Therefore, we will start with the basic scanner first.

Scan The Documents Into PaperPort

Whatever scanner you use to scan images into PaperPort, you need to decide which folder you want the images to go in first.

➤ Estimate How Much Paper You Have And How Much Memory You need

Some of my clients think that they have so much paper that they many need to upgrade or even change their computers to be able to scan all the document. I can tell them hard drive space is not the usually the problem. Let me explain.

As a rule of thumb, a 25" deep cabinet can store 3000 pages. Let say if you have a 25" deep four drawer cabinet. You have

4 * 3000 = 12,000 pages

The good news is that the size of an image scan with 200 dpi is only 50KB. So that, the total memory for the cabinet is

50 KB * 12,000 = 600,000 KB

It sounds huge, right? Actually it is 600 MB of memory that you need and save it into a cd-rom without compression!

In case you are not sure about all the measurement, here is the chart:

1 GB = 1,000 MB = 1,000,000 KB

If a average size is 50KB, you can save roughly 50,000 page in one GB of memory. You can get a 80 GB (4,000,000 pages) hard drive for less than a hundred dollars! That is the reason why memory is not a problem for the small office.

➢ Prep The Scanner & Document

If you do not prepare the scanner and documents before you scan, you could damage the scanner, your system, hence your business.

- **Do not touch the glass**: In an office environment, touching the glass of a scanner is easily avoidable because most people scan documents. For home use, photo or film may post a challenge. Be honest, I will go a little further than that. If I scan my entire picture in JPEG files, I will buy a set of white gloves. The gloves will not only prevent you from touching the glass of the scanner, but also the pictures itself. Gloves are very useful especially if you have glossy pictures.

- **Clean the glass**: There was a movie call "My Big Fat Greek Wedding", in which, it eulogized the power of an all-purpose household cleaner. They even used it to spray on pimples! It may work but I have never tried it. However, I will suggest that you do not use the all-purpose cleaner to clean the glass of the scanner if you intend to keep your scanner for a while. The best cleaning solution is isopropyl alcohol available at any drug store and it only cost you 50 cents. You can use any kind of soft cloth as long as it is lint-free. When you clean the glass, please do not wipe it in a circular motion. You are not buffing your car.

- **Close the cover:** Simple. Mostly, you use the ADF (Automatic Document Feeder) anyway, why would you like to open the cover and let the glass collect dust?

- **Prep the document:** Prep the documents. Believe it or not, most bad images come from bad originals! If you have a lot of dirt or dust, they will show in the images. It is more difficult to clean in the image rather than the paper. It will make the job easier later, if you dusted the photographs. For invisible tape, if you use 300 dpi, it will not show. Secondly, unfolding or straightening up the documents will save you a lot of time. By unfolding a corner and making the paper straight, you can get a much better image result especially when you need the OCR later.

- **Put a white backdrop:** This is the most useful when you are doing a transparency copy. Just put a piece of regular, letter size, white page of paper behind the transparency and your job is done.

- **Eliminate staples:** Check the documents for staples or destroy your roller. In an office environment, especially in the initial phrase, you will scan client's files and most of the files have more than one page. That means you will use the ADF more than the flatbed. You must check for staples! The best solution for staples: total elimination. Remove the staples in the office and use clips instead. I do not mean wire paper clips; I mean the paper clips with a spring system. By using spring clips, you save time and money; spring clips are reusable. In addition, I found that the spring clip does add some agony for the assistant because it does not lie in the file stand without getting in their way. Therefore, you should try to eliminate all clips so you can get the job done QUICKER.

- **Align or you need to adjust later:** Flatbed alignment is a no brainer. I really do not see any reason for not aligning the paper. However, if the text itself is slanted, align the paper rather than trying to fix the text. PaperPort will help you align the text from the screen with very high precision. I assume that you will also align the direction of the documents, do not make it upside down, all right. The ADF is also a no brainer. In an office environment, you may feel rushed and you do not align your documents; that could be a problem. I believe the only short cut in life is "Do the right thing right at the first time" even if it may take a little bit longer to get it done. If you do not have time to do it right the first time, you certainly do not have time to do it again. That should also be one of the reasons for you to buy this book because I am going to save you a lot of time and money by getting all those painful trials and errors done for you.

➢ Beginning From Where The Images Are Going To

1. **Start PaperPort by clicking Start/ Program/ ScanSoft/ PaperPort/PaperPort OR
   click on the PaperPort icon on the desktop**
   This brings up the PaperPort Desktop. Depending on what you were working on the last time you used the software, you may see PaperPort desktop Panels, they may be Scan, Get Digital Picture, Search or Folder panel. If PaperPort is not in the Folder pane, click the Folder icon in the command bar.

2. **Highlight the folder you want the image to go into**
   I will high light the Tax subfolder for illustration purposes.

Figure 7.1 High light the folder to scan into

➤ Scan With The PaperPort Desktop

I will start all the functions of PaperPort from its Desktop. I do not usually use the function, ScanDirect; ScanDirect is a small tool bar that can be used to work the software. I do not use ScanDirect because I leave PaperPort on all the time.

For the purpose of demonstration, I use a typical business document: the bio of David Lam. This sample is a great photo of David Lam and the rest are text. I will show you how to scan it with different kinds of resolution. You should have selected the folder you want this image to go into.

1. Click the Scan icon in the Command bar
This will bring up the Scan Pane

Figure 7.2 Go to the scan function

2. Select the scanning choices from Scan Panel
If you have more than one scanner, choose the scanner of choice from the pull down menu.

Figure 7.3 Select your scan source

3. Highlight Document button and click Setting

This brings up the Setting- Dialog box. You can use the default file name or check the Custom box and type in the file name that you want.

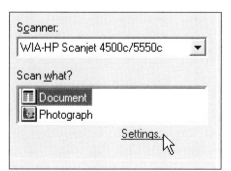

Figure 7.4 Select type of image source

4. Select the file type to scan in

This selection depends on what you want to do with the image. The rule of thumb is selecting PDF for text and JPEG for picture.

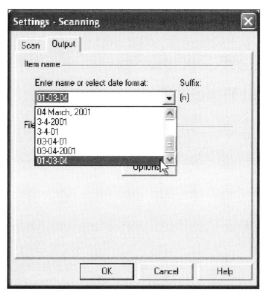

Figure 7.5 Enter name or select date format

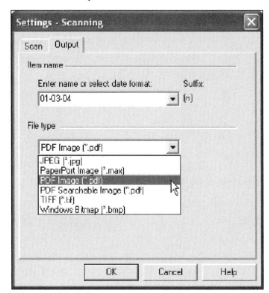

Figure 7.6 Select file type to save as

5. Click OK

This will start your scanner or the software that come with your scanner. Most likely, the scanning software will prompt for settings. There are a few settings that you need to set them right, let me share with you.

Advanced Scanning
1. Should I Prescreen?

First of all, PaperPort does not have a prescreen function, that is the function of the software that comes with your scanner. Some scanners do not have that either.

Mostly, in an office environment, you DO NOT need to prescreen it. The purpose of prescreening is to help you define the screen area. That will help you save time to scan the document if you need a high resolution scan or save the space of the hard drive. Scanners are not that smart yet. White spots on a page are still considered to be part of an image for the scanner and it still occupies space on your hard drive. I do not suggest prescreening in the office because you do not usually need a high resolution scan. For a regular archive purpose scanner, 200 dpi is good enough even for OCR later. Second, the hard drive memory now is so cheap that you can buy one GB of memory for $1.00. Third, if you have a stack of paper in one client's folder, it will not be too much fun to prescreen all of these documents.

However, for home projects like archiving your pictures, unless you have a photo scanner that will scan only the photo, then you really need to prescreen those pictures.

2. Choosing The Resolution

I assume that you are in a regular office and you work mostly with text. In that case, 200 dpi is detail enough for you to do most functions. The higher resolution you set, the longer the scanning process.

This is the resolution I will recommend for different purposes:

Common DPI	True DPI	Purpose of use
200 * XXX	200	Scan most text document
300 * XXX	300	For a better result in OCR of text document. A standard resolution for graphic archive, such as JPEG
600 * XXX		Good enough for every thing
1200 and higher		Unless you need to print a professional picture, it may be a waste of time

Table 7.1 Resolution

3. Setting the color depth
Two methods of measuring color depth.

1. Number of discrete colors in the image
The low end is 256 color (8 bits); the high end 16 millions color (24 bits).

2. Number of bits of data needed to present a single pixel (Bit Depth)
The low end is 8 bit and the high end is 24 bits.

For text documents, 1 bit or 8 bits is enough. Office documents usually have 2 colors only. As for the choice of resolution, the more color you set, the longer the scanning process.

If you need to work on color images, I suggest:

Bit Depth	Purpose Of Use
1 bit or 8 bits	Most text document. I usually use 8 bits.
16 bits to 30 bits	General color scanning
36 bits	Almost every situation
42 bit and up	Professional graphic projects

Table 7.2 Color depth

The Overview Of The Scan Process

Assume you have some paper documents that you need to scan and archive, then, you need to email it out to a friend by email in PDF. Again, I assume you created Office Data folder in My document folder to centralize the data and you link this Office's Data to PaperPort program. The whole ideas is selecting or creating the folder that you want the scanned image go into and then scan the image. Just like the paper document management. You create a manila folder and then file the document into the folder.

1. Start PaperPort

2. Open Folder Panel.
Go to the Command Bar and click on the Folder icon, pick the folder that you want to save the image to.

3. Create or select A Folder.
If you need to create another folder for the new images, then right click on the folder you want, create a sub folder, create a folder name, and select the folder color. In my case, I create a David's In Tray folder inside the Office Data folder.

If you have a folder that you want the image to scan to, simply highlight that that folder.

4. **Click Scan.**

   Go to the Command Bar and click the Scan icon. This brings you to the scan pane.

5. **Select the scanner and document type.**

   Click and highlight the scanner from which the text documents will be scanned. Also highlight the document under "scan what?"

6. **Click Setting ...**

   This bring up the Settings-Scanning dialog box. You can select the format of date or check Custom button to create a name for your folder. Select the format of the scan image.

   The rule of thumb is use PaperPort max extension for document that you need to edit.

   If you know the image is only for archive purposes, you should scan it to PDF.

7. **Click OK**

   This closes the dialog box

8. **Click scan.**

   What occurs next should depend on your scanner software. The resolution should be set at 200dpi or higher if you want.

9. **Double click on the scanned images**

   After scanned the document, double click on the scanned image and PageView window will appear. You can put any annotation or any additional items on to the image. We will discuss more about editing in the chapter.

10. **Click File/ Save as**

    This bring up the save as box. You can save it in the folder that you brought up or you can browse for another folder. You can save the documents in PDF, TIFF group 4 or multi-page group 4 formats. One the other side, save picture in JPEG formats. All these formats are open standards and you can be sure that you can see the image ten years later. I will explain different formats in greater details in next chapter.

Create PDF Files Without Using Acrobat

Since you have a engine in PaperPort that can convert file any text and image documents into PDF, you can now use PaperPort to create PDF without purchase Adobe Acrobat. That is a $300 program. By changing the print to function of PaperPort, you can print anything to PaperPort folders and save them as MAX, PDF or text searchable PDF.

The trick is very simple.

1. You first select or create the folder that you want the image to go.
2. Select the format that you want and
3. Print the document form its source program, such as MS Word.

1. **Start PaperPort and go to Tools/ Options/ and go to Item Tab.**

   Pick the format you want the print to file type to be. Once you set it, it will be this one until you change it.

Figure 7.7 Select format to convert

2. **Go to the Command Bar and click on the Folder icon OR create A Folder.**

   Pick the folder you want to save the image to. The Desktop Panel should show the content of that files. Or if you need to create another folder for the new images, then right click on the folder, you want to create a sub folder and create a folder name and select the folder color. In my case, I created a picture folder inside the Personal Data Folder. I further created another folder called David Lam inside the sub folder pictures. Then highlight the folder you want the image to download to.

3. **Open the file in the source program**

   Let say I received a fax in a FXM extension in WinFax Pro and I want to add some annotation onto that, I need to open the file in WinFax Pro first.

Figure 7.8 WinFax desktop

Click File/ Print, select PaperPort and click OK

If it is a color file, you select PaperPort Color. For B/W documents, you choose PaperPort

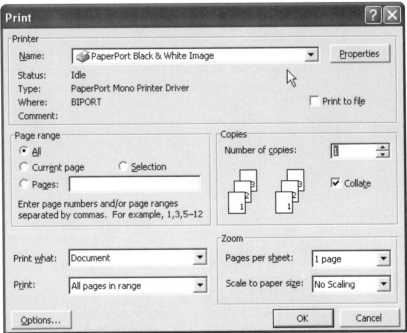

Figure 7.9 Print dialog box

4. **Close the program and go back to the PaperPort Desktop**
   Double click on the file in the PaperPort Desktop to open Page View and put some annotations onto the picture. We will discuss more about managing images in Chapter 8.

   I found that it is a very good conduit method for me to update some proprietary image files into the generic files. I print those files to PaperPort as described and save them in PDF files for text image or Jpeg files for pictures. So that, I do not have to worry about those files becoming obsolete once the source program becomes unavailable.

Download From a Digital Camera

For most offices, graphics and pictures may not be that important. However, for the advertising business, P&C insurance, real estate office, etc., digital graphic solutions are an important part of your business.

Let us say that you are a property insurance agent, you may need to take some pictures of the property and the surrounding area, and you need to send the information to your underwriter; you may need to put an annotation on the image, circle a part of the building, point to a certain area to get attention, if all of this is necessary, you will find that a digital camera could be a great help.

Let say you are property insurance agent, you may need to take some picture of the property and the surrounding and send to the underwriting. You may need to put annotation, circle some part of the building, point to certain area to get attention, then you will find the digital camera to be a great help to you. PaperPort can also help you process the pictures and send them to the underwriter.

In this part, you will learn how to download digital images from your digital camera into the PaperPort Folder.

1. **Go to the Command Bar and click on the Folder icon**
   Pick the folder you want to save the image into, or create a folder with the following steps: right click on the folder you want, create a sub folder, create a folder name, and select the folder color. (In my case, I created a picture folder inside the In Tray Folder.) Then high light the folder you want the image to download into.

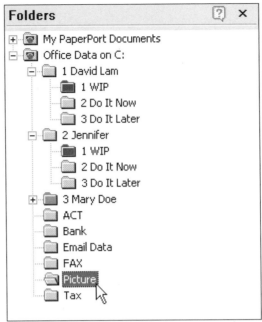

Figure 7.10 Select a folder to scan image into

2. **Open Get Photo Panel.** Go to the Command Bar and click on the Get icon, the Get Photo panel will appear.

Figure 7.11 Go to get photo desktop

3. **Select data source.** Click and highlight the digital camera or scanner from which the photos will be downloaded.

4. **Click on Settings**
   You can create a name for your files and the format you want. The rule of thumb is, using JPEG extension for graphics. This file format allows you to both annotate and touch up the picture in the PageView page.

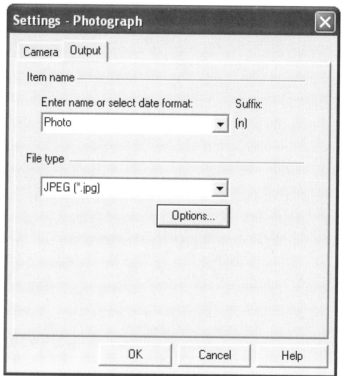

Figure 7.12 Select the name and format

5. **Click OK for your selection**

6. **Click on the Download button in Get Photo Pane to connect to the selected camera.**
   A data source window will pop up and load the thumbnail image of the picture into the PaperPort desktop panel. This process depends on how your camera software works. The key is download the photos into your folder.

If you use Window XP Operating system, you may find a XP window pop up and ask you to download the pictures. I will suggest you close the XP pop up window and use the program comes with your digital camera. It is because your camera usually will give the each picture a different file name every time when you download; whereas Window XP will start a set of name every time. You will have a different to file the pictures in a same folder later if you use Window XP download.

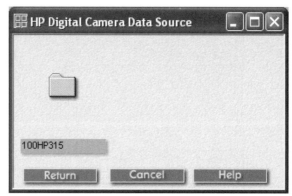

Figure 7.13   Sample of digital camera dialog box

7. **Select pictures to download.**
Again, this step depends on the camera's software. You may choose the pictures to download.

8. **Click the Return button in the data source pop up**.
The selected pictures will be downloaded into the folder you selected or created in step 2.

The pictures are saved in the folder you created or selected earlier. You can now double click on the picture to make annotations or to touch up images in the page view window. We are going to cover that in the next chapter.

Capture And Archive Web Pages

I love reading and I love to use Internet to research my various
interests. I don't think I am the only one!

If you find a great web site for research, you can save it and read it
off-line. In Internet Explorer, all you need to do is save the site in
Favorite. Right click the site icon and check "Make Available
Offline".

However, website may be changed anytime. In additional, if you
want to further manage the information, then, you can export it
into PaperPort in MAX format, PDF, and JPEG, etc.

1. **Go to the Command Bar and click on the Folder icon**
   Click and highlight the folder you want to save the image
   to. If you need to create another folder for the new images,
   then right click on the folder you want, to create a sub-
   folder, create a folder name, and select folder color. In my
   case, I create an "Internet" folder inside the Office Data
   folder. Then highlight the new folder you want the image to
   download to.

**Figure 7.14 Select or create a folder to capture image
into**

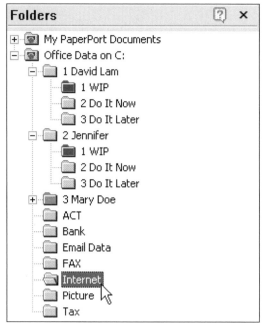

Figure 7.15 High light the new folder to put the web page image into

2. **Click Tools/ Web Capture in the Menu Bar of PaperPort**
   This step actually setup the web capture function and it is running as a background task. As other background task, you can find the Web Capture icon appearing in the Window Task Bar located at the lower right hand corner.

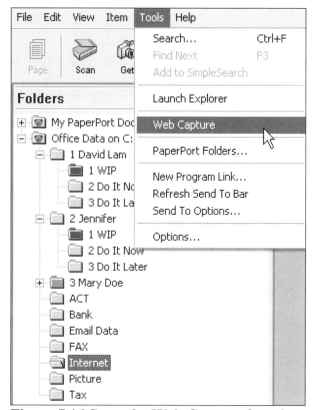

Figure 7.16 Start the Web Capture function

Figure 7.17 Web capture icon at the right lower corner of the computer

3. **Start up IE or Netscape.** Surf the web and you can save the page anytime you like.

Figure 7.18 Surf to your favorite web site :)

4. **Right click the Web Capture icon at the Window Task Bar**
    This brings up the pop up menu options.

Figure 7.19 Right on the Web Capture icon

5. **Select Options.**

   Check "Launch at Window startup" and also check "Display the Web Capture Menu" By checking both of these boxes, Web Capture function will start when the computer startup. You also have a choice if you like to capture just the visible web page or the entire page. For the File Type, unless you would like to modify the web page image, save it into PDF. If you also have OmniPage 11 or later, you can save it in PDF Searchable Image.

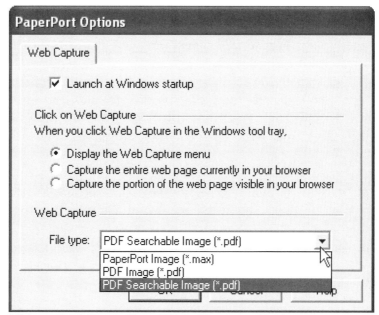

Figure 7.20 PaperPort Web Capture Options

6. **Click OK.**

   Now, you are back to the website.

7. **Right click the Web Capture icon and select either "Capture Visible Portion" or "Capture Entire Page".**

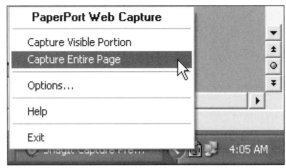

Figure 7.21 Select how you want to capture

If you select Capture Visible Portion, PaperPort will only capture the visible portion. If you select Capture Entire Page, PaperPort will rollover the whole web page and save the whole image in multiple pages.

8. **Go back to the PaperPort Desktop panel**
   Now, the web page is captured in PDF format and you can do the following:
   a. View the page in Page View Window, put annotations or touch up the image
   b. Send the page by email or fax
   c. OCR the page and send to other programs like MS word, Excel, etc.
   d. Print a hard copy (But why? Your goal is to become paperless)
   e. Save the image in other formats

In case you need to convert the file to other format.

Convert File Formats

Let us say, you save the file in PDF and you want to save the image into some other format, such as TIFF Group 4 compressed to save space.

1. Right click the thumbnail of the PDF file in the PaperPort Desktop
   This brings up a pop up menu.

Figure 7.22 Right click the PDF

2. Select Save as
   This brings up the dialog box. Browse the location to save, type in file name and select other format.

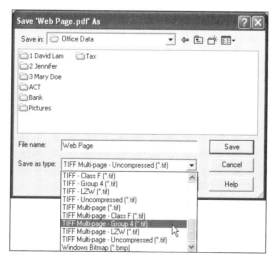

Figure 7.23 Save As other format

3. Click Save

   This will bring you back to PaperPort. You will see that there is a TIFF with the same name. Right click to delete the PDF that you don't want to have two same image.

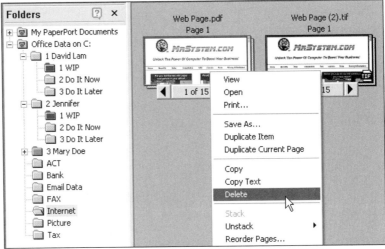

Figure 7.24 Folder pane in PaperPort

Although there are so many different formats that you can save the image of your documents, try to keep it simple. The rules of thumb are:

- Save text document in PDF or searchable PDF
- Save graphic document in JPEG

I understand this is a long section and long chapter, you did do a good job to read up to here. Now, let's see how to annotate and edit the digital images.

CHAPTER 8

Annotate And Edit Digital Documents Like Paper

****

In this chapter, you will learn:
- ➢ **Basic Annotation And Picture Editing**
- ➢ **Annotate Digital Images**
- ➢ **Add Your Hand Signatures**
- ➢ **Let Us Have Some Fun With The Pictures**
- ➢ **Send To Bar**
- ➢ **OCR (Optic Character Recognition)**
- ➢ **Fill A Form In PaperPort**
- ➢ **Add Attachment To Email**

****

Have you ever put a sticky notes on the document? Have you ever edit your letter on the paper? Have you ever fax a document? The document management software should make it very easy and intuitive to work with the image just like you work on paper. You can put various annotations on the images, edit the images or even send the document to other programs like, Outlook Express, Fax and MS word, etc.

To use PaperPort or any other document management softwares effectively, you need to imagine that you are working with paper when you are working on the digital image.

What you need to know is that there are certain limits of the files that the Image Annotation and Editing tools can work on. In PaperPort Deluxe 8.0, most of the functions can only perform on the Max format. In Deluxe 9.0, you can use the editing and annotation pretty much on any formats. However, if you have original PDF file, you need use Save As function to save it into PaperPort PDF. That will change it to the PaperPort PDF format and you can put annotation on the image.

Basic Annotation And Picture Editing

First, when you need to work with a document image, you need to find the document with the PaperPort Desktop Pane by either using the search function or simple retrieval. We will use the Hawaii page in My PaperPort Documents/Sample folder to illustrate how to work with an image.

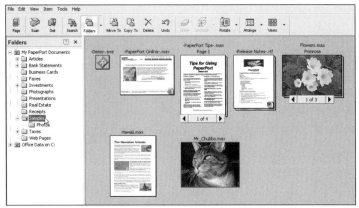

Figure 8.1 PaperPort Desktop Pane

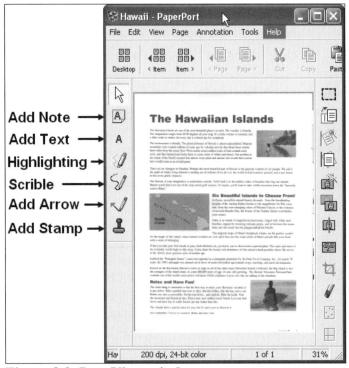

Figure 8.2 PageView window

Second, you double click on the item and that will open the Page View window of PaperPort. The window enables you view the item in full-size.

Third, You can add notes, texts, highlight, free handwriting, line, and even stamp mark with the tool bars on both side of PageView.

➢ Select Annotation:

To select, move and resize the annotation of an item

Add Note:
This function adds a digital sticky note onto your image. You can resize the note and move it around on the image to make it easy to read.

Text:
TYPE a line of text with a transparent background onto the image. You may also change the font, size, color, etc.; to do this, you right click on the icon.

Highlighter:
You can highlight any part of the image; it is just like holding a highlighter and marking the paper document.

Scribble:
This is the fun part; this is where you add freehand writing. It is very easy to create your signature and add information to the document.

Arrow or Line:
You can create a straight line or an arrow line with this tool. You can modify the width, color, and whether you would like to have an arrow at the end of the line.

Stamp:
Have you ever put a stamp on a document? It is the equivalent tool in digital format. It has a selection of very common stamps, such as urgent, received, etc.

All of the annotation tools work very similarly. You select the item; view them in the Page View window. Then you click on the tool and work on the image. If you want to change the properties of the tools, you can right click on the icons of the tools on the left Tool Menu. This brings up the mini menu and you can alter the properties from there.

In the old day when you had a stack of paperwork or documents, you may need to restack it, re-orientate the papers, put annotations, highlight certain words, circle certain sections, write some notes or post a note, and stamp the word emergency on the document.

Now, you can do all these things with your computer and we will do one sample together. .

➤ Select The Document

I am going to show you all the editing tools with the Hawaii.

1. Open PaperPort by clicking Start/Programs/ ScanSoft PaperPort/ PaperPort or click the icon on Window desktop
This brings up the PaperPort Desktop

2. Go to My PaperPort Documents/ Samples and double click the icon of Hawaii.max

This will open up the Hawaii file in the Page View window

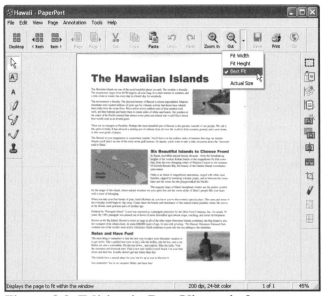

Figure 8.3 Editing in PageView window

3. Adjust the size of the Hawaii file with the zoom buttons in the Menu Bar

You can also pull down the mini menu from click the small triangle besides the Zoom Out icon and, select Fit Width, Fit height, Best Fit and Actual Size.

Now, we can modify and edit the picture.

Annotate Digital Images

Each tool shares the similar steps. You select the tools and then work on the item image.

➢ Add a Yellow Pad Note

Have you ever put a yellow sticky note onto some of your documents and pass to your assistant to do the work? The only difference in the office now is that you do it digitally.

1. Click the Note pad icon on the left Tool Bar.

2. Go to the area on the image that you want to put a note and left click

3. Type the note that you want to add.

In case you want to change the font, font style, color, size, etc., you can go to the Add Text Icon and right click on it to make a selection.

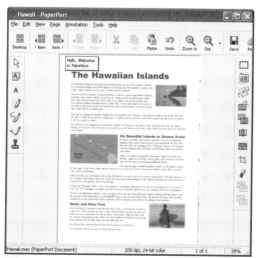

Figure 8.4 Yellow pad in PageView window

If you want to change the size of the yellow pad that you just added, you need to right click on the yellow note. This brings up a pop up menu and you can change the font, colors, etc.

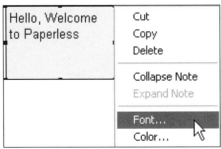

Figure 8.5 Change the font of the note

➢ Add Text

You may want to put a text in the document and PaperPort makes it a breeze.

1. Click the Add Text icon on the Annotation Tool Bar.

2. Drop on the spot where you want to add the text and click on the spot

You can now type in one line of text. You can only do one line at a time. After you finish the first line, you can now click on the space below and type in your second line.

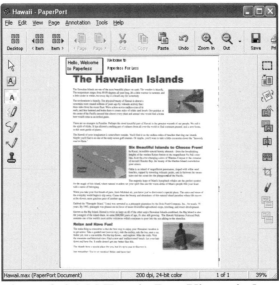

Figure 8.6 Add Text in PageView window

➢ Add a Highlight

You can highlight any area on the image. Let us highlight the text that we just added.

1. Click the highlight icon on the left Tool Bar

2. Click and drag the mouse to cover the area of the text you want to highlight. Release the mouse.

Now, the text area is highlighted.

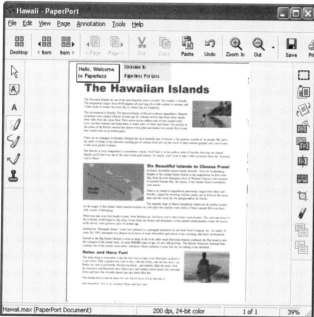

Figure 8.7 Add highlight in PageView window

You can change the color of the highlight by right clicking on the Add Highlight icon or the highlighted area itself. This brings up a mini pull down menu and you can make your selection there.

➢ Add Scribble

This is the fun part. You can sign your name and save it for future use. Let us talk about how to add your handwriting into a document. In our example, you can use it to add notes or circle the important point. Let say we want to circle the title word- Hawaii.

1. Click on the Scribble icon on the Annotation Tools Bar.

2. Drop and drag to circle the title word Hawaii

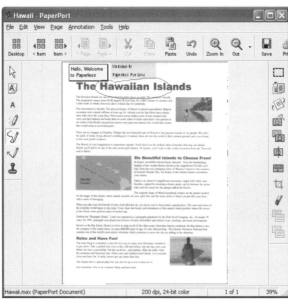

Figure 8.8 Scribble/ Pencil tool in PageView Window

➢ Add an Arrow Or Straight Line

You will have to decide if you want to have a straight line or a straight line with an arrow at the end. Let say you want to have a line with an arrow pointed at the word Hawaii.

1. Right click on the Arrow or Line icon on the Annotation Tool Bar
This brings up the mini menu and you can select your choice of color, line width and arrow direction.

2. Hold the mouse to draw a straight line and drop it close to the word, Hawaii.

Figure 8.9 draw line function in PageView window

➢ Add a Stamp Mark

It is a very simple process.

1. Click on the Stamp icon in the Annotation Tool Bar.

2. Drop the mouse at the spot that you want to have a stamp.
This brings up a window for the selection of stamps.

3. Click an the one you need and click Open.
You should see the stamp is printed on the spot that you clicked on.

If you need to move and resize the stamp, you need to click the Select Annotation Icon first to get the tool to change it. Then you need to click on the Stamp mark. This will bring up a box around the stamp. You can move the stamp by drag the box to other spots on the page. You can also change the box size and hence the size of the stamp.

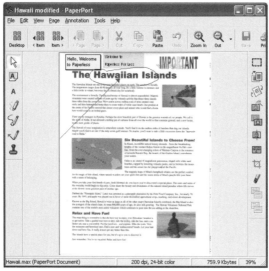

Figure 8.10 add stamp

Add Your Hand Signature

You may find it will leave a more impressive image if you could add your signature in the letter or email. Here is how to do it.

1. File/ New Item
   Right click the Scribble tool
   This brings up the mini menu and you can select your choice of color and line width

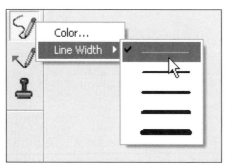

Figure 8.11 Select the signature line

2. Click on the Scribble icon on the Annotation Tools Bar.
Use the mouse to sign your name. If you have a digital pen, the result will be much better.

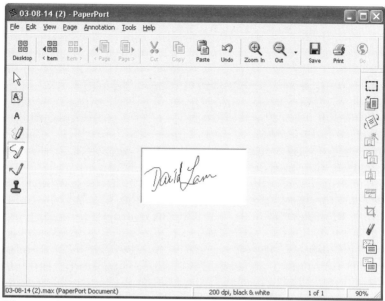

Figure 8.12 Signature with the Scribble Tool

3. Click File/ Save as
Save your signature in TIFF (Group 4) and you can now add this signature into most of the word processor and email softwares.

Let Us Have Some Fun With The Pictures

The process between text editing and picture editing is very similar. The Image Editing Toolbar is located on the right hand of the Page View.

Figure 8.13 Mr. Chubbs

You can use the tools in the Imaging Editing Toolbar to edit or rearrange text document. You click on the picture on the PaperPort Desktop, that brings you to the Page View window, and we can work on the image. In this section, you will use the My PaperPort Document/ Sample/ Mr_Chubbs.max

1. **Start up PaperPort by clicking on the icon on the Window Desktop or click Start/Programs/ ScanSoft PaperPort/ PaperPort.**

2. **Click the Folder icon in Command Bar if the left pane is not the Folder pane.**
   This will bring up the Folder pane.

3. **Click on My PaperPort Documents/ Sample.**
   You should see the picture of Mr_Chubb in the PaperPort Desktop

4. Double click on the thumbnail of Mr_Chubb (the cat)
This will open up the Page View window with Mr_Chubb's picture right in the center. You can now arrange it in a different manner.

The Image Editing tools are very simple and easy to use, plus most of your documents will be text. Therefore, I am not going into details, but I will show you share with you the overview of the tools.

➤ Overview Of The Image Editing Toolbar

The lay out of the PageView in PaperPort is very similar to any other graphic editing programs. You have the tool bar on the right side. If you like to change the position of the bar, just simply drag the bar to they area that you like and drop it. To edit the picture, you can click on the tool that you need. You use the digital tool work to work on the digital image, it is just like picking up a paintbrush to work on canvas. The process is very straight forward and simple.

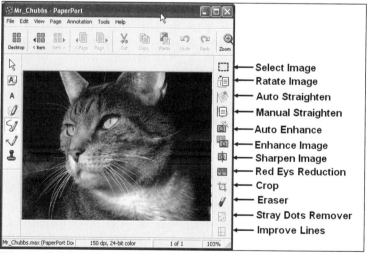

Figure 8.14 Mr. Chubbs in PageView

Select Image or Image Par:
The first square icon is used to select the part of the image that you would like to work on.

Rotate:
It is the button that enables you to turn the image 90 degree clockwise. You can make yourself look like you are standing on your head if you like.

All you need to do is click on the Rotate icon and the image will rotate clockwise 90 degree.

Auto and Manual Straighten:
It aligns the image with the edge of the frame.

1. Click on the Straighten icon.

2. To straighten the image manually, drop a line that you think should be parallel to the edges of the screen and across the image. Release the mouse when you are done.

Auto Enhance:
This function can improve the quality of the image automatically.

Enhance Image (Manually): When you click on it, the dialog box with the adjustments of Brightness & Contrast, color, and tint appears.

Sharpen: This function brings up a dialog box to either sharpen or soften the image.

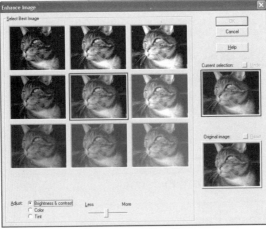

Figure 8.15 Sharpen The Image

Remove Red Eye: If you have some pictures with flashlight, this will be a great help. You can remove the red eyes easily.

Crop: You click on the Select Image button and select the part of the image that you like to keep. Then you click on the Crop button and cut the rest of the image.

Erase: You can use this just like you would use an eraser to erase the pencil mark off the paper.

Remove Stray dots: Sometimes, you may find the document is not clean, or the paper is so thin that you can see through the other side. Either conditions will make the scanner copy have some kind of small dots all over. This function can remove those dots on the image. The problem is that it also erases some details on the image.

Enhance Lines: This function is most useful when you scan forms into the computer, but the lines are not that clear. This function is smart enough to fill up some broken lines. It is especially useful if you scan form and form typer.

Send To Bar

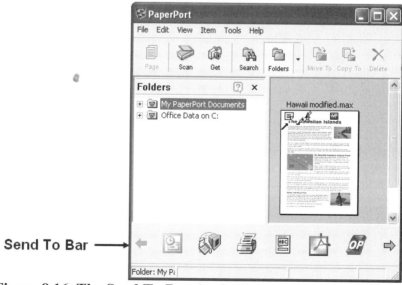

Figure 8.16 The Send To Bar As the linkage

Send To Bar is located in the bottom of the PaperPort Desktop. It is equivalent to the tool Bar on the Window desktop. This is a short cut to various programs and also a conduit to start the programs with the PaperPort files. You can consider Send To Bar ad another way to manage the image items.

It is very simple to open an image in other programs if you are using Send To Bar. All you need to do is just drag the image in the PaperPort desktop and drop it into the program icon in the Send To Bar. PaperPort will do any necessary conversions if required. The selected program will startup and you can use the program just as usual.

When you use PaperPort the first time, the program will search for the software in Drive C: and populate the Send To Bar with all the compatible programs automatically. However, sometimes, not every program is linked and I will show you how to add a program manually.

➢ Add a Program On The Send To Bar

If there are any programs that are not on the Send To Bar, you can add them manually. If you do not know where is the executive of the programs that you want to add, you can find it by the following these steps.

1. Click Start/ Programs
Find the program short cut of the program that you want to add to Send To Bar.

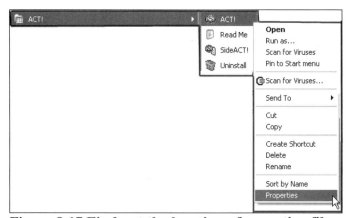

Figure 8.17 Find out the location of executive file

2. Right click the programs executive icon and select Properties from the pop up menu.

This brings up the Properties Box. Remember or copy down the path of the executive command in Target or Start In. There will be a minor differences between different Window versions. You can copy the path digitally by highlight the path, right click, and choose Copy. You will need it later. In my case, I will add Quicken to the Send To Bar.

Remember not to include the quotation marks if there are any.

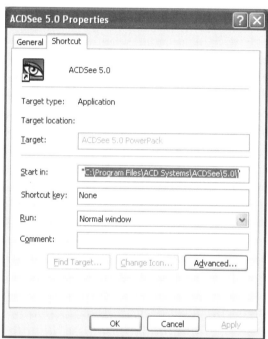

Figure 8.18 Sample program properties

3. Click on Cancel and go back to the PaperPort Desktop

4. Go to the PaperPort desktop, click Tools/ New Program Link ...
(if your are using Deluxe 8.0 or older version, it will be Add To
Send To Bar)
Add to Send To Bar dialog box will pop up

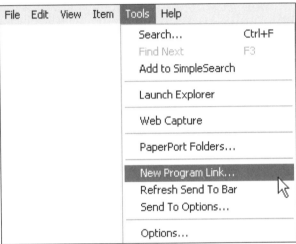

Figure 8.19 New Program Link or Add to Send To Bar

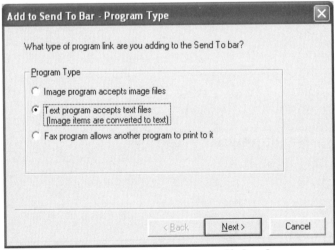

Figure 8.20   Add to Send to Bar dialog box

5. Choose the Program type of the software and click Next
This brings Add to Send to Bar – File Name dialog box

6. Locate the executive file
You can find it by browsing or pasting what you copied earlier
Remember do not include the open and close quotation of the path

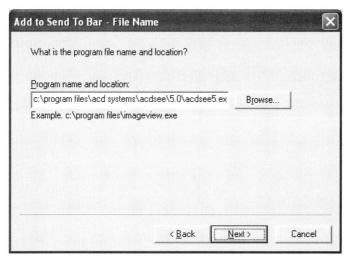

Figure 8.21 Find the executive file to add to Send To Bar

7. Click on Next
This will bring the Add the To Send To Bar – Program Name dialog box. The Program name space is filled either automatically or manually. You may type in the name that you prefer for this program.

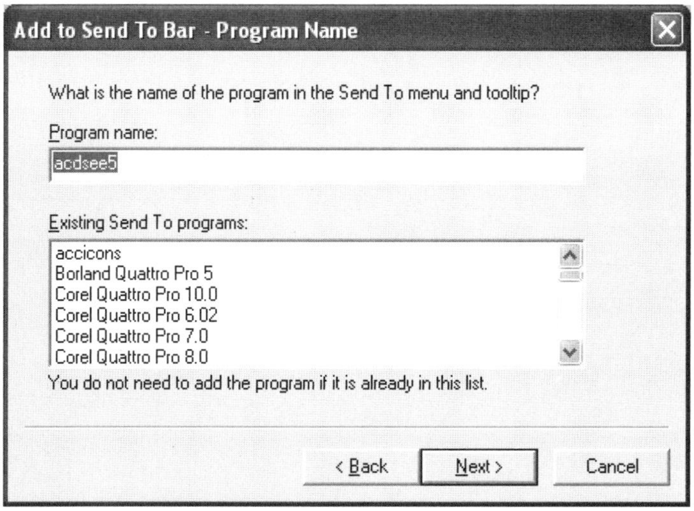

Figure 8.22 Program name

8. Click Next

There are two different dialog boxes depending on if PaperPort 'knows' the program. If PaperPort knows the program, it will go straight to the icon selection, step 11. If PaperPort does not know the software, it will ask for instruction. If you do not know which one to use, pick Tiff first and finish the process. If you cannot link the item to the program later, repeat the process and try another format. I have to warn you, not every program can be placed in the Send To Bar successfully.

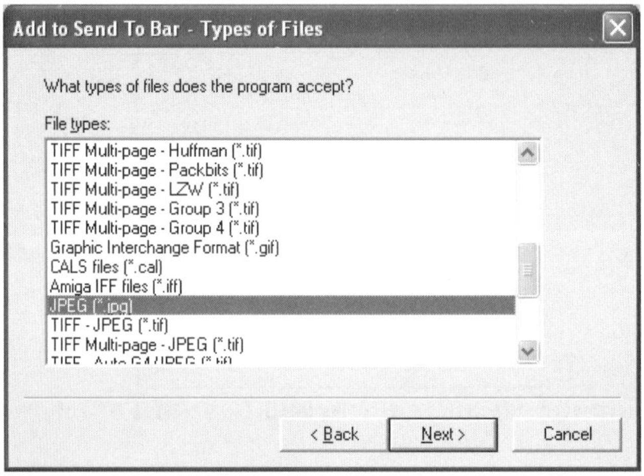

Figure 8.23 Type of file

9. Click on the Next Button

This will bring up the Add to Send To Bar- Program Close box. I suggest that you delete the temporary file to avoid too many junk files in your folders.

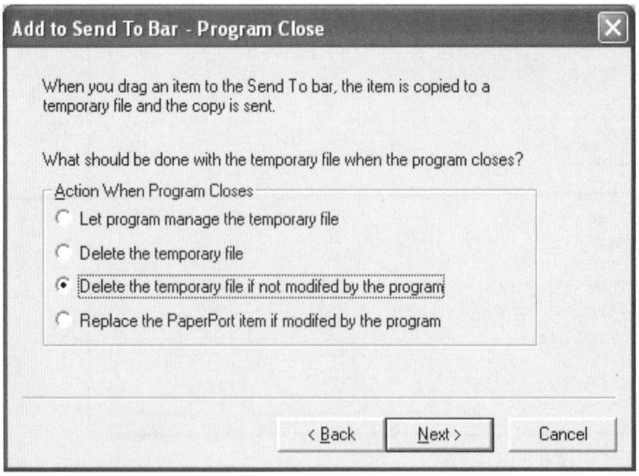

Figure 8.24 Close Program

10. Click on the Next button

This brings up the Image Resolution dialog box. Leaving it blank is the most secure way.

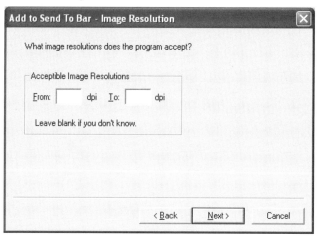

Figure 8.25 Image Resolution

11. Click on the Next button

That will bring up the icon source. Most likely, you should use the one provided by the source program itself; select to use the icon form the program.

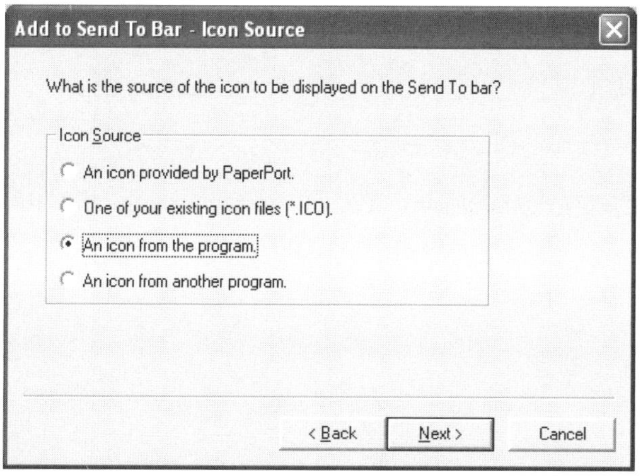

Figure 8.26 Icon Source dialog box

12. Click on the Next button

This bring up the Add to Send To Bar – Program Icon, highlight the icon you want. Use the default one if possible. This will keep the icons congruent in the computer and avoid confusion.

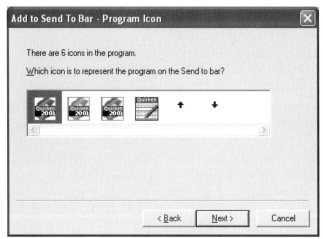

Figure 8.27 Select Program Icon

13. Click on the Next button

This is the last step and just click. The process sounds like a lot of work. However, most of the steps are very much self-explanatory, it is not as difficult as it seems to be.

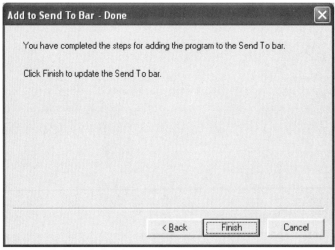

Figure 8.28 Finishing add to Send To Bar

➤ How To Change the Properties Of Send To Bar Items

As PaperPort automatically populate the Send To Bar, you may want to change some of the setting to fit your need. Generally, there are a few choices that you have:

- The file format that PaperPort sends the item to the Send To Bar.
- What process PaperPort should go through before sending to the Send To Bar program.
- Whether you like to have the program in the Send To Bar.
- Resolution change
- Should PaperPort send the file as image or text

I will advise you not to change the setting, unless you do not want to have the program in the Send To Bar. However, you may have a unique situation that you would have to change the original setting. The following are a few examples.

➤ Rearrange The Send To Bar icons

You probably would like to arrange the icon, so that, you can drag and drop the icon into the Send To Bar more conveniently. PaperPort does a good job in that. It makes the process just so much more intuitive and easy to manage.

You can easily rearrange the icon by holding down the **ALT** key and drag the icon you want to move to the where you want it to be.

➤ How To Use The Send To Bar

PaperPort provides a conduit function with the Send To Bar. It is a linkage between the image items and the programs to manage or alter that file. It is very intuitive to use this function.

All you need to do is find the file that you want to manage, and then drag and drop it to the icon on Send To Bar accordingly. This will start up the program automatically.

There are a few built in functions that may be benefit you in a paperless environment.

OCR (Optic Character Recognition)

OCR (Optic Character Recognition) is the process that a software 'read' the document. It is a very useful function if you do not want to retype a document. You can easily convert a scanned text document image back into text.

In case you need to convert the whole document, this task is very simple. All you need to do is find the image in the Folder Pane and PaperPort Desktop. Then, you drag and drop the image into the word processing program icon on the Send To Bar.

In addition, you can also convert part of a document into text. It is especially useful if you need to copy the text from a magazine. I will use the Hawaii file again.

1. Start PaperPort
Make sure you are in the Folder Pane

2. Go the My PaperPort Documents/ Sample

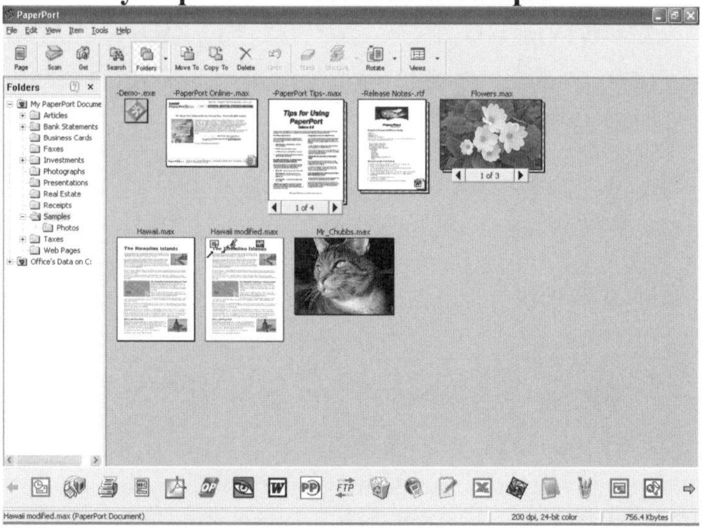

Figure 8.29 PaperPort desktop

3. Double click on the icon of Hawaii.max file
That will bring up the Hawaii.max file in Page View.

4. Click on the Select Image Tool on the Image Editing Tool Bar on the right hand side.

5. **Draw a box to capture part of the file that you want to copy into the word processing program.**

Figure 8.30 Open file in PageView

6. **Right click anywhere in the captured text**
   Highlight Copy Text in the pop up menu. PaperPort will then automatically start the OCR function. The built in OCR function of PaperPort will automatically convert the copied text and copy to the Window Clipboard. You can now start the any word processing, database, or even spread sheet program and Paste the converted text to those programs.

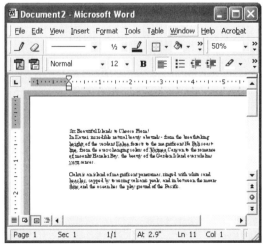

Figure 8.31 OCR convert image into editable text

If you want to convert a whole image into text, simply drag the image item into the word processing program in the Send To Bar. The build in OCR function will automatically convert the whole image into editable text. .

Fill a Form In PaperPort

If you use the Add Text Tool in PageView to fill in a form, you may encounter some challenges. It is very difficult to put the text exactly where you want it with the Add Text Tool.

There is a built in function that can help you in fill the form much easier. It is the ScanSoft Form Typer. Follow the first four steps in the previous example.

1. Drag and drop the form into ScanSoft Form Typer
The program will automatically decide where the blanks are and, underline the space. You can now type in the information. The positions are all aligned.

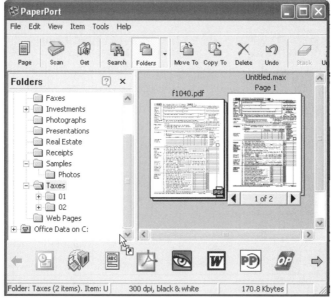

Figure 8.32 Convert the image into a fillable form

Figure 8.33 Convert the image into a fillable form

2. After you have completed the form, you can save it either in a PDF file, MAX or any other formats such as TIFF, GIF, etc. I suggest that you use PDF for archive purpose.

You can use either the Form Typer or the Add Text Tool to get the job done. Form Typer, however, is easier to fill the form because the form is ready to be typed in. You do not need to measure and adjust where you should type. The Form Typer program does all the adjustment, alignment and highlight automatically.

Add Attachments To Email

Adding attachments to email is a very simple process. Just drag and drop the PaperPort item into the email icon located on the Send To Bar.

However, the key concern is if the receiver is able to view the attachment. You should make sure that either the receiver has PaperPort program or you will need to send the attachment in the format that the receiver can read.

You can do so by saving the item in the PaperPort self-viewing executive file (.exe) or other universal formats. Examples are PDF, HTML, TIFF, GIF, etc.

This chapter have given you a clear understanding how to create a folder, capture the image, manipulate the images, and save the images into the correct formats.

Just remember it does take time to get used to a new way of working. The simple fact that you build a document management system has already differentiate yourself from the other who don't. You are heading the right direction of office operation, or on a bigger scope, the way of living. In the information age, it is so much easier to get back the control of life with the assistance of technology. In this book, I want to offer you enough technological tools to help you to take control and accelerate whatever goals you have in mind.

In the next part, we will discuss a few programs that every business should have.

Part IV: Achieve High Efficiency With Low Cost Technology

I Have a Dream That One Day ...

226

LAM Chart™ Of Digital Operation Center
(**L:** Learn **A:** Acquire **M:** Master)

	David: "Good people are like diamonds. The real good ones are not made, they are found. The bad news is that you need to go through a lot of people to find a few good one. The good news is that it pays handsomely when you do."
Setup A digital mail room	1. Setup digital fax with Window built in fax server or use WinFax 2. Setup at least three different email accounts for different purposes. You can get free email accounts from Hotmail.com, Yahoo.com, etc. 3. Setup email accounts in Outlook Express and setup rules to sort email automatically
Purchase a CRM/Client Relationship Manager	ACT! 5.0/2000 : Cannot send HTML email direct but only cost about $50 in second hand markets ACT! 6.0: Easy to use but limited to 50,000 contacts ($199) Goldmine 6.5: Automatic sales processing but longer learning curve ($199)
ACT! 6.0	1. Centralize data into My Document or Office Data folder 2. Setup security measure 3. Create fields and customize the lay out to fit your business needs. 4. Create a lot of templates and use the internal communication tool, such as letter, email, fax to contact clients 5. Block out time for importance 6. Schedule activities with CRM 7. Synchronize your PDA with CRM daily
Virtual Financial Manager	For business use, you may use Quicken Premier Home and Business. 1. Centralize Data 2. Setup security measure 3. Setup online banking 4. Link to tax record 5. Automatic Categorize
Continues digitalize your life	There are a lot of other productivity softwares that can help you to digitalize your workflow and hence improve your productivity. Microsoft® Office is a good example. Keep on using the technology and you will get more comfortable with it. I have never seen a baby quit learning walking even they fall so many time, why shouldn't we have that kind of tenacity?
Never forget human contacts	We try to digitalize the work process and become more productive. However, it will be all in vain if you forget your clients are basically human being. You need to create personal touch either in person or in technology to incubate the TRUST relationship. The is the real bottom line of business.

CHAPTER 9

Build A 24/7 Digital Mail Room

****

In this chapter, you will learn:
- ➢ What Is a Digital Operation Center
- ➢ The Two Powerful Free Programs In Your Computer
- ➢ Turn Your Computer Into A Digital Fax Machine
- ➢ Save Your Faxes
- ➢ Basic Email Program Functions
- ➢ Centralize Your Email Database
- ➢ Create & Your Manage Identity
- ➢ Manage SPAM Effectively
- ➢ Set Up an E-Mail Accounts
- ➢ Build an Automatic Sorting System
- ➢ Subscribe To Newsgroups

****

Chinese proverb says:" If you cut the weed without dig out the root, it grows again when spring comes."

The simple fact that you are able to scan all your documents into the computer will only turn your office into a paper free environment for a few days, if you do not stop the inflow of paper and change the way that you work.

You need to digitalize your workflow and reduce the information into digital formats, you can manage the information right on computer. You can eliminate paper as the medium for the information. You can stop the overflow of paper. You can save all those time wasted in paper management and become more productive.

You can achieve that by building what I call a Digital Operation Center (DOC).

What Is A Digital Operation Center (DOC)?

The purpose of a DOC is to reduce the incoming and outgoing paper communication and into digital information. That will eliminate the media, paper, itself and we can manage the information in its more pure form, electronic data. We can then processes and manage the digital information through a centralized digital information center.

If you use digital technology to communicate, you can easily centralize and manage the information. You do not need to duplicate any paper documents and make the system a huge time saver. The good news is that you are doing that already. Most likely, you did not take it to the maximum level. My job is to point out functions that people often overlook. I hope that these ideas will help you to further eliminate the need of paper, improve your productivity, and for you to make and keep more money.

Depend on your industry, there are many other productivity softwares that can create and manipulate digital information; I will discuss the listed universal softwares. For your own particular software, there should be many different manuals in the market place.

There are a few basic office productivity softwares that are pretty universal to any business and you need them for to build your own DOC:

- Communication program such as Email Software, and fax software
- Client Relationship Management Software (CRM)
- Personal or Business Management Software (PFM or BFM)
- MS Office that has Word, Excel, PowerPoint, Publisher, Outlook with business contact manager

The Two Powerful Free Programs In Your Computer

Have you got any junk fax or SPAM? If is quite a wastage of resource to take care of that. In this chapter, I will show you show you how to build a digital fax machine inside your own computer and delete the junk fax with a click.

I will also show you how to create a few different email accounts with Portal like, Hotmail.com and sort the emails, 24 hours a day!

The fax function in Window 2000 and XP is probably is the one of the most frequently overlooked program. We have used the stand-lone fax machine for so long, we just think that we have to do that way. We overlook the built in function in Windows because of habit. We may complain, on occasion, about the junk faces we receive and wish that we can eliminate them. Well, now, we can. If you receive a fax in digital format, you can eliminate that easily or even block that particular senders' fax.

Ninety-nine percent of the time, your computer should have a fax modem installed already. If you do not have one, just go to any computer or office equipment store and purchase a brand name 56K fax modem and instill it yourself. Again, ninety-nine percent of the time, the Window operating system will recognize the modem and install it automatically. For the one percent unlucky situation, go to Start/Setting/Control Panel and use the add/remove hardware wizard to install the fax component.

If you have Window 98 and any earlier versions, you need to buy a fax software. The most popular is WinFax Pro. You can go online and buy the OEM version that cost you only about $25 compared to $90 for the regular full version.

You see, I always keep your pocket in mind.

Turn Your Computer Into A Digital Fax Machine

There are different methods to access the fax console from different Window versions. I will focus on Window XP, but this instruction apply to Window 2000, too. If you have Window 98/ME, you need to buy software like WinFax Pro as we discussed earlier.

In window 2000:
1. **Click the Start / Programs/ Accessories/ Communications/ Fax/ Fax Service Management from the pop up menus.**

In Window 2000/XP
1. **Start/ All Programs/ Accessories/ Communication/ Fax/ Fax Console in Window XP**
   This brings up the Fax Console window

Figure 9.1 Fax Console

2. Go to Tools/ Configure Fax

The Fax Configuration Wizard will appear.

Figure 9.2 Fax Configuration

3. Click on the Next button

This brings up the Sender Information window, type in your information.

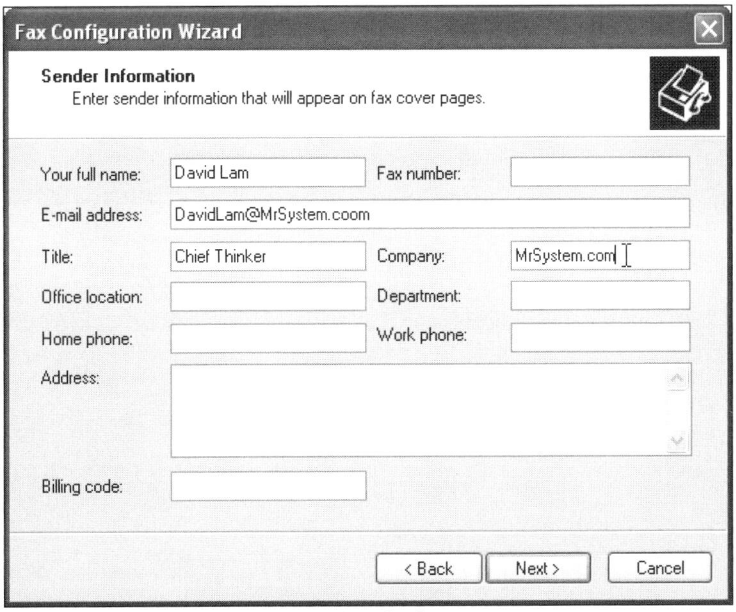

Figure 9.3 Fill in the sender info.

4. Click Next

This is an important step; select what you would like to use the fax. I will enable the send and receive function. I will select answer fax after one or two rings unless you really like the sound of faxes.

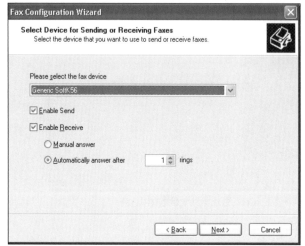

Figure 9.4 select the modem

5. Click Next

The Transmitting Subscriber Identification (TSID) box will appear. Do not get intimidated by this jargon. All it means is type in your name and your fax number. By the way, it is not necessary for you to fill it up either.

Figure 9.5 Fill in the TSID

6. Click Next

The Called Subscriber Identification (CSID) will appear. CSID used to identify you when your computer receives a fax. You do not have to fill this one in either.

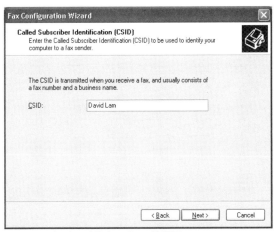

Figure 9.6   Fill in the CSID

7. Click Next

I attempted to print the fax to PaperPort directly, but I was not quite successful. Unless you can do it successfully, I will suggest that you should leave the two spaces blank. I will share with you how to save the faxes by printing to PaperPort in the next section.

Figure 9.7   Routing option

8. Click Next

Check the configuration and click finish to close the window.

Figure 9.8 Finish up

Save Your Faxes

As all the other functions, I always emphasis on centralizing the database. In this section, we will create a Fax folder in Office Data folder and instruct the fax console save the incoming and out going fax into this folder.

1. Start/ All Programs/ Accessories/ Communication/ Fax/ Fax Console in Window XP

This brings up the Fax Console window again

2. Go to Tools/ Fax Printer Configuration

This bring up the Fax Properties dialog box.

3. Go to the Archive tab

Check both 'Archive all incoming faxes in:' and 'Archive all successfully sent faxes in:'. Then, click browse button to bring up Browse for folder dialogue box.

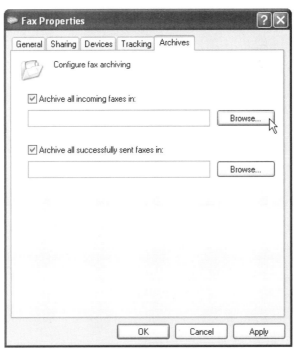

Figure 9.9 Add New Folder

4. Go to the Office Data folder

Use the hierarchy in the Browse for folder dialogue box to find your Office Data folder. The path is C:\Documents and Settings\Your user name\My Documents\Office Data. Check the Make New Folder Button.

Figure 9.10 Make New Folder in Office Data

5. Type in Fax

Create a new folder Fax in Office Data folder, then highlight the just created Fax folder and click Make New Folder again to create a Incoming Fax folder

Figure 9.11 Name the new folder Fax

6. Click OK to finish your creation of Fax and Incoming Fax folders.

This bring you back to the Fax Properties and you need to repeat the steps to create a Outgoing Fax folder.

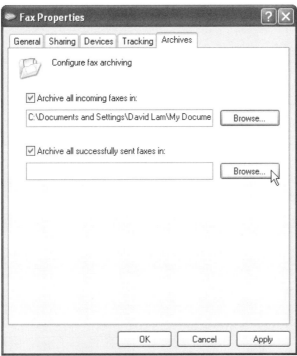

Figure 9.12 Repeat the steps to create Outgoing Fax folder

Figure 9.13 Creating Outgoing Fax folder

It is very simple to set up a digital fax function right from the Window 2000/XP. Although it is a simple setup and it is come with Window 2000/XP. Sometimes, you have to purchase a fax software like WinFax Pro. It will be necessary if your database software cannot fax to a group of clients.

The reason is: if you are in business, you can use the WinFax Pro for mass faxing and send out tons of fax automatically. You can export the contact database into the WinFax and send mass faxing to each of your clients or prospects. You should do it at night if you have a long list of contact.

Besides, you should have a stop faxing request contact for receivers in case they do not like to receive your marketing fax. You must provide a toll free number for the receivers to call in to delete their names from you contact lists. You should do some homework to find out any legal issues in mass faxing your states. I know there will be some work, however, who says business is a easy thing to do. However, every effort that you invest into your business will be handsomely rewarded at the end.

Keep you original fax machine
One thing I need to remind you of is that you should keep your stand alone fax machine as a stand by fax.

The best way to do it is going to buy those one to two telephone converter and connect both of the fax machine and computer fax modem into one jack.

If you have a multifunction printer or a stand alone fax machine, the trick is setting them pick up after 4 rings and setting up your computer fax pick up after two or even one ring. The faxes that are not received by the computer fax function will then be received by the other fax machine.

If you receive any junk fax, you just need to delete it with on click.

This concludes the faxing portion of this book. Now that you have read this chapter, I hope you can eliminate more paper, which brings us one step closer to our journey towards attaining a Highly Efficient Office.

Basic Email Program Functions

There is an email program called Outlook Express which comes with Window 98/ME/2000/XP. This is a basic email program, but you can still do a lot of different things with the program. You may hear about another program called Outlook, which is a comprehensive version of Outlook Express. It comes with a lot of more management functions. I prefer to use Outlook for all the extra functions. You may also use another email software, Lotus Note.

The basic concepts of all email softwares are similar. The most important for our discussion is how to use the email functions to streamline your work and improve your efficiency.

Let us geek around with the free email program, Outlook Express.

As all the other programs mentioned earlier, it is difficult to describe all details of this email software. However, 20% of the knowledge of this software should solve 80% of the problems. I will only share with you the parts that you need the most. The good thing about Outlook Express, when compared to the web e-mail program of your ISP, is that you can download your e-mails into Outlook Express and read them later. It is especially important when you are on the road and you do not have time to read all of your the mail at once. You can also consolidate all your e-mail accounts into one place and manage them together. Many of my clients have more than one e-mail account and each one is used for a different purpose. By using different mail accounts, you can prioritize your work more systematically and be more productive. To reduce even more paper, you should contact all of the companies that you deal with and ask them to communicate with you via e-mail instead of snail mail. I will share with you the following ideas:

> ➤ Centralize your email database in one folder
> ➤ Create and manage identities (It is the user level security)
> ➤ Send and receive email for different e-mail addresses. It is a great tool for integration if you have different email addresses.
> ➤ Subscribe to news groups
> ➤ Setup email folder, rules of reception to organize the email

Centralize Your Email Database

By now, you should know what I will be suggesting you to do. I will suggest you to create an Email Data folder in your Office Data folder. If you did not create an Office Data folder in My Document folder, read Chapter 5 to create one.

The path of your folder should look like this:
C:\Documents and Settings\Your User Name\My Documents\Office Data\Email Data

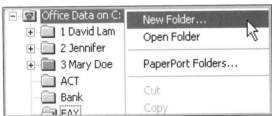

Figure 9.14 Create a Email Data Folder

The next step is to setup Outlook Express so you can save all the messages into the new Email Data folder.

1. Go to Start/ Program/ Outlook Express and start the program
Outlook Express will appear on the screen.

2.Go to Tools/ Options/ and go to Maintenance Tab

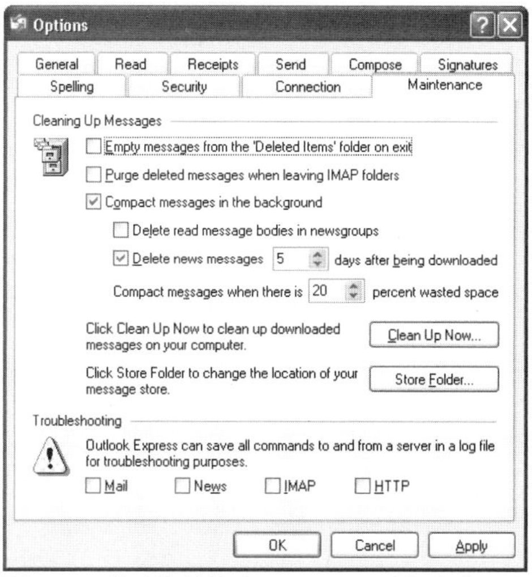

Figure 9.15 Maintenance Tab in the Option dialog box

3. Click Store Folder button

This brings up the Store Folder dialog box

Figure 9.16 Browse the Email Data folder that your create

4. Click Change

Find the Office Data in My Document (Created in Chapter 5) and click OK to confirm.

The benefit of a centralized folder makes backing up data and administrative duties easier for you and your staff.

Create & Manage Your Identity

I know that you know who you are. If other people use your computer, such as your spouse and your kids, you may want to separate your email accounts from theirs.

The purpose for setting up an identity is that different people have different interest and priority; any users can setup e-mail accounts and news group according to his/her preferences. In addition, you can also setup password protection and no other people can read your emails.

In other cases, you may also want to create different identities to separate different sets of email addresses, such as business and personal. You may need to set up different identities just like setup different mail boxes. However, Outlook Express may not know you if you do not create an identity for it to recognize you.

If you are the only one who uses your computer and you do not plan to share your computer with anyone, you can skip this section.

➤ Creating a New Identity

Create a new identity in Outlook Express is very straightforward.

1. **Click Start/ Programs/ Outlook Express** (You could create a shortcut to the desktop by right click Outlook Express icon and click Send To Desktop)
   This will start Outlook Express

2. Click File / Identities/ Add new identity
This will open the new identity dialog box.

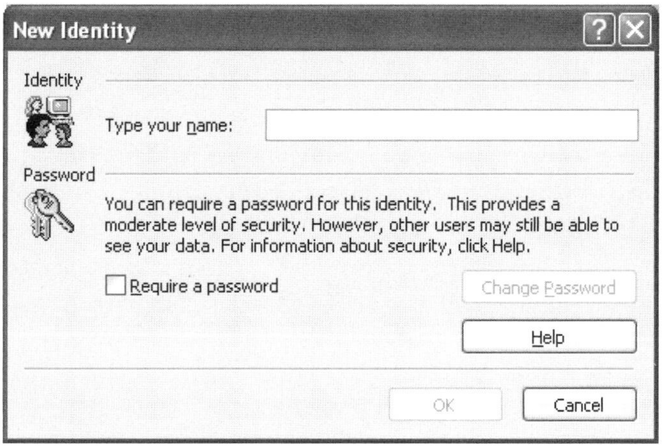

Figure 9.17 New Identity

3. Type in the name of your identity
The identity is just for the identity/user name for the program, it will not show up in any email that you send)

4. Check the Require A Password box
Enter Password box will appear. You need to type your password twice.

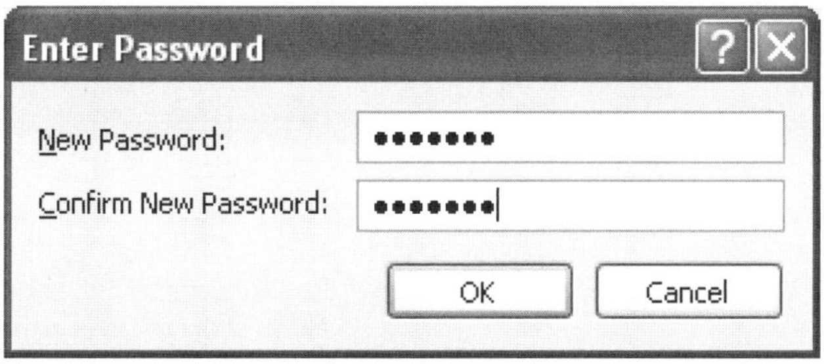

Figure 9.18 Enter password

5. Click OK to confirm your new identity.
Outlook Express will ask you if you would like want to switch to the new identity. Say no for now and close all the dialog boxes.

➢ **Managing Identities**

If you have created multiple identities, you may need to add, change or remove it sometime. Modifying an identity or identities is a simple process.

1. **Go to Start/ Programs/ Outlook Express**
   This will start up Outlook Express.

2. **Click File/ Identities/ Manage Identities**
   This opens the Manage Identities Box.

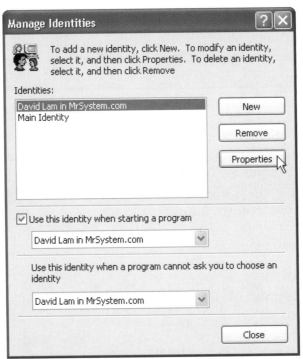

Figure 9.19 Manage Identities

3. **Select the identity that you want to change**
   You can remove any identity, except for the main one.

4. **Click on the Properties box and make the changes.**
   If you want to remove any identity, just highlight it and click on the remove button. Confirm the selection by clicking YES to the pop up box.

Manage SPAM Effectively

Because of the low cost of email marketing, there are a lot of companies using unsolicited email to market their products and services. In the CAN-SPAM ACT of 2003, it is legal to send out unsolicited email if the emails:

- Clearly identity the email is a piece of advertising, e.g. putting ADV in the subject line
- AND include the companies' physical addresses
- AND include an email address to unsubscribe

Unfortunately, I still receive a lot of junk mail without comply with the regulation. Since you cannot escape from junk email, you need to find out ways to manage that.

The spammer use different address to email you, they use address guessing to find your address. The worst nightmare is after you unsubscribe the email, they now know your address and they will SPAM you even more!!! I used some SPAM stopper kind of software, unfortunately some of them are not very accurate and they even eliminate the mails you need.

Remember, you receive junk email because you use your email address some, where it was being extracted or being sold. Even though the websites may claim that they will never sell your email, you cannot really prevent that from happening. Some spammers may use program to guess your email but you know those right away when your read the Send To email address.

The tricks of managing email effectively are:
1. NEVER unsubscribe SPAM unless there is a physical address in the email.

2. I will suggest that you setup at least three email accounts:
   - One email address for your family only and never give it to anyone else
   - One email address strictly for business communication with someone you already know.
   - One email address for general use, such as online shopping, subscription, etc. This one is the one that tend to get a lot of SPAM. You can sort email sent to this address separately

and simply abandon this one when the volume of SPAM get out of hand.

3. You can sign up for free email from hotmail.com, yahoo.com and tons of others. Yahoo.com will charge you for downloading to your email program like Outlook Express but hotmail still provide free email accounts.

4. Use Outlook Express to create the email accounts and download the emails regularly. Outlook Express can help you to centralize and manage your email accounts.

5. Use the sorting and rule functions of Outlook Express to sort and manage the email. I will show you later in this chapter.

Set Up an E-Mail Accounts

In the small business environment, the owner has to do everything himself or herself. If you have a web presence, it will have a better corporate look if you set up different e-mail addresses for different functions. You may set up marketing@yourdomain.com for marketing and admin@yourdomain.com for administrative questions. Contact your Internet Service Provider (ISP) to see how many e-mail addresses you receive with your web hosting service. A lot of ISP offer 100 email addresses with unlimited auto responders.

1. Start Outlook Express

2. Go to File/ Switch Identity to get into the identity you want to add the email address.
If you did not add an identity, you can skip this step.

3. Click Tools/ Accounts

The Internet Accounts dialog box will appear.

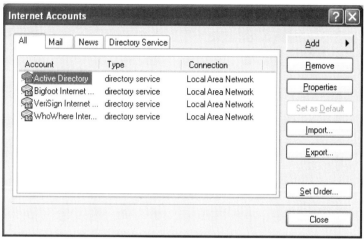

Figure 9.20 Internet Account setup

4. Click on the Add button, select the Mail ...

This brings up the Internet Connection Wizard dialog box.
Once it appears, type in the name that you want to appear as the sender.

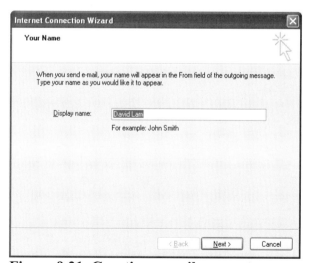

Figure 9.21 Creating e-mail account

5. Click Next

This will bring up the Internet E-mail Address section. Type in your e- address.

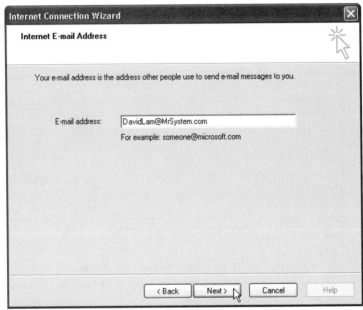

Figure 9.22 Type in your e-mail address

6. Click on the Next button

The Internet Server Name section will appear . You can get this information from your ISP.

You will get all these information from you ISP (Internet Service Provider).

If this is a free account from www.Yahoo.com, your answer should be like this:

My incoming mail server is a POP3 server
Incoming mail server: pop.mail.yahoo.com
Outgoing mail server: smtp.mail.yahoo.com

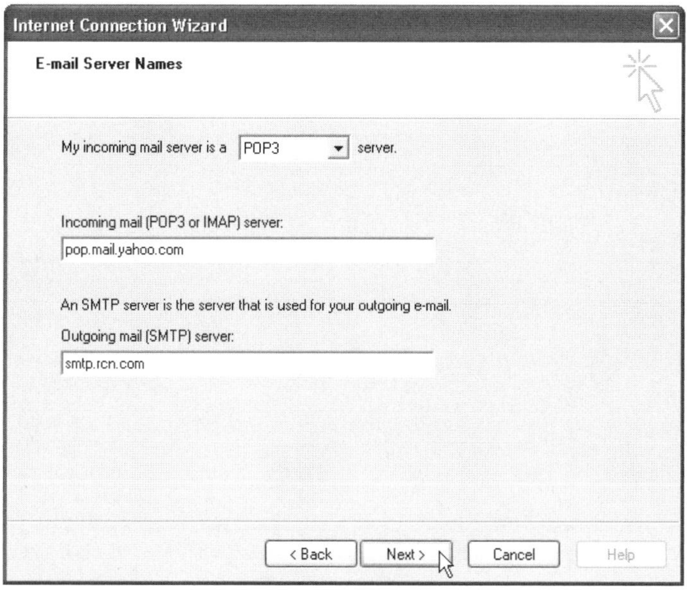

Figure 9.23 Setup Mail Servers

However, even if you set up everything correctly in Outlook Express, you may not be able to download your email if you have not paid Yahoo the premium service fee! Yahoo started to charge user about $30 annual fee to download email from its server.

Some ISP do not allow subscribers use third party out going email server. You may need to use the ISP's SMTP server to send email. However, the mail still can be the third party email address, e.g. DavidLam@MrSystem.com. You can try to put the third party SMTP email server first to send out email to see if it works. If it does not work, call your ISP technical support to check if you must use their SMTP servers. Example of ISP SMTP servers are: smtp.rcn.com, smtp.comcast.net.

Another very popular free e-mail account provider is www.hotmail.com that was bought by Microsoft in1999. It is very sensible that Outlook Express has a simplified setup for Hot Mail accounts. Select HTTP from the pull down menu. If you pick HTTP and Hotmail, you do not need to fill the server names.

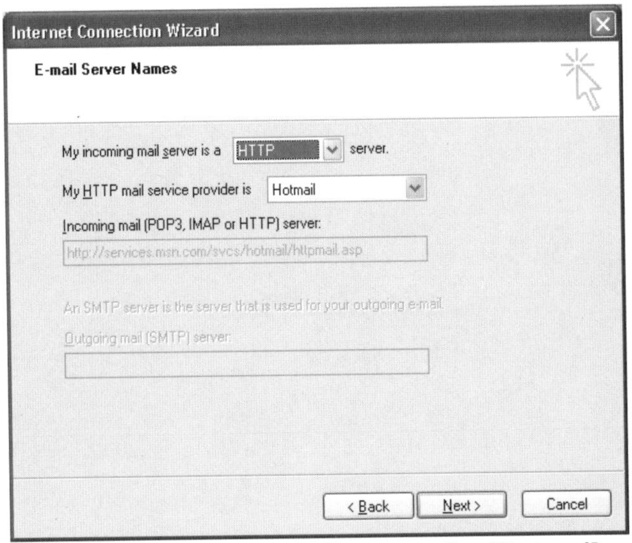

Figure 9.24 Select HTTP server for Hotmail accounts

7. Click Next.

You need to type in the Internet mail Logon information. You ISP may require that you put the whole email address as the account name sign in. Some ISP only require the name before the @yourmain.com. You do not need type in @yahoo.com for Yahoo mail account. You need to type in the whole account name, such as yourname@hotmail.com for Hotmail email account. Enable the remember Password. Check with your ISP if it use SPA log on.

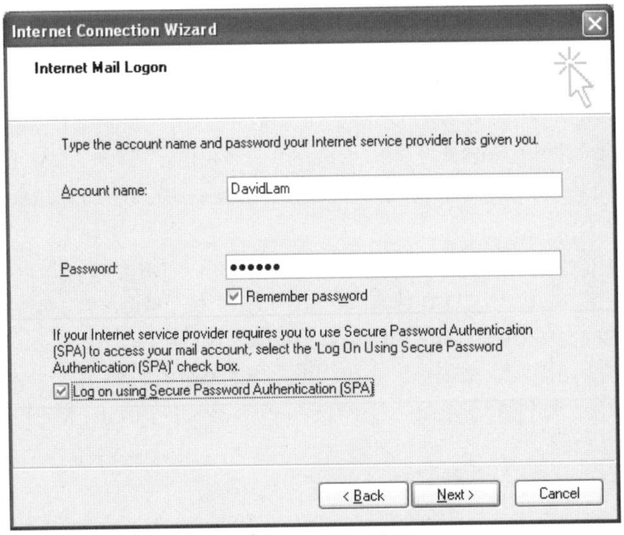

Figure 9.25 Type in account name

8. Click Next, and then Finish

This brings you back to Internet Accounts dialog box

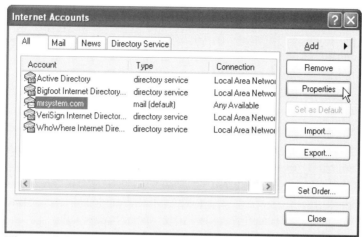

Figure 9.26 Back to Internet account dialog box

9. Highlight the new e-mail address and click Properties.

This will bring ups the General tab of the new mail account properties. Select the name that you want to appear in your e-mail.

Figure 9.27 Correct the mail account name

10. Click OK and finish adding email account

Build an Automatic Sorting System

The heart of an automatic mailing system is to create different folders and a set rules for the email software to sort the incoming email automatically. The software acts like a mail worker who can help you sort the email automatically according to your instruction. You can color the folders or you can even enable the software to notify you when the mail comes. That is our digital mailroom system.

➢ Create Folder And Rules In Personal Outlook Express

Earlier in this chapter, I mentioned that you can eliminate SPAM effectively by setup a few different accounts. One for business, one for family, and one for anything else. I will show you how to set rules so that Outlook Express will help you to sort the emails according to the your email addresses.

1. Right click on the local folders

Figure 9.28 Local folder pane

2. Select New Folders from the menu
This bring up the Create Folder dialog box, type the name, Business, as the name of the new folder.

Figure 9.29 Create a folder

3. Click OK
This close up the Create Folder dialog box and bring you back to Outlook desktop

4. Go to Tools/ Messages Rules/ Mail
This brings up New Mail Rule Dialog box will appear. Check 'Where the To line contain people' and 'Copy it to the specified folder'. A paragraph will appear in the third box and there will be two highlighted selections, contacts people and specified folder.

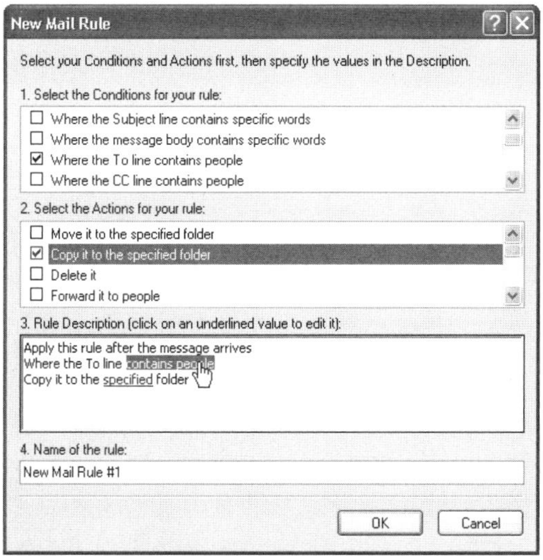

Figure 9.30 New Mail Rule

5. Then click <u>contains people</u>

This brings up Select People dialog box.

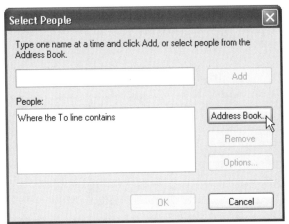

Figure 9.31 Select People who receive email

6. Click Address book

This brings up Rule Addresses. If you name is not in the address book, click New Contact button and fill in the information especially your email address. Then click OK.

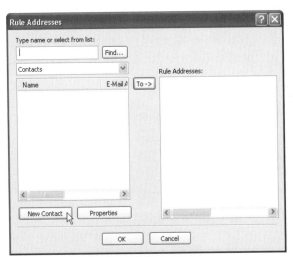

Figure 9.32 Rule Addresses

You will then go back to the New Mail Rule box to click specific folder and select the newly create Business folder. The result is all email sent to the address your selected, let say your business email address, will be sorted into this Business folder. You can create other folders to fit your needs.

➢ Setup an Email Receipt Notice

If you want Outlook Express to notify you when there is new mail, all you need to do is going to Tools/ Options and bring up the Option dialog box. You can then choose different notification methods and interval.

Subscribe To Newsgroups

Newsgroups are news or messages grouped by topic and they are posted in News servers. The news is composed by any person who is interested in that particular topic. If you ask what are the topics, I will say any thing conceivable. This is another way to research and keep up to date of your interests with no expenses.

The good news to you is that you can use Outlook Express to subscribe to the groups that you are interested in.

I am going to share with you how to find the group that you like, subscribe to them, how to download. Of course, you may also become a contributing member to the groups and start to reply and post messages. Outlook Express also makes the process simple and easy that you can start right away. This is another step where you can collect information without using paper.

➢ Add a News Server

I assume that you have either a DSL or a Cable connection. The first step is connecting yourself to a news server.

1. Start Outlook Express

2. Click Tools/ Accounts
   This brings up the Internet Account Box

3. Click the Add button and then Click on the News button
   This will bring Internet Connection Wizard dialogue box. Type in the name you would like to appear in the news group. I will suggest you put an alias here.

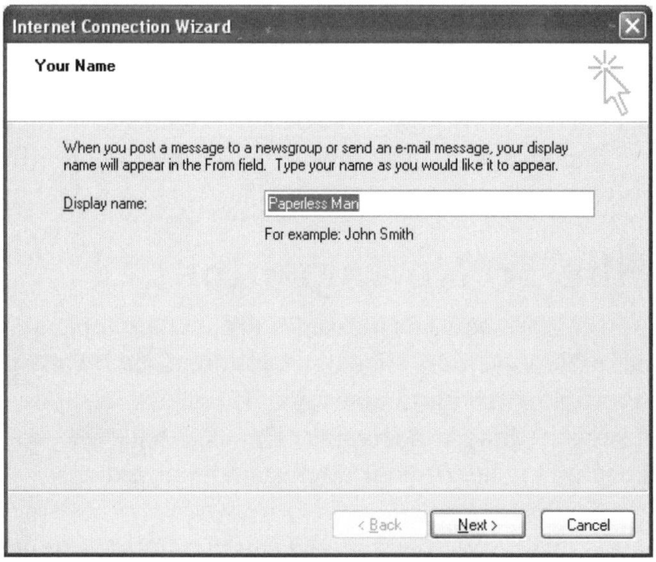

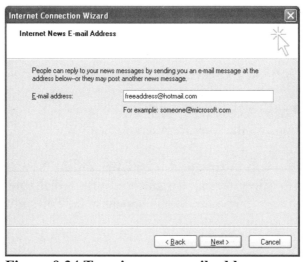

Figure 9.33 Internet Connection Wizard

4. Click Next

Type in you email address. I will suggest that you get a free email address first, and then put it here. There are a lot of marketing companies that canvas email addresses from news groups and send out Spam e-mail. If you put your real name and personal e-mail address in the Newsgroup, you will get a lot of email that you may not want. With a free email address with alias, you can change that any time.

Figure 9.34 Type in your email address

5. Click Next

Fill in the Internet Server Name from you ISP.

Figure 9.35 Type in news server name

6. Click Close and then Finish

There will be a dialog box asking if you would like to download newsgroups from the news account you added. If you use a DSL or a Cable Internet connection, you can click YES any time. However, if you use a dial up, you will be better off wait until you do not need to work on the computer. It is because downloading the list will take a long time.

➢ Search & Subscribe Newsgroups

There are unlimited numbers of newsgroups on the Internet. The challenge is how you can find the one that you are interested in? Outlook Express has a search function that help you do a title search on the newsgroups. As an example, I will search for a newsgroup that discusses clothing. We cannot just think business all the time.

1. Start Outlook Express Start/Program/Outlook Express

2. Click on the entry of the newsgroup in the left pane

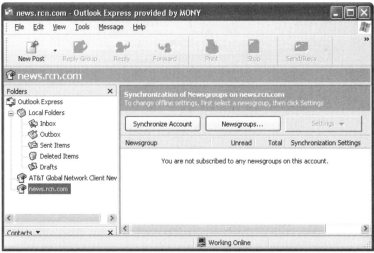

Figure 9.36 Select your newspaper to synchronize

3. Click on the Newsgroups in the right pane
This will bring up the Newsgroup Subscriptions box.

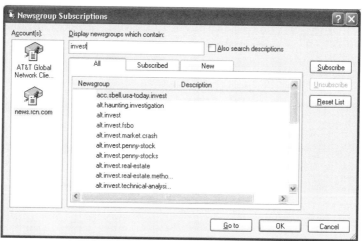

Figure 9.37 Select the newsgroup

4. Type in a key word of your interest in the blank space under "Display Newsgroups Which Contain'.
It is quite impossible not find one that suits your interest.
Contact your ISP if nothing appears.

5. Highlight the group that you like and click on the Subscribe box.
Until now, setting up a newsgroup was similar to setting up an email account. The difference lies in how you download the newsgroup messages. You can only download the messages manually. There is no automatic synchronization in Newsgroups subscription.

Outlook users may ask why there is not any news group in Outlook. The answers is that there is a conduit link to the NewsReader, you just need to look at the right place. In Outlook, go to View/ Go To / News and you will start up the newsreader in Outlook Express.

➢ Download The e-mail Or News

1. Start Outlook Express

2. Click the entry of the newsgroups or mailbox that you want to **synchronize with the news server.**

3. Go to Tools/ Send and Receive
You can choose all to send and receive all email or you can pick a particular action to perform.

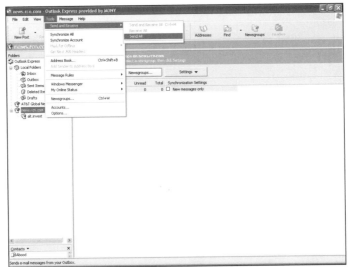

Figure 9.38 Pull down the Tools Menu

All these email and fax tools could be setup in a short period of time and you can use them right away.

In the next chapter, I would like to discuss about a very important software that every business should have, that is the Client Relationship Management program (CRM).

CHAPTER 10

Use a Digital Personal Assistant Who Never Forget

****

In this chapter, you will learn:

> ➢ **Client Relationship Management program (CRM)**
> ➢ **Which CRM To Buy**
> ➢ **Centralize Your Data**
> ➢ **Create a New Database**
> ➢ **Import Data From Other Database**
> ➢ **Setup Security**
> ➢ **Customize The Database**
> ➢ **Setup Fax, Telephone And Email Preferences**
> ➢ **Budget Your Time**
> ➢ **Instant Messaging**

****

Have you ever feel overwhelmed? Have you ever feel you got trap in life? I could not help you to analyze you inside problems here, but I could show you a simple technology that can help you to get organized and get thing done in a much more efficient manner. This solution is so simple and easy that anyone can do it.

CRM is the client relationship management software. It can help you to centralize you contacts' information, schedule your activities, and keep track of what you did.

If you learn how to use a CRM program, synchronize with your PDA and work with discipline, you will always have your schedule in hand. You will be in control again and you will never be late for anther appointment.

Client Relationship Management Program (CRM)

Being a business owner means that you will have to take some risks. You will have to spend some of your own money and there is a chance that you may not have a lot of income during your first few years of business. It also means that you will have to wear many different "hats" simultaneously.

You need to keep track of your appointments, meetings, phone conversations, and clients' records, etc. Besides, you also need to take care of marketing, finance, and operational work. That is a lot for one person to manage. That translates to the need of carefully planned schedules and very precise execution of your plans. That is quite a challenge but it will be easier if your have a Client Relationship Management program (CRM).

Unless your business is not client oriented, CRM should be your most important program. To build a Highly Efficient Office, I can hardly imagine it being done without a CRM; the CRM should be very versatile. It should be able to:

- Keep clients' information and history
- Correspondence via letter, email, and fax
- Schedule your activities
- Mass marketing

Depending on your business, each function will have a different importance value to you. However, some issues are universal. Imagine that you communicate with outside parties and that you do not keep records. You may lose valuable information such as, information on your vendors, suppliers, and clients.

By storing and centralizing the information about your clients in their record, you can make more timely contacts with them. You can also design your marketing and operation plans from all of these data. So that, when you open their record, you can have their data in your hand.

The second role is communication. The better the software, the more the communication functions it includes. For example, you should be able to write, email and fax right from your CRM. You may also call them and type notes in the note pad. Therefore, you can keep track of all of the communication history with your clients. You can also able to use your computer to receive fax and paste them back to you CRM. That could help you to centralize the history. The best part of that is the process is all digitalized and you eliminate the paper handling ;and human intervention. It saves time; you do not have to file and it saves you from administrative work. If you are using any CRM, you should explore the communication functions of the software.

Most likely, the CRM will have fax and email functions. However, they are acting like a conduit functions. That means those CRM actually uses Window default fax and email software to do the actual jobs. They are able to initiate the function and most of the time they link the received and sent communications to the contact information. We are not going to discuss each CRM here. I will discuss the functions that you need to know to make your CRM work harder for you.

Even if your CRM has faxing and email functions, you still need to set it up to use and they are only to send. You do need to know how to receive the fax and email and link them back to your CRM to centralize the data.

In addition, it is also very important to use CRM to schedule our activities and contact with clients. That alone should also be able to synchronize with PDAs, such as Palm and Pocket PC. It should also able to print out various calendars for your planner if your use one.

Since you have all of your clients' data, it makes sense to contact them on special days (such as birthdays, anniversaries, etc) to develop a closer relationship or you can mass email every one on a regular basis.

If you need to invoice your clients or keep the accounting with them, your CRM should be able to work with your accounting program too.

The general and popular are softwares such as ACT, Goldmine, and Maximizer. There are also many industry specific softwares that can handle even more business operations.

For financial business, you may have EZ-data, FDP, dbcam, etc. For law firms, you may consider AbacusLaw or Amicus Attorney. etc. For accounting firms, you may take a look of White Paper from Creative solutions Practice and File Net. You need to do your own due diligence to find out what software package fit your needs the best. Most companies allow you to download their trial versions. Visit my web site, www.MrSystem.com, and you will have their websites handy in your web browser.

Which CRM To Buy

For home office user and small business, I find you may find ACT! and Goldmine to be very useful and affordable.

ACT! 2000 or 5.0	ACT! 6.0	Goldmine 6.5
$50	$199	$199
Easy to use	Easy to use	Longer learning curve
No HTML email	HTML email but still a contact manager	Automatic Sales Process
Up to 50000 contacts	Up to 50,000 contacts	Unlimited

Table 10.1 Comparison of CRM

If you have fewer than 50,000 contacts and you do not need to have built in automatic sales process (send out email in a scheduled time frame …), then ACT! is a very good choice. It is the most widely use contact manager. It is very easier to use and there are a lot of add on software to fit your needs.

One major challenge to today's computer users is integration, how to make the software to work together. If you use a widely used program, integration would be a less problem because there are so many companies would build the supporting systems around that software. ACT! is one of the popular program.

Goldmine on the other hand is more on the automatic sales management software. It is a little bit more complex but it can handle unlimited size of database and it can handle scheduled automatic sales cycle. You can create a tripping sales process and the software can take care that for you.

Both softwares selling for about $150 - $200 and you can download the trial versions of both softwares. If you still feel it is expensive to use these software, you can buy the ACT! 5.0 on ebay or other used software market. The price will be about $50 and there's not much difference with the later versions. The major down fall of ACT! 5.0 or 2000 is that they cannot send out HTML email.

In this manual, I will use ACT! to illustrate certain functions that you should know to manage your database program. I am not attempting to replace a software instructional manual; I could not possibly fit it into one chapter. However, there are a few steps that you need to take to ensure your CRM work well.

1. Centralize you data (I suggest to save it in the Office Data folder)
2. Setup a new database
3. Input or import data from other database
4. Setup security
5. Customize the entry fields and the lay out to your business
6. Make sure you use all the communication functions that fit to your business, such as telephone, letter, fax and email
7. Schedule your activities according to the importance and urgency

Centralize Your Data

In the earlier chapters, you know more about filing system. You will also need a great backup system. However, I would like to remind you that centralization and backing up data is extremely important and crucial to your business. Therefore, we would like to make it simple and easy to locate and back up data. I would like you to back up to in the Office Data Folder (the folder that we create in Chapter 5; or wherever and whatever name your like to name it. The key is that you know where it is.) under your My Document folder.

Some of my clients choose to use the My Document Folder as the master folder for all other folders, instead of creating Office Data folder inside My Document. That is absolutely OK and that is your own preference. Just remember I created a Office Data folder in My document folder in this book.

Because there are so many different CRM in the market place, I will use ACT to illustrate my point.

➢ **Where Should I Place My Database?**

I always mention the importance of centralization of data. I repeat it because I believe it and I want you to do it. The best place for you to centralize is the Office Data folder that we created in chapter in your main computer.

1. Go to Start/All Programs/ScanSoft PaperPort 9.0/Paperport and start the program.
   Click the folder icon in the menu.

2. Right click the Office Data folder and select New Folder

Figure 10.1 Create a ACT folder in Office Data folder

3. Type in ACT and click OK button
   You just created a ACT sub-folder in Office Data folder

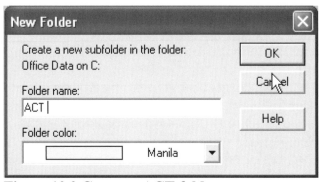

Figure 10.2 Create a ACT folder

4. Go to copy all of the FOLDERS in the ACT! 's directory to the ACT folder in Office data folder.
You can find the directory by going to Start/ Explore and then follow the path C:/Program Files/ ACT. Select Edit/Select All/Copy

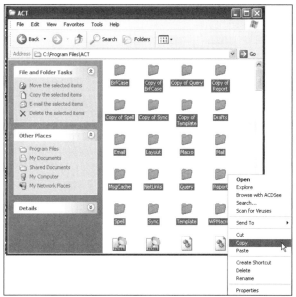

Figure 10.3 Copy the data folders of your CRM

5. Go back to PaperPort Desktop
Highlight the ACT folder and select Edit/ Paste

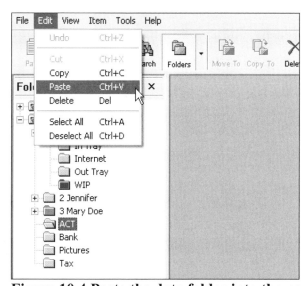

Figure 10.4 Paste the data folder into the new folder

6. Start ACT by clicking on the icon on the desktop or go to Start/Program/ACT6/ACT

7. Open the demo database or any database of yours
The path is C:\Documents and Settings\your user name\My Documents\ ACT\ Database\Demo

8. Go to Edit/Preference
This brings up the Preferences dialog box

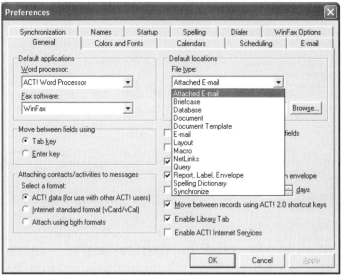

Figure 10.5 Preference dialog box

9. **Pull down each file type and browse to the location of the respective folder in your new ACT folder. Repeat the process for each of the files.**
Browse to this path C:\Documents and Settings\David Lam\My Documents\Office Data\ACT

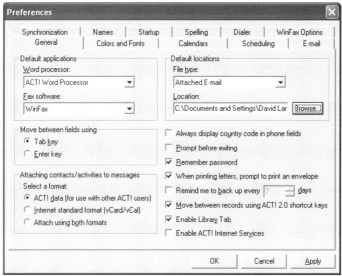

Figure 10.6 Change to location of the files

10. Go To the Startup Tab

Select your layout you like to use at start up and check the button for Last opened under Startup Database. Unless you have a database that you like to open every time at startup, I found this option useful.

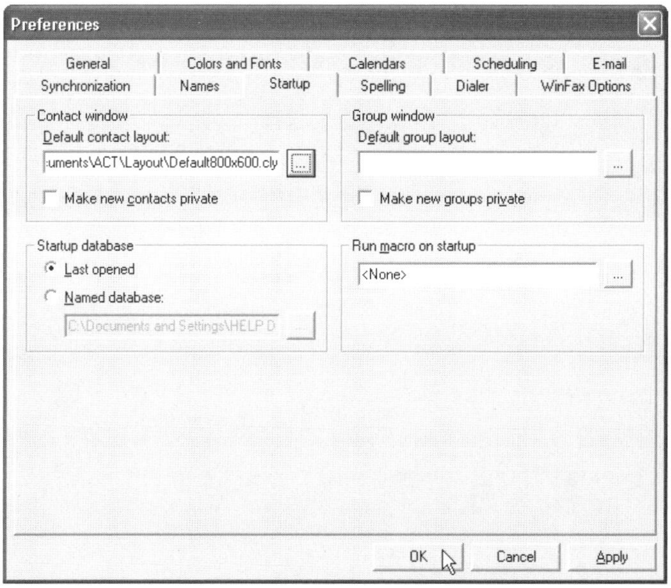

Figure 10.7 Set up Start Up Preference

11. **After you change the default directory of each folder, click OK**

This brings you back to the Demo contact view. Leave the database by going to File/Exit.

Create a New Database

Creating a new database is a very straight forward process and the program will pretty much guide you through each step.

After you installed ACT!, it will ask you to registered and create a new database. You can work from there or you can create a database later with the following instruction.

1. **Start ACT! by Start/All Programs/ACT! 6/ ACT.**

The program will start. Go to File/ New and click OK at the New dialogue box.

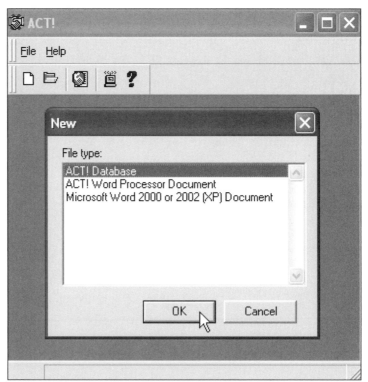

Figure 10.8 Create a new database

2. **Find the directory of the database folder in the new ACT! that we just created.**

   Depend on how you create the new older earlier, the path should look like: C:\Documents and Settings\Your user name\My Documents\Office Data\ACT\Database. Enter the name you want and click Save button.

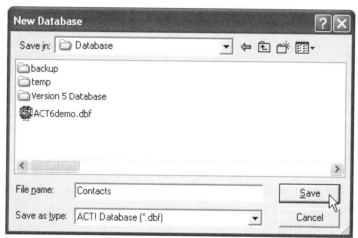

Figure 10.9 Name the new database

3. **ACT! will create a new database and a Enter "My Record" Information dialogue box will pop up.**

   Type in all the information about you. It will also be the return contact information if you send out your communication

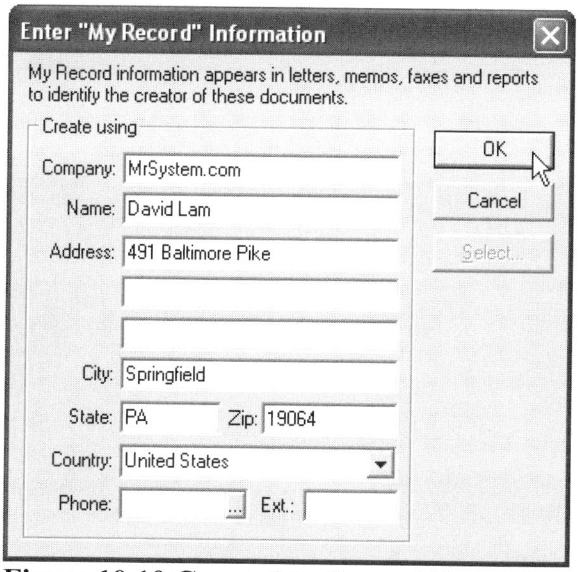

Figure 10.10 Create My Record Name the new database

4. Click Yes and confirm

If this is the first time you set up ACT!, it will also ask you to setup

　　i. Email software

　　ii. Important data from Email program or Palm Desktop.

The process is very straight forward. You can also follow the rest of this chapter to setup all those.

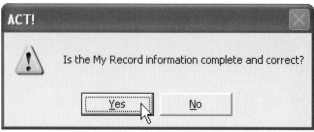

Figure 10.11 Confirm your information

Import Data From Other Database

You may be using Palm or Outlook Express already. You probably want to import the address book, activity and other data into your new ACT! database. It could save you a lot of time.

1. Open ACT! by Start/ All Programs/ ACT! 6/ ACT

This start the program. It should open the Contacts database that you just created.

2. File/ Data Exchange / Import/ Browse to the database

Figure 10.12 Data Exchange

3. Select the database you want to import
Most likely, it should be either Outlook or Palm. If you have both, you need to import each at a time. Click Next.

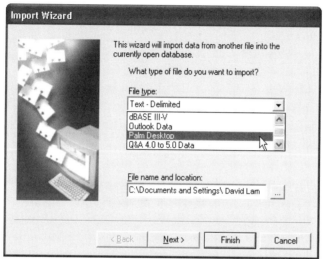

Figure 10.13 Select The Database To Import

4. Mapping the field
You may have your user defined fields and different arrangement of fields. This is the way for your ensure the data from other database will match what you have in ACT! Just make sure each of the import fields match the fields in ACT! Click Finish button.

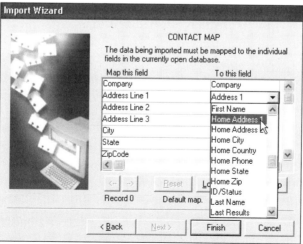

Figure 10.14 Import Field mapping

Setup Security

The simple way to set up security for the database is to setup password. If you have more than one user of the database, then you should different users with different passwords that will limit the access to your database. That is what we call "User Lever" security. Even if your database is stolen, the person will not be able to open your database without knowing the password.

1. Go to File/ Administration/ Define user

This brings up the Define User dialog box. If you never setup password, leave the old password blank. Type in the new passwords and click OK.

Figure 10.15 Set Password for yourself

2. Go to File/ Administration/ Define user

This brings up the Define User dialog box. Click add user if you need to and setup password. Set up User name, password, Security level, and others. For a small business environment, you may consider giving your staff Administrative power so that they can help you get the job done. Click OK

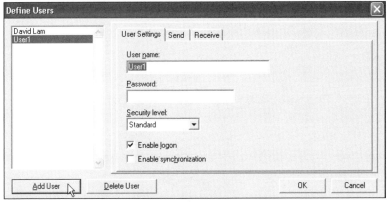

Figure 10.16 Define Users dialog box

Customize The Database

For a general database like ACT, you may need to add certain fields and design the layout to make it easier for you and your staff to work. In ACT, you can use more than 10 user fields for your unique data. However, I suggest that you do not change the user field. You will have many problems when merging databases if you change the user fields. You will be better off adding new fields to suit your unique situation.

➢ How To Add a Field

1. Go to Edit/ Define Fields

This brings up the Define Fields dialog box

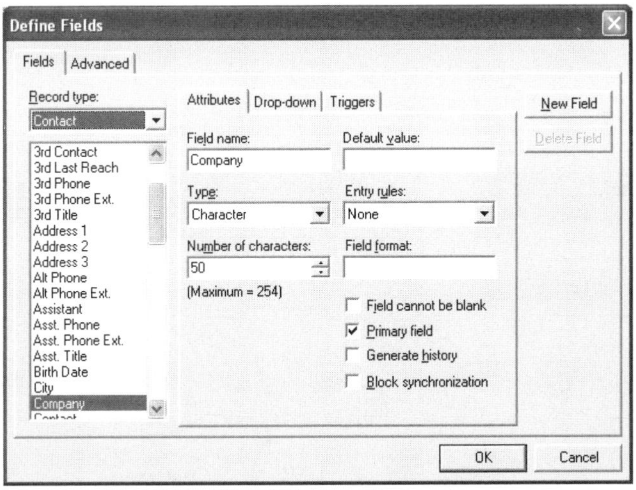

Figure 10.17 Define Fields dialog box

2. Click The New Field Box
   Type in the Field Name you want. You may even create a list
   of choices in the Pull Down Tab.

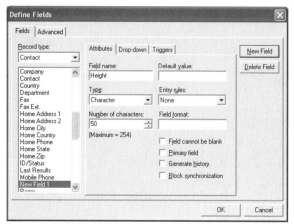

Figure 10.18 Add a new field

3. Click Ok after you finish

➤ How To Change The Layout

After you add the New Field, you may want to put it in the desktop
for your convenience to fill or change the new field. You may also
change the layout to fit your needs more.

1. Click the layout button at the bottom of the screen
   Select the basic layout you want to change.

Figure 10.19 Change the lay out

2. Go to Tools/ Design Layout
This open up the design layout window

Figure 10.20 Design layout

3. **Select View/ Show Palette**
   This is the step just for the cast that the palette does not show up.
   This brings up the Palette tool box. You can click on the Arrow
   icon and point to field that you like to delete or move.

4. **Select the Field tool by click on the field sign. Drop and drag
   the cursor and you will make a new blank field.**
   Select the field definition you want the blank field to be.

5. **Rearrange how the tab key jump between fields**
   Click the number of the fields that you want to rearrange its
   numeric order. The number will disappear. Then click the empty
   number box in the order you want to TAB to.

6. **You should click the red dot box (the box besides the number
   box) to set up the order that the cursor is going to jump.**
      7. Click File/Save As
   The Save As box will pop up and you will need to name the new
   layout.

8. **Click OK**

Setup Fax, Telephone And Email Preferences

1. Go to Edit/ Preference.

ACT makes the setup extremely simple and easy. Go to the tabs and setup the fax the way you want it.

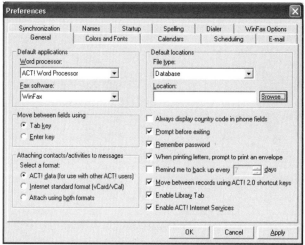

Figure 10.21 Preference dialog box

2. Go to the WinFax Option

Here is how I centralize my data and keep records of my fax communications with my contacts. Simply check all the empty boxes.

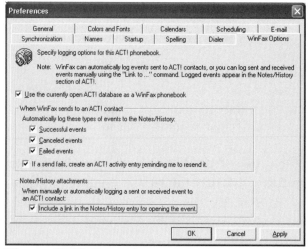

Figure 10.22 Fax setup

Regular WinFax will cost you about $100. Go to websites like www.Yahoo.com and you will find WinFax OEM version (bundle version) for only $20 or you can buy those older versions, like version 10.

➢ Setup Telephone Preference

If you want to have both the fax and telephone function working with your CRM, you need to have two modems installed. You can simply go to any office supply store or computer store and ask for a fax modem and it will work fine. You can use ACT to dial out a call and it will never make a mistake. In addition, you can have both hands free and type in the conversation. One more bonus is that you can set up the timer pop up automatically and you can control your time much easier.

1. Go to edit/ Preferences
   This brings up the Preference dialog box.

Figure 10.23 Does it look familiar now?

2. Go to the Dialer tab

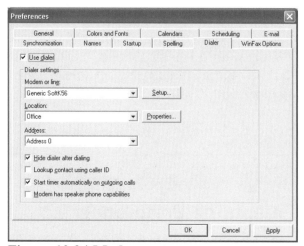

Figure 10.24 Modem setup

3. Check Use dialer and other boxes accordingly

4. Use the pull down menu to select your telephone modem; setup is usually automatic.

5. If you did not setup calling location, click the Properties box
This bring up the Phone and Modem Options box

Figure 10.25 Phone and modem setup

6. Click the New button

This brings up the New Location dialog box.

Figure 10.26 New location setup

7. Type in the name of this location

Fill in the space accordingly

8. Click OK

There is a very common mistake in setting the communication ports if you have more than one modem. Remember to setup your two modem ports either as 1 and 2, or 3 and 4. If you setup your modems as 1 and 3, or 2 and 4, the modems will not work probably.

Keep Your Hands Free

There are still some people thought that hand free telephone set is a privilege of big corporation. If you are in marketing business and you need to call people everyday, I will suggest you sit in front of the monitor and working on the CRM when you are calling. You need to work very proficient because you need to talk, to type in what you say and schedule the follow up all at the same time. If you don't do it, your follow up will be out of hand very soon. The only way for you to do that is using a telephone with headset and using the auto dial function of your CRM. The good news is most CRM has built in auto dial function already and a headset is available in most office store for less than $100. Just plug the telephone line from the wall into the Line In slot of the modem; and plug the line of the telephone set to the Telephone Line slot of the modem. You are good to go.

➢ Setup e-mail Preference

1. Go to Edit / Preference

2. Go to the E-mail Tab

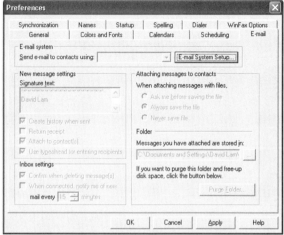

Figure 10.27 E-mail system setup

3. Click the E-mail system Setup button
This brings up the E-mail setup Wizard.

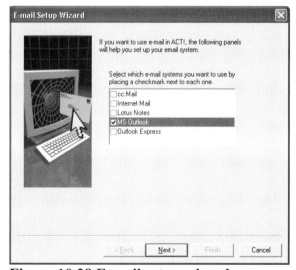

Figure 10.28 E-mail setup wizard

4. Check your E-mail software that you use

5. Click Next
This brings up the confirm page. Unless you want to change the default e-mail setting of your software, check the box of Always use Default.

Figure 10.29 E-Mail Setup Wizard

6. Click Next and then click finish
That brings you back to the E-mail tab in the Preference dialog box. Here is an important setup step or you may lose your email attachment.

- Type in your signature; what you want people to see at the end of every email you send
- Check the box of Create history when sent
- Check Attach to contacts
- Check Always save the file
- Browse the folder you want the e-mail message to save in

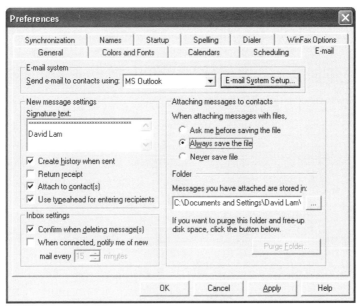

Figure 10.30 E-mail Preferences

7. Click apply and finish the e-mail setting

By setting up the fax, telephone, and email functions, you should be able to communicate digitally with your clients and keep all the record at the same time. You just took another important step towards a Highly Efficient Office.

If you still to send out letter to your clients, you should also use the internal word processor to do your word processing. The key is create a lot of template for your business and use merge function as much as possible instead of type a new letter every time.

Every time after your merge a letter or letters, remember to schedule follow up activities. You should also setup alarm function for the schedule activities.

You should have a habit of synchronize your PDA and ACT!, or your other CRM, daily. In case you need to find your contacts and note, they are all at your finger tips.

There is a list of email services here. If you use Outlook Express, just check the box and move on. If you use Outlook then you may encounter a problem: the option of Outlook may not be there!

Usually, there are three possibilities causing the problems in setup:
- Your firewall software blocks the linkage
- Your anti-virus software blocks the linkage
- Bad installation of your e-mail software

Stop the firewall and anti-virus software and restart ACT to see if you can see the option of Outlook.

If you are not able to fix the problem, you will need to find the Outlook or Office installation disk. Start Outlook, go to Help/ Detect and repair and check the box of Restore my short cuts while repairing. Click Start to proceed and insert the installation disk when asked for. You should then solve the problem and see the option of Outlook in ACT E-mail setup Wizard.

Figure 10.31   Detect and repair in Outlook

Budget Your Time

Adding a new contact to ACT is a simple step to go to Contact/New Contact and type in the fields.

If you have a group of people with similar background, you can speed up the input process by using Contact/ Duplicate Contact/ Duplicate Data From All Fields. However, the simple fact that you have a lot of name does not guaranteed your success in a business.

For most small businesses, time and capital are two limited resource. I know most business owners have budgets for their money, however, many do not have a budget for their time.

Most of us are to do many things at one time and hope that we could finish all. I was there. As time goes by, I learnt that most of the time I was major in the minor thing. It is very important to prioritize our task and allocate the time accordingly.

Don't jump into the hoop of planning your day. Find our what is important to your and block out those time slot first in your calendar first. If you do not do the exercise in chapter one, this is the time to go to finish it.

It takes discipline and time to do the important things such as prospecting, calling, setting up appointments, etc. It also takes time and multiple interactions with your contacts to establish a trust relationship. That is the place where you can use the help of a CRM budget your time. Let the CRM to help you to make it easier to follow your plan.

➢ Block Out The Time For The Importance

I will say you should do monthly planning and block out the time according to the importance of the activities. Let's say you want to block out 2 hours of calling time Monday to Friday.

1. Start ACT! and go to Contacts Database.
This brings up your My Record data.

2. Select View/Calendar/Monthly Calendar.
This brings up the monthly planner.

3. Right click anywhere on the calendar
Select Schedule/Call and bring up the Schedule Activity box.

Figure 10.32 Schedule Activity

4. Fill in the time, period, priority of the block of time.
Click Recurring Setting tab

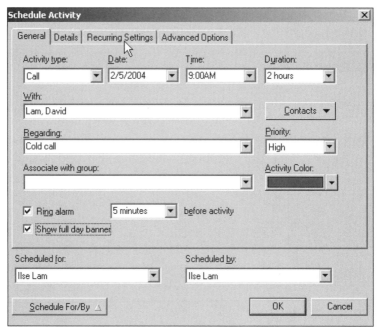

Figure 10.33 Fill In Activity Details

5. Click the Custom button

Click on the pull down calendar of "Until" box and select the end of the month. Then highlight the date of the you want to block out the time that you want to repeat.

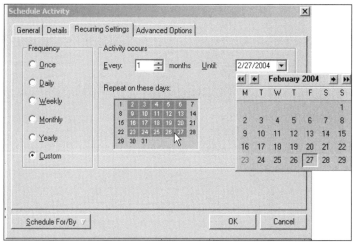

Figure 10.34 Block Out Time

6. Click OK.

This will bring your back to the monthly calendar. You should see the time is blocked out.

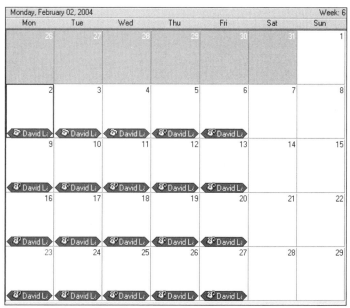

Figure 10.35 Confirm The Schedule

➤ Find Your Contact & Schedule Activity

After you prioritize yourself, the next step is how to arrange your day and hour. I will show you an example of how to schedule a lunch meeting with your contacts. The first step is looking up your contact in the database, and then schedule an activity and alarm.

You can search your database by any criteria. I will use Last name here.

1. Start ACT! and got to Contacts Database. Select Lookup/Last Name

Figure 10.36 Look Up By Last Name

2. Type in the Last Name of the person. Click OK button
This bring you back to the Contact Page.

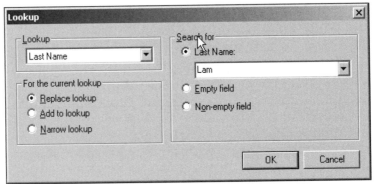

Figure 10.37 Type In Last Name

3. Select View/ Contact List

If you can look up exactly the person you want, you can skip this step and the next one.

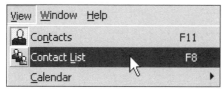

Figure 10.38 Chang e To Contact List View

4. Locate you contact

You can click on the Head of column to rank the contacts by the each field. You can also right click the column head to add column to view. Double click the box on the left hand size and ACT! will bring you back to contact view of the selected contact

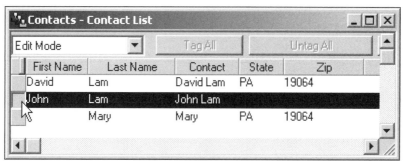

Figure 10.39 Select The Contact

5. Select Contact/ Schedule Meeting

This bring up the schedule

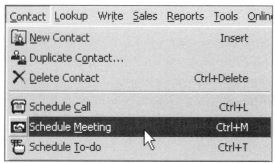

Figure 10.40 Schedule Meeting

6. Schedule the activity

This Schedule Activity is a universal tool to schedule Meeting, Calls and Work To-do. If you click Contact/ Schedule Meeting, the Activity type will automatically select Meeting and use the default setting. (The default setting can be changed Edit/ Preference/ Scheduling) You can type in all the information about the meeting. Check the box of Ring Alarm and select how much earlier for the alarm to go off. Click OK button to get back to the contact view.

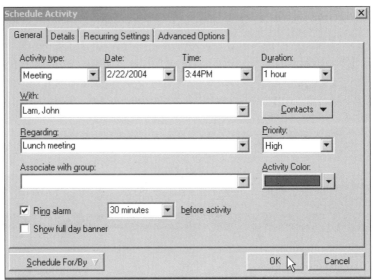

Figure 10.41 Type In Details

7. **When the time comes, you will see a pop up alarm in your program**

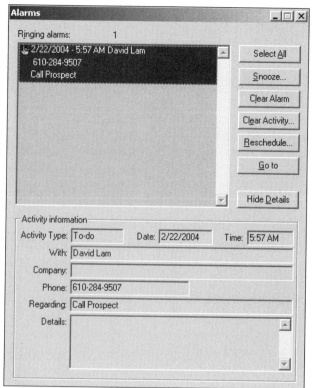

Figure 10.42 Set Alarm

8. Click Clear Activity and bring

Instant Messaging

You may heard that there are a lot of young people using it for chatting. However, you may use it for business It is actually a instant email box that is open all the time on your computer once you sign it. You will get your email in a message format. The difference is that you can exchange message with your associate at real time.

If you have a few employee in your office, or you have some associates whom you need to keep close contact, instant messaging service is very useful. In addition, you can sign up with MSN.com or Yahoo.com and use their for free. Of course, you may be force to look at some advertising but at least you don't have a monthly fee to pay for the service.

Both sites have very clear instruction to show you how to sign up and use the service.

If you really don't know, go to either site and search for the word, Instant messaging, and you will find they list their own service in high priority.

It concludes the discussion of the use CRM. Let's talk about the green matter.

CHAPTER 11

Hire Your Own Virtual Money Manager

****

In this chapter, you will learn:

> ➤ Selection Of Financial Manager Software
> ➤ Centralize The Data
> ➤ Keep Your Data Safe
> ➤ Online Banking
> ➤ Simplify The Tax Record Keeping
> ➤ Memorize And Categorize The Transactions

****

If there are stacks of paper in your office, you should examine what kind of paper could be eliminated first and convert that into the digital format.

The first one that probably will come to your attention is the number of bills and statement. . It is very easy to reduce various bills and statements into digital format with the help a good financial management software.

There are two kinds, the PFM (Personal Financial Management software) and the BFM (Business Financial Management software). You also need to have Internet access to use the program to its best performance.

Selection Of Financial Manager Software

If your business files separate tax return and involves with lots of invoices and receipts. You would need the QuickBooks. It is a very sophisticated BFM and you can link the financial record to your particular CRM.BFM such as, QuickBooks, offer more business functions such as managing invoices, account receivables, account payable. It can also create payroll checks, set aside employment tax and prepare tax-filing reports.

If you only need to centralize your financial data, then, Quicken or Money will be good enough for you. Both of the programs are very popular PFM. I will take PFM instead of QuickBooks if I do not need all those business functions. If you work by yourself or you do not need to generate invoices, payroll checks ... etc. I will suggest you to save some money and get a PFM with business accounts.

You first need to decide what version to keep or to upgrade to. If you have a business, I will strong suggest you to get the PFM with personal and business entry. It will save you lot of when you can have both personal and business on the same screen and look at your financial health status in one shot. Either the new Quicken 2004 Premier Home and Business, and Microsoft Money 2004 Deluxe and Business are very much convenient to use.

There are a lot of neat functions in these two softwares. I would like to keep our focus on those functions that can save eliminate some more paper. I will use the new Quicken Premier Home and Business to illustrate a few crucial steps.

1. Centralize the data
2. Security setup
3. Setup on Online Banking accounts
4. Link the item to the tax form

Centralize The Data

As you will know later, I always suggest centralization of data. Open a new folder, Quicken Data or whatever name you like, in the Office's Data that we create in Chapter 7. You can easily accomplish in PaperPort desktop.

1. Right click the Office Data folder that we created in Chapter 5 and select New Folder
This will bring up the New Folder box.

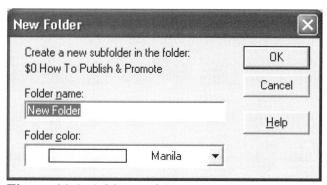

Figure 11.1 Add new folder through PaperPort

2. Type in any name you like for Quicken, I will use the name Quick here

3. Click OK

If you are new to Quicken, simply indicate in set up to save data in this Quicken folder. If you are Quicken user, you can move the data here by File/ Save As and browse to save in this folder. You should delete the old one to avoid any confusion of folder.

Keep Your Data Safe

Since this is a very sensitive data, you may want to limit the access to this folder. The most simplest security measure is setup a password in the PFM itself.

1. Go to Start/ Program/ Quicken/ Program/ Quicken/ Quick2003

This opens up the Quicken folder.

2. **Go to File/ Passwords/ File**
   This will bring up the Quicken File Password.

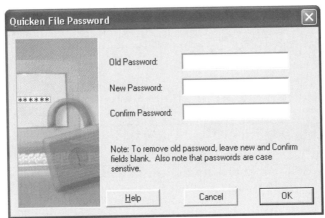

Figure 11.2   Setup the password

3. **Type in the password you need and click OK**

Online Banking

There are two types of online banking. Web-base online banking and online banking with BFM or PFM.

You can go online and use web-base online banking to send check, check balance or transfer…etc. However, you do not own the data and
you can only look at your accounts while you are online. you cannot categorize your transactions in the software. It is not quite useful if you want to use it with you tax software. If you have more than one accounts, the web-base service could not help you to consolidate the accounts either.

We will focus how to work the online banking with the PFM This is a much better option. The advantages are:

- It can download of detail transactions from your bank account, credit card and investment accounts if the institution support that. It save a lot of time in data entry
- It enables online payment, direct deposit and integrate to the data
- It enables categorization every transactions according to type of spending and tax provisions

- It help you to file tax very easy if you categorize every transactions and link them the tax item on tax return
- It can do different budgeting and planning
  Online banking or download is a very powerful function of PFM if we use more of it. You might have used PFM for a while already. I hope you did do all the following:

- Did you set up all your bank accounts, investment accounts and payment accounts with automatic download?
- Have you set up direct deposit with your paychecks?
- Have you set up automatic payment for all the regular payment accounts that offer monthly email bill and automatic debit?
- Do you write MOST your checks with the automatic check pay with your bank?
- Have you use your check card for MOST of your purchases?
- Have you categorize your expenses?
- Have you link your expenses to tax form?

If you do not do any of the above, you create a lot of unnecessary mail and hence paper sent to your on a regular basis. You are wasting the power of online banking and you waste a lot of your valuable time. I will show you, with Quicken, how to do the essence of using online banking to streamline your banking activities.

➢ Setup Internet Connection

1. Go to Edit / Preferences/ Internet Connection Setup

This brings up the Internet Connection Setup dialog box.

Figure 11.3 Setup internet connection

The rest is very self explanatory. Unless you used dial up(telephone line), you should enable Quicken's link to you default internet setup. If you use dial up, choose the first one and follow the simple instruction.

➢ Add Accounts For Internet Download

Most likely, you bank, credit card and investment company off online banking with data download. You will find it when you go to setup online account in Quicken. If any of those company do not offer this service, then you really need to consider change those company or keep on dealing with unnecessary papers.

On of the challenge I wrote this book is there are so many readers at different stage of their office automation projects. In real life consultation, I can adjust my instruction to different but I am not able to put all the different approaches in the volume of this book. I will assume you need to need to set up a new online account. If you have an account you use Quicken or Money for a while and you do have existing account setup, just simply edit the existing accounts.

1. Go to Online/ Online Account Services Setup
This bring up the Online Account Setup window

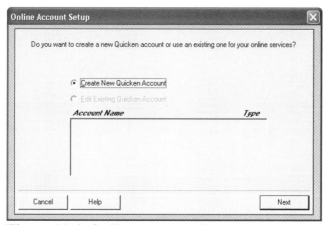

Figure 11.4 Online Account Setup

2. Depend if you have an account setup already

3. Click OK
This brings up Create New Account dialog box.

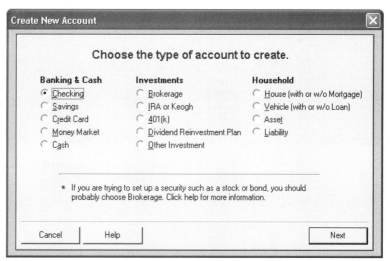

Figure 11.5 Create New Account

4. Click the account you need
Assume you open a new checking and check Checking here

5. Click next button

Checking Account Setup, show window will pop up. Type in a nickname for your new account and select your bank.

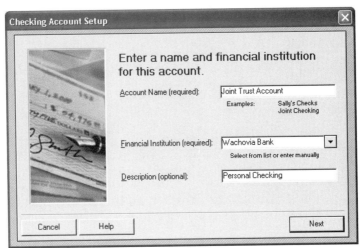

Figure 11.6 Checking Account Setup

6. Click Next

If you are unsure about the account, you do not need to fill anything. Just leave the spaces blank.

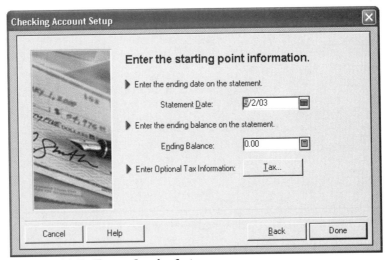

Figure 11.7 Enter basic data

7. Click done

It will bring up the Online Account Activation

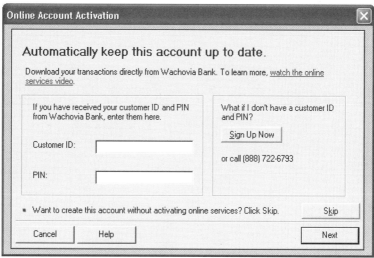

Figure 11.8 Activate online account

8. Type in the Customer ID and PIN

Even if you do not have an Customer ID, you can very quickly
check it out from the web site or call the number.

9. Repeat the process with all the financial accounts you have.

Even if you setup online download with all the account you
have, it will not work very well unless you do centralize all
your payments. I will suggest you to do the following

- Have you set up direct deposit with all of your
  regular deposits, such as paychecks.
- Set up automatic payment for all the regular
  payments accounts, such as utility bills, that offer
  monthly email bill and automatic debit
- Use credit card to pay those accepts credit card
  payment
- Use the checking writing ability of you PFM to
  send check

➢ Write a Online Check

1. Click on the Cash flow account that the check is send from left pane and click write check on the account page
This brings up the Write Checks box of the account that you select.

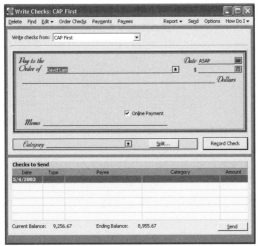

Figure 11.9 Write a electronic check

2. Type in the payee's name
If it is a new payee, the Set Up Online Payee box will automatically pop up. Just type in the information. The bank will send out a check the payee directly.

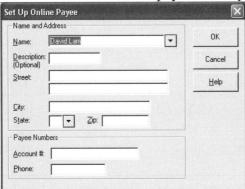

Figure 11.10 Setup online payee

3. Click OK and confirm the information in the second window.

With all the accounts set, centralize you bill payment and deposits. We need to download the accounts on a regular basis. The new Quicken 2003 even enables automatic schedule download.

➢ Schedule Regular Download Update

Quicken makes this step so much easy and intuitive to setup.

1. Go to Online/ Schedule Updates

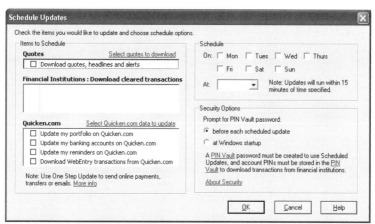

Figure 11.11 Schedule automatic updates

2. Click PIN Vault

You need a PIN for every online accounts to setup download.
However, you probably would not like to put every PIN every
time when you do a download. A PIN Vault enables you have a
overall PIN and download all the accounts at once. Just type in
the number you can remember.

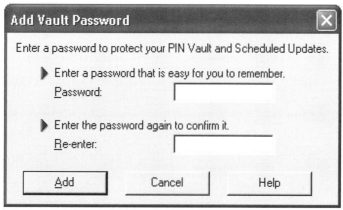

Figure 11.12 Add Vault Password

3. Click Add and then check the time you like a download to be done.

I should have already given you enough bullet us to make your PFM to help you to centralize your data and eliminate those paper statements, bills and invoices.

Simplify The Tax Record Keeping

Do you know what is the greatest fiction created by mankind every year? Take a guess.

AND THE ANSWER IS…….. TAX RETURN 1040!

I learnt this joke back in the time when I was studying my accounting degree. The person told me this joke explain to me that it was very difficult to keep track on all the expenses. Therefore, most of the taxpayers just took some educated guess to fill their tax return.

However, the educated guess may cause you money because you did not take all deductions that you are entitled. It is especially important if you have your own business.

With the power of computer and the help of your PFM, we probably should give a much more clear picture of our deductible expenses.

To link the expenses to the line in tax form, you need to create the deductible business expensed categories. Then, you link the expense to the tax item and assign the expense to the categories. After that, your whole database will be ready to export to those tax filing software.

➢ Create Business Categories

1. Go to Tools/ Categories list

This will bring up the categories list and Quicken already did a great job in setup the personal items. I will show you how to create a entertainment account.

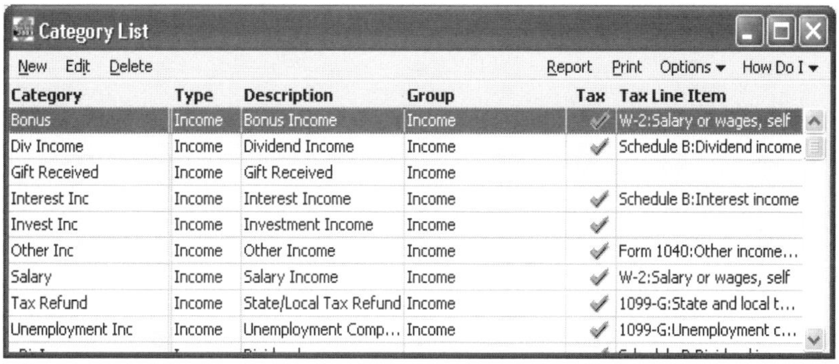

Figure 11.13   Categories list

2. Click New

This brings up the Set Up Category. We will create a new overall categories of business expenses. It is an overall categories and you do not need to link it to any tax line.

Figure 11.14 Setup category

3. Click OK

This send you back to the Category list

4. Go to New and create a new category of entertainment
Fill in the blanks as the Figure here.

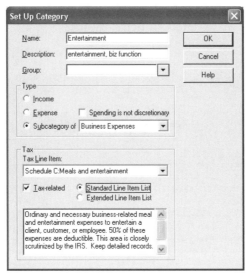

Figure 11.15 Link category to tax line

5. Click OK and create all the business expense subcategories
You may need your accounts' help in creating categories.
Another very convenient way is take a look of your own
schedule C to see your expenses and create the categories line
by line. You can also create a overall category of business
income and the subcategories accordingly depend on your
business.

➢ Assign The Categories To The Download Transaction

1. Go the transaction you download and right click the categories space
It will pull down the whole list of categories.

Figure 11.16 Assign category to transaction

2. Find the category and click on that.

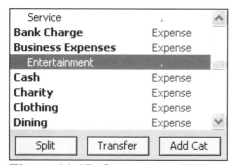

Figure 11.17 Category pull down menu

3. Jot down the other required tax deduction item.
With the help of Quicken, you have the Location, Amount of expense and payment type. However, for tax purpose, you need to fill in two more information in the Memo Space to make it a legitimate tax-deductible activity:

- Name of the attending person
- The business reason of this expense

Memorize And Categorize The Transactions

You may find yourself spend money on the same place a few times or a lot of times. You can enable Quicken to memorize the transaction. Quicken then will remember the payee and assign the categories to the transaction automatically.

1. Simple right click anywhere on the transaction and select memorize transaction.

There are a lot of instruction books out there designed to explain each software in great details. If you want to learn more about the program, you should consult those manuals.

My purpose here is showing you the potential of PFM to eliminate paper as an information carrier, streamline your work process and be more productive. In addition, I also try to help you to integrate the software into your operation and multiply the value and effectiveness of your existing computer system. I hope I have given bullets to you. Let us to shoot down more of the paper.

In this chapter, I just show you a few functions of a PFM. There are a lot more that you can do with the software. I would like to show you that it is not difficult or complicated at all. You just need to take a little bit of initiative to learn. I am sure you will have no problem in learning and find the softwares very useful.

Part V: Protect Your Investment

Always, Expect The Unexpected ...

LAM Chart © Of Computer Security Measures
(**L:** Learn   **A:** Acquire **M:** Master)

(image) ™	*David: "The most important principle in risk management in business is NEVER trade your financial risk with character risk."*
Protection From Intruders	<ul><li>Control physical access</li><li>Setup Window log on password</li><li>Make personal file private</li><li>Automatic update Window OS</li><li>Install antivirus program</li><li>Install anti-spy program</li><li>Purchase paper shredder</li></ul>
Backup	<ul><li>Setup Restore Point</li><li>Backup with CD-RW, DVD-RW, external hard drive</li><li>Uninterruptible Power Supply (UPS)</li></ul>
Maintenance Plan	<ul><li>Automatic disk clean up</li><li>Defragmentation of hard drive</li></ul>

CHAPTER 12

Security Is Not A Dirty Word

****

In this chapter, you will learn:
- ➤ **Physical Access Control**
- ➤ **The Basic Log On Password**
- ➤ **Something For Your Private Viewing**
- ➤ **Automatic Window Updates**
- ➤ **Install Antivirus Program**
- ➤ **Install Anti-Spy Program**
- ➤ **Paper Shredder**

****

It is time to discuss a scary thing in the digital world: Security.

PaperPort does NOT come with a security system. In a small business environment, you probably would not mind if your staff get into the clients files and obtain the information they need. This allows you staff help you to get thing done.

Even if you decide to have open access to office files for all your staff, you may want to set up some access control in case your files got stolen. Additionally, you may also have certain files that you do not want any other people to get into except yourself. Luckily, Window 98/ ME/2000/XP has certain security levels that you can setup.

Beside losing files, you also need to be careful about viruses and hackers.

How much security is enough? That is a great question and the answer is depends on you. I believe there are some basic steps you must take to protect your valuable business information. There are also some options for your own preference.

I will assume that you setup a peer-to-peer network. If you set up a Client/Server network, your technician should be able to share with you how to set up a centralized security of your system.

Physical Access Control

It is obvious. The challenge is that we take it for granted. In an office environment, there should not be too many strangers wandering around. However, it is a good idea to remind your staff to log off of the computers after work. As a business owner, you may leave by nine o' clock at night. However, there may be a chance that someone comes in after you have left. You will be better off if you do not leave your notebook computer in your office over night.

The Basic Log On Password

In a small office environment, mostly, productivity of the office is on a higher priority than security. Therefore, there are a lot of businesses do not setup any security at all in their computer system. However, certain security setup will help to secure the business data without interrupting the operations of business.

With the booming usage of network in business and even homes, privilege in using a computer becomes a more important issue. Privilege means what a user can do to the computer such as setup password, set up security level, getting into certain folders, etc.

The first setup of Window should be the password to access window desktop. The fancy name of this process is "User Level Security". If the computer is stolen, the person cannot start up window and transfer your data easily. He or she of course can do an image of your hard drive and use some other methods, but it is not a simple or cheap process. The last resort that the thefts can do is erase the whole hard drive.

Second, you must enforce a policy that states that your staff must setup log on password and turn off their computers when they leave their office. This will force them to log on their computer every morning. I will show you how to setup log on password.

➢ Log On Password Setup For Window 98

In Window 98/ ME, you can setup a password to access Window by following the steps:

1. Click Start/ Settings/ Control panel and click on Password Icon
    This brings up the Password Properties box

Figure 12.1 Set a User password

2. Click Change Window Password button
    Setup your window password here

➤ Administrator And User Setup For Window 2000

In Window 2000/ XP, you will have better security set up, the systems comes with a different Administrator and users setup.

The default user is the administrator; who has all the privileges to change every setting on the computer. You may want to setup certain limitations for your staff. To do that, you need to setup a user account for your staff to log onto the computer.

To add a user and setup a Window password in Window 2000, use the following steps:

1. Click Start/ Setting/ Control Panel /Administrative Tools This brings up all the administrative tools.

2. Click the icon of Computer Management
This brings up the Computer Management dialog box

3. Go to Local User and Groups/Users
There will be a list of users on the right pane.

4. Click on the user name.
Most likely, you are the administrator. Set the password.

5. Click OK
That will bring you back to the Computer Management window

6. Double click your user name
That will bring up the administrator Properties dialog box and you can fill in the type of security level that you want. That is your basic security policy setup.

You can get a lot of options by going to Start/ Programs/ Administrative Tools / Local Security Policy. However, I think it is a little bit too complicated for small business environment.

Something For Your Private Viewing

If you have any folder or file that you do not want other people, including those in your office to see, you may encrypt it. Encryption actually means adding something to your files that other people will not understand. This is the "File Level Security" and this will help ensure your privacy.

Do not be scared of the technology jargons. You and I are at the end of the technology user spectrum; we only need to know what technology does and how we can use it to our best interest.

1. **Right click the file or folder that you want to encrypt.**
   This bring up the pop up menu

2. **Select Property and check the Advanced button**
   The Advanced Attributes dialog box will pop up

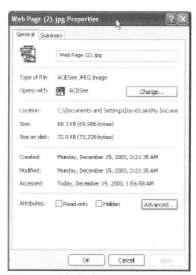

Figure 12.2 Change the security options

3. **Check the box for Encrypt Content to secure data and click OK**

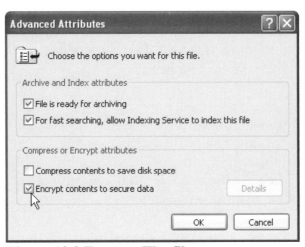

Figure 12.3 Encrypt The file

Now, no other machine could read your file or folder if they try to read you file from other computers. One reminder is that the source program of the file may decrypt the file if you do any modification. Therefore, you need to encrypt your files after each modification.

Automatic Window Updates

On August 11th 2003, there was a virus called W32.Blaster that attacked all the online PC with window 2000 and XP operating system. As most of the corporate has download the service pack for their computers. The home users become the group that was seriously affected.

Actually, rumor and warning about the worm were out there for more than a month. Microsoft also posted a service pack to solve the problem. Therefore, it does make sense to update your Window operating system. Your Window XP is preset to update itself on a regular basis. If there is an update available to install, you should see a balloon notice the corner of Window desktop. It is a good idea to install all critical updates and Window XP updates. However, you should skip the Driver Updates, that usually mess up your computer, and download the updated drivers from the manufacturers' websites.

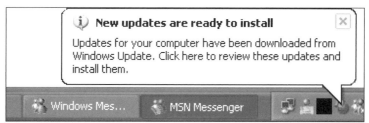

Figure 12.4 Update And Install Service Pack

If you need to reset the update options, following the instruction bellow

1. Click Start/ Control Panel/ Performance and Maintenance
This brings up the Performance and Maintenance dialog box

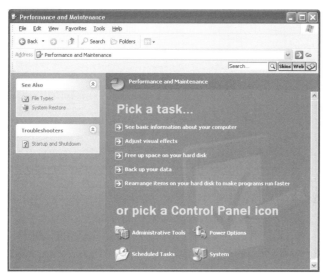

Figure 12.5 Performance and Maintenance Dialog Box

2. Click System
This brings up the System dialog box

3. Go to Automatic Updates tab, and check the box next to Keep My Computer Up to Date

Figure 12.6 System Dialog Box/ Automatic Updates

4. Select Automatically download the updates, and install them on the schedule that I specify.

This is the option that I prefer. It enable the computer to install the update automatically. Remember to set a time when the computer is turn on. I like to choose those odd hour like 3:00am or 4:00am. I hope you do not need to work that late every day.

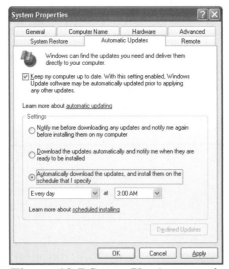

Figure 12.7 Setup Up Automatic Schedule

Install Antivirus Program

Even Microsoft and Federal Government network have been successfully attacked by viruses and that alone should be a lesson. We do not have the money like those two institutes, but we could use a standard protection. We can Install antivirus software in all your computers.

It is vitally important to setup the program right. You must set your computer to scan every disk, downloads and emails coming into your computers. New computer virus appears every day. It is also a good idea to setup automatic updates of the antivirus software.

There are a few very popular antivirus programs:
McAfee VirusScan, Site: http://www.mcafree.com
Norton AntiVirus, Site: http://www.symantec.com

Install Anti-Spy Program

Spy software is a program that can track EVERY websites that you visited, and EVERY keystrokes of your keyboard. You may accidentally download it when you are surfing. It will make you extremely vulnerable especially if you use broad band Internet access. The software will send your personal data back to the company that produce it. You will lose your privacy. In additional, there may be many spy softwares running in your computer at the same time and that will tremendously slow down the whole system.

You can install a anti-spy program like Anti-spy software from www.McAfree.com to eliminate the spy program. It costs about $40.

There is a great anti-spy software that you can download for free from http://security.kolla.de. There are many anti-spy programs cost about $30, and they are not as good as the one from this website. If you like, you may help out this website by donating money to it.

There are two steps to use anti-spy program. It scans the whole hard drive, show you a list of suspicious programs. Then, you need to check those programs to delete them. As long as it is not something like c:\window, that indicates the file is a system files , you may go ahead to eliminate those listed programs.

Paper Shredder

Well, I think I shared enough security measure in regard to the softwares. However, all these will be in vain if you leave your data in pieces of paper and throw them into trash. You probably have heard that some con artists may go to recycle center to find some companies' important data.

Your personal and business information to you, should be as important as those of the big corporations. Therefore, no office should be without a paper shredder.

There are two main kinds of paper shredder, cross cut and strip cut. Cross cut will be more expensive and cut less sheet of paper at a time. I will say for regular small business and home office, strip cut shredder with 10 sheet cutting power should be cost effective.

However, you should test the cutting power of the shredder before you buy it. It is because the data the company provide is not necessary accurate. I have bought a well known company's seven sheets capacity shredder but it always jam even with three sheets of paper. When you are in your own business, you always need to be extra careful.

All these security measures are pretty simple and should not disrupt your business operation. Have you setup all of them yet?

CHAPTER 13

Always Have A Backup And Maintenance Plan

****

In this chapter, you will learn:
- ➤ **Backup Options**
- ➤ **Select Backup Solution**
- ➤ **Uninterruptible Power Supply (UPS)**
- ➤ **Basic Maintenance Procedures**
- ➤ **A Brief Summary**

****

No one thinks that computer crashes happen until it happens to them. I was one of those people; and pretty much, I believed that I deserved the disaster.

That was a couple of years since I had been planning to get an external hard drive. It was a regular office day, I left my notebook computer in my office and went to lunch. I came back from lunch and could not start my computer. To make a long story short; I lost a lot of data, especially my writings. I luckily did backed up My clients' data in another computer. If I lost my clients' data, I would have lost my career's work. It is a real horrible computer experience. Imagine that you have built a DMS and lost **all** of your documents and data inside your computer. What do you feel now? There should be a chill up your spine.

Most computers are sold with a standard 40 G or 80 G hard drive nowadays, that is a lot of memory. If it fails, it will take every file down with it. The potential disaster of the computer makes backup data a mandatory step in any computer operations.

I assume that you have a computer in your office already. I also assume that you have a back up solution. Therefore, I will keep it short and explain a few different backup ideas to you. So that, you can compare each of them and decide if there is a better alternative solution for you.

Backup Options

There are two kinds of back up solution.

The first one is an on site backup. That simply means that you leave your backup data in the same location as where the original data is. Most likely, that is your office. However, if your office gets broken into, a fire occurs, or a natural disaster happens, your backup data will also disappear. I do not that the on site backup alone is a great way to protect your data.

The second type of solution is called off-site backup. It simply means that after you finish the back up, you keep the backup data somewhere else. Actually, it should be very easy to accomplish, but a lot of people just do not have the discipline.

One day, I was watching news on TV about a bulgur in an office campus. There was this extremely desperate looking business owner with tears in his eyes, he said to the news reporter, "All my hard work in the last 6 years are all gone now. They took my computer and all my back up disks." I could understand his pain deeply. For a person to build his business in six and lost all the data in one night is a big trauma to any body.

My friends, do not be the next one.

For your back up purpose, you should take the back up away from your office every day. If you work from home, you can put the disk in your car or use a Internet storage service.

Besides, there are full backup and other incremental backup methods. Since you centralize all your data in Office Data folder that we created in Chapter 5, you should use the full backup and backup all the data folders.

➤ Floppy Disks:

You can copy your entire file into a stock of floppy disks. The challenge is that each disk can only store up to 1.44MB data. It becomes a very time consuming process to back up even if you have mere one gigabytes of data. I really do not think floppy disk is a feasible backup solution.

➢ CD-Rom Or DVD Rom

It is a very popular solution for backup solution. A CD-Rom can store about 800 M data. With the compression feature of the backup function of Window, you can store about 32 G data in a disk. If you have a DVD-RW drive, you can backup in a DVD. The regular storage size of the disk is 4.7 GB. It is a very good size for a day's backup for most small business.

Advantage:
- CD-RW drive is a standard for all computer systems sold.
- Relatively large memory for a small office.
- Least expensive disks.
- Easy to backup and carry the disk away. Most likely, you leave the machine running and you pick up the disk the next day.
- It is very easy to organize the disk. It is especially important if you need to back up data for a long period of time.
- If your do not use the compressive, you can access the data any time with random access.
- Since the Disc are covered by plastic, it is very resistance to dust, finger printer or other office damages

Disadvantages:
- DVD-RW is still an optional hardware in some computer models. Internal DVD-RW cost about $200. The external one is about $400.00. You may need to buy one if you do not have one already.

➢ Tape Backup (DAT) :

You may have an internal or an external tape drive. Either way, the tape drive is large enough to store all the data in sequential order on the tape. Let say something happened to your hard drive, you can easily put back all the backup files into the computer. However, it is not very convenient if you need find a particular file on the tape. Since the files are in sequential order, you may have to wait awhile until the tape drive reaches the files you need. Besides, the tapes, Dec-tapes, are not as durable as disc. Tapes are more bulky to store and organize. It is a very common backup solution but I do not recommend this backup.

➤ Other Magnetic Media:

There are some other removable magnetic media, such as Zip drive, Ditto, Jaz unit. They are relatively small in size but the media are generally bigger than Dec-tape. The disadvantage challenge of all these drive are that they are not very large in memory and you do need a special drive for each media. It could be a very good solution to store some files to carry on the road, but they are not good solution for backup.

➤ Mini External Hard Drive

It is the solution without disk. The advantages are the simplicity in using and you can backup different date of data into this external hard drive and bring it with you when you leave the office. However, by putting all your data in one place, you also run into a small chance of disaster if both of the computer and the external hard drive are damaged or lost at the same time. I like this solution for the simplicity but you must remember not put the external hard drive with your computer.

One of my friend use a notebook computer and backup with the external hard drive. One day he put both of his computer and external hard drive in his car, and his car caught fire. He lost all his files.

➤ Internet Rental Spaces

Some companies lease their memory storage and you can rent it for a fee. You can upload your data through the Internet. Most of these companies claim that they will back it up in at least two different locations. The challenge is the high cost of rental space.

➤ RAID

This is the most sophisticated solution for small business's backup. However, this technology is still too expensive at the moment. For the descent RAID 5 tower, you need to spend about $5000.

The RAID 5 system is actually a combination of software, multiple hard drives, and a tape drive solution. It is a optional equipment of a server computer. The computer has a few hard drives and all of them run simultaneously. There is an overlap of memory of each hard drive. The less the overlap, the more duplication of the data and the more secure the backup.

If one of the drives goes down, you can simply replace it with a brand new hard drive while the computer is still running. Your computer does not even need to stop and your office is running as usual 24 hours.

In addition, you back up whatever files you need into the internal tape drive and take the tape away from the office every day.

So that, the system provides you a non-stop on-site backup system with multiple hard drives; and off-site backup with the tapes.

The system sound all well except the price tag of such a server computer starts at about $5,000.

Select Backup Solution

If you do not have a backup solution, you really need to get one quick.

It is the insurance for all of your hard work. Do not wait until it is too late. The experience of losing data is too painful and it is going to hurt for a long time.

To make it easier on you to select the backup ideas, ask yourself a few questions:

1. What is my budget?
2. How much memory of data do I need to backup?
3. Do I need to use the backup data, or do I just need to back it up for safety? If you just need to back it up for safety purpose, you can compress the data to save memory if you need to.

In most situations, I find CD-rom, DVD-rom portable hard drives are the great backup solutions for small business.

Both CD-Rom and DVD-RW are great choice because of the thin size of the disk. Which one you use depends on your budget and size of data.

The other is the portable hard drive. It is not as secure as the disk because you will have to store all of backup in ONE external drive. However, its small size and big memory does make it very convenient.

Data Size	Small than 700 MB	Between 700 MB and 4.7 GB	Larger Than 4.7 MB
Solution	CD-Rom	DVD-Rom	External Hard Drive
Budget	Most likely, there is a CD-RW drive in your computer CD-RW disc is less than 50 Cent each	External DVD-RW Drive is about $300 DVD-RW disc is about $5 Each	120 GB External Hard drive is about $200 200 GB drive is about $300

Table 13.1 Comparison Of Back Up Options

There are a few different software solutions.

1. You can use the backup function comes with Window 98/ME/ 2000/XP to backup the specific folders and files.

2. Backup softwares, such as Norton Ghost, Backup Executive and Arc Serve. For small business solution, Norton Ghost is a better solution because it only cost about $60 whereas the other two softwares will cost more than $500 each.

I will show you here how to use the FREE function comes with your Window 98/ME/ 2000/XP.

1. Click Start/ Accessories/ System Tools / Backup
This brings up the Microsoft Backup dialogue box.

Figure 13.1 Backup wizard

2. Click Next
This brings up the Backup or Restore dialog box. Select Backup files and settings.

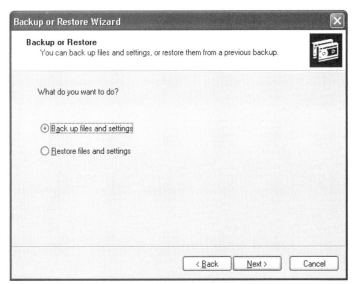

Figure 13.2 setup backup preference

3. **Click Next**

   This brings up What to Back Up dialog box.

   If you listen to my advice and create the Office's Data folder in My Documents folder, that is just a matter of a few clicks in this step. You can check My documents and settings, and then the Backup Wizard will do the backup My Document folder, Cookies, My Favorites and Desktop file automatically.

   However, it may be necessary for you to check 'Let me choose what to back up' if there are some files some else where.

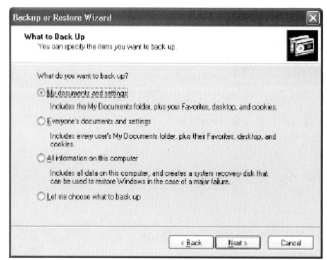

Figure 13.3 Select you backup option

4. Click Next

This brings up Backup Type. Here is where you can choose your backup media. Just simply browse for the media and click on the Next button. The software will do the rest for you.

Figure 13.4 Select a location to back up

You may wonder how long your should keep your backup. The answer depends on your business and the legal requirement.

Big corporations will save certain data online and some data off line in a storage area. For example, if you want a copy of check dated a few years ago, you may need to wait for a few days (if you are lucky) for the bank to do the "research". It is because the banks have limited online. They store the older files in microfiche in other locations.

For small business, I seldom see a need to save data in different locations. Most likely, you should leave all your data saved in your hard drive and keep two weeks of full back up in cd-rom or other media in some place else. You then can keep recycle the cd-rom to backup your hard drive.

Uninterruptible Power Supply (UPS)

It is very different to have instant back unless your have a RAID tower that will cost your at least another couple thousand dollars.

What we can do about unexpected electricity interruption without big expense is installing a UPS. A UPS is just like a battery. All you need to do is putting the plug of the USP into the wall outlet, and put the plugs of equipment into the UPS. If you power get interrupted because of any reason, your can run on the power of the USP for a short period of time. It is usually less than 30 minutes. You should finish and save your work in that short period of time.

Most UPS will have built surge protector and current regulator. It should able to protect your system in some minor abnormality of current flow.

One reminder is that UPS is not built for high voltage variation. That mean it is not a fool proof machine to shield your from very voltage, such as lightning.

You should pull the plug of the UPS from the wall jack if there is a thunder storm in your area.

The following is a picture of a regular UPS.

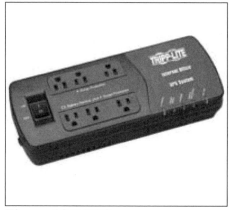

Figure 13.5 UPS

Most UPS have two sets of outlets. One set is just battery supported outlets for your computer, monitor and cable modem in case of power outage. The other set is just surge protect power outlets for other equipment. Remember: make sure which plug goes into the battery supported outlets.

After your charge up the UPS for the first time, unplug the UPS and see if your computer is still on.

There is not much secret in buying a UPS and there is not much quality differentiation either. There are a few things that you need to know:

- Just make sure it has enough outlets for your office
- A warranty cover data and equipments if it fails.
- It is on sales!

Basic Maintenance Procedure

If you want your computer work hard and keep on working hard, your need to keep it healthy and do some maintenance on it. There are three basic maintenance I believe you should perform on a regular basic. Luckily, you can even set a schedule and the computer will automatically do it.

- Automatic Disk Clean up
- Defragmentation Of The Hard Drive
- Setup a Restore Point

➢ Automatic Disk Clean up

You computer will accumulate a lot of temporary files and old files. If you do not clean it up, it will occupy the memory. It is advisable to perform a regular clean up.

1. **Go to Start / All Programs/ Accessories/ System Tools / Scheduled Tasks**
   This brings up the Schedule Tasks Window.

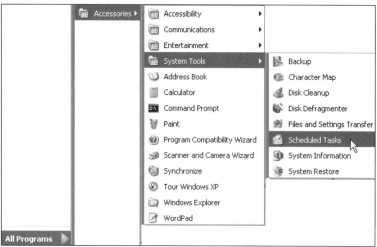

Figure 13.6 Scheduled Tasks

2. **Click Add Scheduled Task**

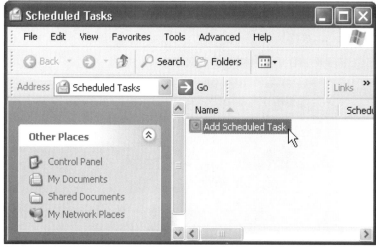

Figure 13.7 Schedule Tasks Window

3. **Click Next**
   This brings up the Schedule Tasks Window..

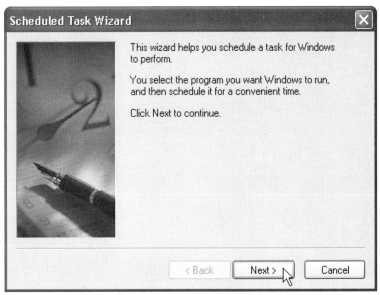

Figure 13.8 Scheduled Task Wizard

4. **Click Disk Cleanup**
   This brings up the Schedule Tasks Window.

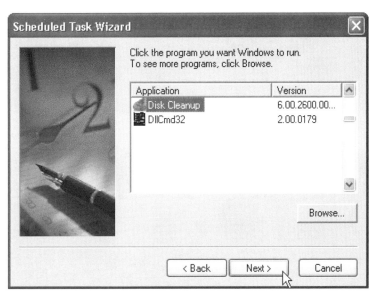

Figure 13.9 Select The Task

5. **Check Monthly and then click the Next button**

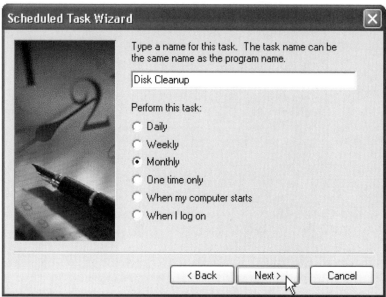

Figure 13.10 Select Frequency of Task

6. **Check the time and day that you won't be using the computer**

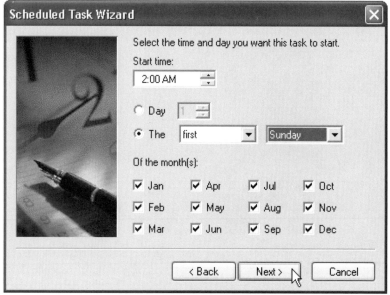

Figure 13.11 Check the time and day of task

7. Check the time and day that you will not be using the computer

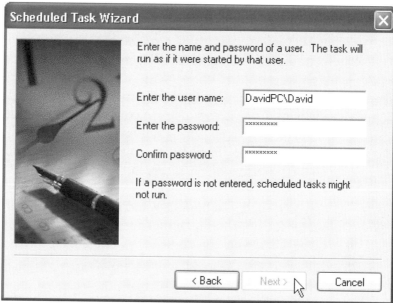

Figure 13.12 Type in your log In password

8. Click Finish button and finalize the schedule task

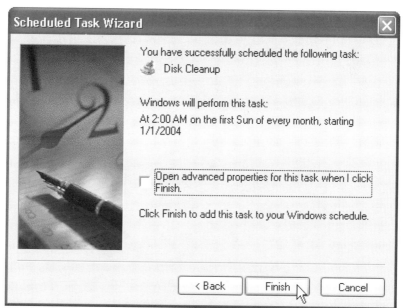

Figure 13.13 Finalize the scheduled task

➤ Defragmentation Of Hard Drive

The hard drive actually comprise of an array of disc. Each disc is divided into millions of sectors that only store a small bit of data. One file has thousand sectors of memory. Unfortunately, those sectors may not be arrange into the same area of disc, or even worse, the sector of a file may be in different disc.

You get the idea? If the sectors contain the data a file scatter in the hard drive, it will take the computer much longer to read or write those sectors. The situation like that is called fragmentation. This is the reason that your computer produce a clicking noise while it is search for files.

Luckily, there is a built in Window software to pull all the sector together and rearrange them continuously in the hard drive. However, you do need to initiate the process regularly. This is what we call Defragmentation.

1. Go to Start / All Programs/ Accessories/ System Tools / Deframenter

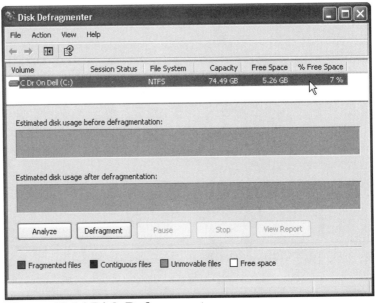

Figure 13.14 Disk Defragmenter

2. **Highlight the hard drive and click Defragment button**
   You should perform this process at least once a month. The first time is going to be pretty long if you have not done it before. You better leave it for over night.

➤ Setup a Restore Point

Have you ever install some new programs and then your computer is not working right?

There are many possibility of what went wrong. You can uninstall the program one by one, or you can restore your computer to the state that everything is alright. This is a nice feature that you should use it.

All you need to do is setup restore stages.

1. **Go to Start/ All Programs/ Accessories/ System Tools/ System Restore.**
   This bring up system restore dialogue box.

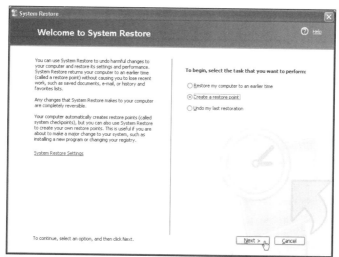

Figure 13.15 Create a restore point

2. Check Create a Restore Point and click Next button.

This bring up system restore dialogue box. Type in the name of restore point. Click Create.

Figure 13.16 Type in the name of restore point

3. Click Close to finish the process.

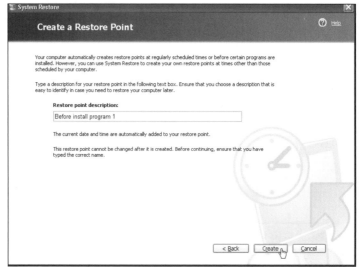

Figure 13.17 Restore Point Created

If there is a unsolved problem with your computer, you can now restore to it to the state of good old time very easier.

Simple go to Start/ All programs/ Accessories/ System Tools/ System Restore and check Restore my computer to an earlier time. It will be a very straight forward process.

By restore the earlier state, you only eliminate the program but not change any documents or database. That is the beauty of this utility.

I know some of the process seem to be trivial, however, it is very helpful to have all these setup. That is a difference between a smooth operation and the daily struggle with the small problems.

A Brief Summary

Finally, we finish all the important parts of a Highly Efficient Office system. You should understand by now, most of the functions that you need to build your Highly Efficient Office system are built in your computer already. You have most of the software you needed either. The challenge actually is taking the time to put them together and setup a new office procedure to run the business.

These are the things you should know:

1. A clear vision of your business and your life

2. A complete infrastructure: It could be an Internet access and local network (if you have more than one computer)

3. Document management system to store, retrieve and manage your files

4. Digital Operation System to manage the information digitally

    a. Digital Mail Room
    b. CRM (Client Relationship Management program)
    c. PFM/ BFM (Personal or Business Financial Manager Program)

5. Setup back up, security and maintenance procedure
   a. different levels of security measures
   b. Setup a backup system to prevent aftermath of disaster.
   c. Schedule automatic maintenance of your computer

6. A determination to continuous monitor and improve

I understand that most business owners are very busy. You don't have to setup all the procedure at one time. It is understandable. However, I do suggest you to setup the part that can improve your productivity immediately and do the rest later.

We always hear a saying: Information Is Power. My opinion is that information is power, only when you have access to the information when you need it.

First, you need to know what information you need. Secondly, you must be able to get it when you need it. Therefore, you need to be aware, you need to organize in the way that you can find it, and you need to access it at the time you need it. This will be only achievable efficiently if your utilize technology.

That is what a Highly Efficient Office™ can help you. Reduce information into digital formation, centralize and organize it in your computer system, and enable you to access and manipulate quickly. This is help you maximize your efficiency and have more free time to do what you want to do. The process is a techno empowerment process. This is what I call DOM™ your business.

As technology evolve and improve everyday, it also becomes necessary for you to learn more new ideas, acquire new equipments, and master the new technologies. This is a never ending cycle and continuous improvement . Visit www.MrSystem.com and sign up for a free membership for latest tips and tricks, plus many other benefits. I will be there to help you along the way.

In the next part of the book, I will share with you more additional resources and strategies that I find useful in a Highly Efficient Office™.

Part VI: Never Ending Improvement

The Happy Benefactors Of A
Highly Efficient Office™

LAM Chart™: Never Ending Improvement
(**L:** Learn **A:** Acquire **M:** Master)

	David: "Every thing has a potential risk, such as driving car, taking air freight, or even walking across the street. However, one real risk that we mostly ignore in life is the inaction because we feel comfortable or scared."
10 More Ways To Eliminate Paper	• Better Use Of Your Client Database Software • Print On Demand • Hand Writing Input And Recognition • More Use Of Net Meeting • Digital Voice Recorder • Voice Recognition Technology • Online Subscription • Build a Website • Use Favorite Folder In Internet Explorer • Keep Your Digital Operation
10 Great Business Resource	• US Government • Wall Street Journal • Local Newspaper Website • Chamber Of Commerce • Trade Associations • United States Small Business Administration • Yahoo Small Business • Amazon.com • Google.com • Technology Review Sites
Last But Not Least	• Visit My website www.MrSystem.com and sign up a free membership. I will keep you update on the new technology that can help you to maximize office productivity and minimize cost.

CHAPTER 14

10 Ways To Eliminate Even More Paper

****

In this chapter, you will learn:
- ➢ Better Use Of Your Client Database Software
- ➢ Print On Demand
- ➢ Hand Writing Input And Recognition
- ➢ More Use Of Net Meeting
- ➢ Digital Voice Recorder
- ➢ Voice Recognition Technology
- ➢ Online Subscription
- ➢ Build a Website
- ➢ Use Favorite Folder In Internet Explorer
- ➢ Keep Your Digital Operation

****

I enjoyed writing this book. It summarized all my effort; pain and a sense of accomplishment to build a fully functional digital office with less money. I did it while everyone around me told me it was an impossible goal.

This is definitely not a closure of the journey. Every day is a learning experience. I would like to share with you more experiences about what I have learnt in the last ten years. This is a summary of all of the trials and tribulations that I have encountered on my path of attaining a Highly Efficient Office system. I hope all the information can help you to operate in a more efficient environment and become more productive. I hope this book will free up some of your time, so you can concentrate on your higher priorities, such as family, education, and marketing rather than getting caught up with administrative work.

Better Use Of Your Client Database Software

I have asked so many business people what is the single most important factor to the success of their business, almost without exceptions, they said that customer relationship is of utmost importance.

Since the client relationship is so important in any business, it only makes sense that you have a good Client Relationship Management software to help you build a strong tie between you and your clients.

If you use certain generic CRM like ACT or Goldmine, you will save yourself a lot of money. These generic CRMs only cost about $200 but they can do so much.

Typical functions of a CRM

- They Manage all your customer information in one location
- Create and send out one or thousands of personalize letters, faxes, and e-mails. In addition, the CRM keeps all of the communication in one location
- Keep all of your daily, monthly, yearly schedule in one place
- Some of the CRM, such as ACT, even have a built in sales goals and training module
- Some are network ready with one user price, ACT supports up to 4 people work group. It saves you the so much agony in sharing and organizing information
- Print out the popular organizer format, so that, your can have the synchronized calendar
- Synchronize contacts and other information with Palm or Window CE PDA, your can have all the data in your finger tips any time, any where
- Able to expend the functionality by add on softwares

If there is a very specialized CRM for your industry, do not pick the one that is least expensive. A great CRM will pay off in the long run, if you select the one that can help you to integrate information and save time. They key is to explore the all of the CRMs available in your industries.

No matter what CRM software you use for your business, you should try to use all of the functions in the software, such as: fax, email, telephone log, that will help eliminate a lot of posted note.

Print On Demand (POD)

POD is the relatively new technology that print and bound one book at a time. This technology not only allows everyone has a chance to express their opinions, but also allow companies print only when they need to and at the time they need to.

Such as some major hotels, using Kinko's national printing infrastructure, were able to print the evening digest of New York Times by 6:00 pm and deliver to their customers around the nation. The process is timely, quick and pervasive. What will your customers feel if you are able to deliver the information to them at the time they need and you can do it faster than everybody else? That is the power of Print On Demand. You can utilize this service to save money and yet provide excellent service to your customers.

How about those forms, applications and brochures that you only use occasionally? If your business needs to process forms, have you ever throw away any forms because they are outdated? Have you ever get the form rejected because you use the old one?

You can also apply the POD concept in your office, i.e. only print out documents when needed.

Unless you want to be in a free storage business, make sure that you do not stock up too many paper documents, such as: applications, forms, and marketing materials, etc.

It already cost you money to have high speed Internet access in your office so take advantage of it. You should not waste the power of that. Use the Internet as a massive storage space for your literature, and save your rental space for better use rather than for paper storage.

Use the concept of Print On Demand, download the documents into your computer and print them out only at the time you need them.

In business, forms are always changing. It is so difficult to keep up with the paper work in a timely fashion. If you discipline yourself to stock up on only the necessary paper for emergency and print the rest of the documents when needed. You are going to save a lot of administrative time and money.

By using Print On Demand, you and your staff will not need to keep track of paper inventory. Most of the documents are in PDF format online and the download process is very fast if you use either a DSL or a Cable Internet connection.

In addition, many forms are fillable forms. You can type into the form directly and save in your computer.

Hand Writing Input and Recognition

This has been a long time that we dream about input data directly into computer. Finally, there are some feasible solutions for that.

InkLink is a image-capturing device. It is a handwriting system that instantly capture our handwriting or drawing into the PC or PDA directly. It cost about $150.

It is good if you need to take a lot of note or need to jog down your thoughts on the road very often.

However, it has no memory capacity and no hand writing recognition function of. You must connect it to you PC or PDA when you use it. Besides, all it does is capture the digital pen movement and transfer that into you PC or PDA.

One of the major disadvantage is it could not convert your writing into text. Another disadvantage is that you need to take it out to use every time.

SmartPad is a zippered noted pad portfolio. The trick is the digital pen and infrared transmission of the pen movement into you PDA. With the appropriate softwares, this device works with both Palm and Pocket PC.

It has no memory ability and it must work with a PDA at the same time. There is no hand writing recognition function either. It is simply a image capture device for PDA. The price dropped to $100.

Both devices are made by Seiko Instrument Inc and you can go to their web site to find detail. Their web address is: http://www.siibusinessproducts.com

You may also get a Wacom Tablet. There are a few different models. I recommend the Graphire2 model that has the Graphire2 mouse, a pen and a tablet. The whole set is about $100.

You can use the mouse, write directly on the tablet and input the text and drawing into the computer.

If you combine it with Tablet PC or installed an hand writing software into your computer, you can also get the hand writing ability.
Hand writing recognition software manufacturers: https://www.visionobjects.com/

More Use Of Net Meeting

NetMeeting is a powerful software that can connect you with other people in real time via Internet or Intranet connection. You can use it to communicate one on one, or you can use it to host a online conference. If you would like to have a video call, all you need is a inexpensive video cam that cost about $30. Since you use the existing Internet connection, the call itself is free! Unfortunately, I found most of people does not take the full advantage of this program.

To start the program, simply go to Start/ All Program/ NetMeeting

You can place a call by type in IP address, computer name, DNS address or telephone number. I do not like to list myself in any directory, therefore, I have to use an IP address to call up people. Since most of us have a dynamic IP address, you may need to find out your IP address.

Click on Help/ About NetMeeting and you will find you IP address at the bottom of the dialog box.

After you type in the IP address of your listener, just click the Place Call icon to call up your listener. He or She will then see a box asking if he/she would like to answer the Internet call. The process is very similar to a telephone call.

NetMeeting is a intuitive program. It is also very easy to share programs, transfer files, chat, and even draw a picture to illustrate. I will urge you to use to its potential. More information can be found in Microsoft's web site.

http://www.microsoft.com/windows/netmeeting/default.asp

Digital Voice Recorder

In our business life, we always try to make the best out of our idle time. I use my digital recorder to record my ideas, instructions or letter for my assistant to type letters, send faxes or emails, and speeches, etc.

I record when I am driving or taking a break, and then download the recording to my assistant's PaperPort folder. So that, she can listen to the recording and type the documents, letters, memo.

If you do not use a PDA phone with recording function, there are so many stand alone digital voice recorder models. The cost depends on the memory size and additional functions. The key features you need to know is length of recording, and if it comes with a USB download ability. You should never buy those recorders without download ability, or use a serial port to download. The benefits of a USB download is that it does not require reboot your computer and it can download the voice files quickly.

Voice Recognition Technology

Imagine, being able to talk straight into the computer and transform your verbal information directly into the digital format or transform the information on the paper directly into editable text. Imagine how much time you can save!!!

It is a good companion to the digital voice recorder especially if you have a long document to type.

The more popular VRC are Dragon Naturally Speaking and IBM ViaVoice. Both of them have very high recognition accuracy. Unless you have a strong accent like me, you should not have any problem in translate your speech into text without many corrections. You can purchase either of them online or in the local office supply store. You may find out more about these softwares in the follow web pages.

IBM ViaVoice: http://www.scansoft.com/viavoice
ScanSoft DNS: http://www.scansoft.com/naturallyspeaking/

Online Subscription

Do you want to read newspaper in the morning without going outside to pick up the mail? Online subscription is one the easiest way to read. I subscribe Wall Street Journal online and some other trade publications online. Most of the online subscriptions are less expensive than their paper version. For example, Wall Street Journal online only cost about $70 for one-year subscription! Check it out in www.wsj.com.

There are at two advantages to read a newspaper online, they are: You do not need to wash your hand after reading the newspaper and you save a tree – it is paperless; isn't it the original goal? It is also much easier to archive and do research if you use PaperPort web capture, that is mentioned in Chapter 8. You do not need to cut and paste the newspaper clipping. All you need to do is click on the web capture icon and the whole page image is transferred to PaperPort folder. It can save you a lot of time.

To read online, you need a good monitor. I like the 17" flat panel. LCD technology offers a very crisp image and it is easy on the eyes.

Build a website

It is not necessary for every business get a web sites. However, it usually does not hurt to have one to explore the opportunities.

Web site is a very good tool to offer superior customer service at a very reasonable cost. Actually, you can also build your own website when software like FrontPage. I did build my own website in the beginning to save cost. If you hire web designer, it should cost less than $2000 to build a descent website. If you just want to have a very simple web page, you can also use word processor like MS Word to create one. The hosting fee is usually less than $10 a month. You can also get a domain for less than $10 a year.

Since you should know most of your customers' questions, you may post the answer on the web and refer your customer your website to find the solutions. You can develop it to be your customers' resource center.

Web site is also a great promotion tool to build name recognition.

Use Favorite Folder In Internet Explorer

Internet is the best low cost, or even free in most cases, research resource. There are so many web sites that have useful information. In my line of business, I need to keep my eyes open and always look for a good idea to improve my clients' businesses. It is vital for me to able to research, organize and save the information collected.

Research in Internet is not a problem. The actual challenge is how you are going to organize the information. In Chapter 6, we mentioned how you can use Web Capture function in PaperPort to record the image of a web page. How about those web sites that you need to book mark and go back to research when needed? It is where the favorite function comes into place.

It is very important for you to decide what your interests are. Then you can click on the Favorite icon on the tool bar. Click Add button on the Favorite menu bar and Create different folders according to your research topics.

When you want to remember the URL of the web site, all you do is click the URL address and drag it into the folder in the Favorite side tool bar.

Keep Your Digital Operation

Human is an animal of habit. We do what we do, sooner or later, we feel comfortable and we do not want to change. It is natural but we need to remind ourselves what is the purpose of doing business. The bottom line of a business is profitability. Digital approach will make a business more profitable because the system saves man power, save time and save space. It save all the scared resources in business.

When you first begin the digital operation, you will feel uncomfortable or even inconvenient. You may take more time to finish a simple than before. However, all these it takes is just some discipline and determination to execute the system.

If you are the owner of the business, you must embrace technology first to lead your staff. If you can keep the vision of a more effective and efficient office operation, you will get there with the my setup.

CHAPTER 15

10 Great Business Resources

****

In this chapter, you will learn:
- ➢ **US Government**
- ➢ **Wall Street Journal**
- ➢ **Local Newspaper Website**
- ➢ **Chamber Of Commerce**
- ➢ **Trade Associations**
- ➢ **United States Small Business Administration**
- ➢ **Yahoo Small Business**
- ➢ **Amazon.com**
- ➢ **Google.com**
- ➢ **Technology Review Sites**
- ➢ **My Last Few Words (In This Book)**

****

One of the challenges that every business owner has to tackle is resource management. There are so many hats that a business owner and we are supposed to know a little bit things about a lot of things. It is a crucial skill to be able to attain the information at the right time.

The following is a list of 10 best resources that I believe could help you to get what you need.

US Government

Do you pay tax? If so, how much government benefits do you receive? You do not need to wait until retire to receive government help.

US Government is the largest institute in the world and it has many resource available for you and me. The challenge is that it is such a huge organization and it is very difficult to find what we need. Luckily, it finally comes up with an online solution that everybody can use.

www.FirstGov.gov is the US Government's office web portal and it has every government available at your fingertip. The web site is very well organized and divided into four categories: for Citizens, for Business and Nonprofit, for Federal Government and Government to Government. It is only reasonable if you get the best out of the government.

Wall Street Journal

It is hard to be in a business and not affected by the economy that we are in. Unfortunately, I see a lot of businessmen get too busy in their day-to-day operation but ignore the major factors in their businesses' growth.

As a small business owner, we cannot do a lot to change the macroeconomic environment. However, the basic knowledge and the sense of economic direction will help us to adjust our businesses to the changing environment . The economic knowledge also help you to invest our hard earn money for a better than average return.

Chinese proverb says: when you sail in a sea, you better ride with the wave. We need to see the wave to be able to ride with that. Out of all those web sites in the net, I still found Wall Street Journal gives me the best overview of the whole economy. In addition, it also has the business news in Asia, Americas and Europe. the

Go to visit the paper at www.WSJ.com and click on any news title, there will be a pop up window ask you to subscribe the online version. The annual rate is only about $70, just a fraction of the print version. If you can read the economy section every day, it is well worth your money already.

Local Newspaper Website

Newspaper is the best resource to understand a place when we just arrive a new city. It is also the resource to feel the pulse of a city at the lowest cost.

It should be the top priority of a business owner to read the local newspaper everyday. We probably will not see the result immediately. However, if we read it for a few month, we will have a much understand of the place we do business in.

Besides daily news, it is also very important to read the advertising and announcement to know what is happening in the city. What is the dominant business in the city, what new business come into town, what your competitor is doing, etc.

Chamber Of Commerce

It is another obvious choice especially if your business serves the local community. It is very important that you know your local business environment well, develop a network of information sources and take advantage of the local environment.

One the other side, join the chamber and network with the other businesses also help you to keep a wide spread of knowledge.

I will suggest you visit the United States Chamber of Commerce website, http://www.uschamber.com/default, and find your local chapter. After you join the local chapter, it is also a good idea to join an interest group and build a relationship with other members.

Trade Associations

No matter what business or profession that you belong to, you should be able to find the local chapter of trade association that you could join.

It is a tough job to run your own business already, do not make it any tougher by doing it all by yourself. Find a trade association to join to exchange ideas of running your business, or create a cross referral opportunities. If you are an attorney focus in tax planning, you may find a litigation attorney to form alliance to serve your clients. There are many opportunities out there but you need to find them.

You can simply go to www.google.com and type in your industry's association and you should be able to pull out a list.

It is usually not expensive to join. Most of the time, you can attend a few meeting before you decide to join the association. I will suggested that you go to a few different associations before you decide which one to join. You must feel comfortable first.

United States Small Business Administration

SBA is a government agency established in 1953. Its web site has a wealth of information help small business to solve various business problems.

One key contribution of SBA is its ability to help small business get loans to start or grow their business.

In 2002, the SBA has backed over $12.3 billions in small business loans and secured $40 billion federal contracts for small businesses. It is a great resource for small business.

SBA web address is: http://www.sba.gov/

Yahoo Small Business

You may have go to Yahoo and use its search engine to search for information. However, Yahoo has a section for small business to find information about how to run a business. I particularly like the Read Buyer's Guide in Market Place. There are a lot of brief descriptions and tips of buying business necessities from business insurance to a chair.

The URL is http://smallbusiness.yahoo.com/.

Amazon.com

It may sound a little bit odd to you or you may think that I will suggest you to buy book from Amazon. If you find any great book that you like to buy, feel free to do so. However, I have another way to use Amazon.

Reading book actually is a mutual communication if we actively read the book and ask questions while reading. Amazon is a great research tool if you have any business questions.

Select Books and type in your question in the search space. After clicking on the search button, there will be a list of book on the right pane. The first few books are the popular items. The second list is all the book relate to your questions. Select Sort by Avg. Customer Review and the book will be listed accordingly.

You can preview the books by clicking the icon and read the Table of Content. That is the fastest way to preview different ideas on one topic. It is the first step for you to start to form a basic understanding of your question, learn different ideas and decide which approach is the best for you.

The key is by reading different ideas, you can form a unbiased opinions on the topic for yourself.

Google.com

Google is has bypassed both Yahoo and MSN, and becomes the most widely used search engine. There are many reasons for its success. I like the simplicity of the site.

There are not any popup advertisements that try to get my attention all the time and I could focus in what I try to do. Another reason is the easy to use Directory and Business Solution information. Both of these functions offer a direct and quick access to the information when I needed.

In addition, Google now offer free tool bar that has pop up block function that is more accurate than a lot of the other popup blocker that cost me money.

Other search engines are:
www.Yahoo.com , www.MSN.com, www.Excite.com, www.Lycos.com, www.Infoseek.com

Technology Review Sites

Technology is leading our life to a new level of convenience and efficiency every day. However, sometimes it is also very difficult to adapt to the new technology. Although this book is about how to use technology to operate our businesses to a higher lever of effectiveness and efficiency, I do not embrace every new technology.

The purpose of using technology is enable us to be more productive and enjoy life better. We should not pursue technology for the sake of technology. No matter how advanced technology is,

I will still have to face my own mortality. I better use it to enjoy my life.

There are a lot of websites that can help us decide if a technology is good for us or compare different products and prices.

The following is a short list of samples:
www.pcworld.com, www.ZDNet.com, www.tomshardware.com

My Last Few Words (In This Book)

All of the Highly Efficient Office™ components are either built-in or can be purchased at a very affordable price. It is feasible, simple, and easy to setup a digital environment to process the documents.

This is a good start to have all of this in place. However, it is only the beginning. As your business grows, you will find some new challenges that you may need to consider. You may need to upgrade equipments, software or install new procedure. It is a natural process of business growth. By then, you should have equipped yourself with the basic knowledge of how to build a digital business operation. This will help you make an informed decision about upgrading technology in your office.

I spent more than ten years of my life using the traditional method of progress, paying my dues to trials and errors. Finally, I figure out a way to run my business in a more productive manner and help improve the bottom line.

I believe this book will help you build a Highly Efficient Office™ System, generate more business, and yet be able to spend more time with your family. Sometimes, when we get ourselves in a bad situation, family is all we get. I have been there and my advice is: 'They deserve our time.'

All the links mentioned in this book will be available on my website: www.MrSystem.com .

Any comments or suggestion can be sent to DavidLam@MrSystem.com. Thanks for reading. I wish you all the success in your business.

Jargons:

Jargons: Words that keep you confused, intimidated, but more importantly, save some people's job. I have been put down so many times in my life because of my foreign accent, my lack of knowledge in US, and my ignorance in computer. I hope this section can help you to speak some of the technological terms, you will earn some respect and more likely to get better service.

Computer Basis:
1 G(iga) = 1,000 M(ega) = 1,000,000 K(ilo) = 1,000,000,000
1 M(ega) = 1,000 K(ilo)
1 K(ilo) = 1000 (In computer , more exactly 1 Kilo=1024)

bit: short for **B**inary dig**it**. It is the most basic unit that a computer represents. It is either On or Off. 8 bits of signal make up of 1 Byte of data. For example, the letter A is one Byte of data that is made up of 8 bits. It is always written in lower case. Transmission speed of data is usually measured in Mega (000,000) bits per second, i.e. Mbps.

Byte: Eight bits of On and Off signal make up of one Bytes of data. It is used to measure memory of data. It is always written in Capital B. For example, hard drive storage is measure in G(iga)B(ytes), i.e. 1,000,000,000 Bytes.

Broadband: High Speed Internet Access. The main stream examples are cable, DSL and T1.

CPU: The brain of your computer. There are two major manufacturers: Intel and AMD. The faster the CPU, the faster your computer can "think". It's 'thinking speed' is measured in Mega Hertz(MHz) nowadays. If you buy a new computer, it should be faster than 2 G(iga)Hz.

Ethernet Card/ NIC: The circuit board that connect the computer and the gateway, or router if you have one.

Hard Drive: an array of disc that can remember data even after the power is shut off. Most hard drives are measured in GB. Most computers are sold with 80 GB or 120 GB hard drive nowadays.

Gateway : A device that enable access to Internet. Common examples are cable and DSL modem. You can compare it to an antennae, that is the gateway of radio wave.

If you go to a computer store, the salesman ask you what kind of **gateway** you use, you may say it is either **Cable or DSL.** If he say what kind of speed, let him/her know it depends on the **ISP.** If he/she ask further technical questions, let him/her know that his/her manager will know better how to help you instead of using the technical term to intimidate you.

ISP: Internet Service Provider. A fancy name for those companies that host your website or connect your to the Internet, such as AOL, MSN, Earthlink, Comcast, RCN, Verizon, etc.

RAM: Random Access Memory. This is the short term memory of the computer. The memory disappear after you turn off the computer. It is usually measured in Megabyte (MB) and sold in the multiple of 128MB. The minimum you need is 256 MB

Router: A device that get the signal from the gateway(Cable or DSL modem) and **ROUTE** the signals between different computers in the local network. It allows you to share the Internet access between your computers by assign each computer a unique address, and ROUTE the signals automatically. If you don't have a router, you cannot share the Broadband Internet access because the signals will jam the computers in the same network. It is just like the traffic in a intersection.

SPAM: unsolicited email. The legally one are those with ADV in the subject line, with the company name, physical address and unsubscribe email address in the body. The illegal are all the rest. You can find out more about the SPAM by going to http://www.spamlaws.com.

WIFI / 802.11X: It is the standard that how the wireless equipment "talk" to each other. With the speed that wireless technology develop, you will see more a change of the last letter pretty often. There has been 802.11a, 802.11b, 802.11g … The most popular is 802.11 B and 802.11 G. If you buy a new wireless equipment, remember to buy 802.11 G. G standard is 5 times faster than the B standard and the price is just 20% higher.

Index

A Short List Of Suggested Reading

Basic Skills
How To Read A Book (Mortimer Adler)
Art Of War (Sun Tzu) : Register for Free membership in
                      www.MrSystem.com and get a free copy

Mental
The Mask Of Command (John Keegan)
The Lessons Of History (William Durant)

Self Management
7 Habits Of Highly Effective People (Stephen Covey)
First Thing First (Stephen Covey)

Motivation
Think And Grow Rich (Napoleon Hill)
Awaken The Giant Within (Anthony Robbins)

Marketing
Selling The Invisible (Harry Beck)
101 Ways to Promote Yourself (Raleigh Pinskey)

Infopreneurship
The Self-Publishing Manual (Dan Poynter)
Multiple Streams of Income (Robert Allen)

Basic Money Concepts
The Wealthy Barber (David Chilton)
Millionaire Next Door (Thomas Stanley)

Self Employed Knowledge
Working From Home (Paul Edwards)

Environmental
Beyond Earth Day: Fulfilling the Promise (Gaylord Nelson)

If you find any great book that you would like to share, free feel to email
to: booklist@MrSystem.com.

List Of Equipments & Softwares

The Perfect Computer	CPU: Intel P4 2GMHz up or AMD Athlon XP 2200 and up 80 GB Hard drive or bigger 256 RAM and 512 L2 Cache DVD-RW (DVD burner) Window XP Professional 10/100 Mbps Ethernet Card One or Two 56K fax modem Monitor: preferably LCD (Easier on eyes)
Mobile Computing	PDA Phone: ($600) Tablet PC: ($2000)
High Speed Internet Access	Call the local phone company like Verizon and ask about either DSL or Cable modem service. Most company will provide one CAT 5 cable to connect the modem and your main computer.
Router	**Linksys Wireless-G Broadband Router WRT54G (Approx. $80)**
Wireless Adapter	**Linksys WUSB54G Wireless-G USB Adapter (Approx. $70)** For notebook computer, get a 802.11G notebook adapter like: **Linksys WPC54G Wireless-G Notebook Adapter ($60)**
Scanner and Laser Printer	**HP Officejet 5510 ($199)** is a excellent beginner's choice. You may also purchase **HP LJ 1012 LaserJet Printer ($199)**
Document Management Software	**PaperPort Deluxe 9.0 ($90)**
Office Productivity Softwares	**CRM : ACT! 5.0 ($50) or 6.0 ($199)** **PFM: Quicken 2004 Premier Home and Business ($90)** **Microsoft Office 2003 Small Business Edition ($250)**
Protection	**Antivirus programs : McAfee or Norton ($50)** **Anti-spy software: McAfee AntiSpyware ($40)**
Backup	**Uninterruptible Power Supply UPS ($60)** **CD-RW, DVD-RW, or 200G external hard drive**
Local Shopping And Document Service	www.Staples.com, www.CompUSA.com, www.Kinkos.com, www.OfficeMax.com, www.OfficeDepot.com, www.frys.com, www.MicroCenter.com, www.BestBuy.com, www.CircuitCity.com, **Many other resources will be listed in www.MrSystem.com**

368

More Services From MrSystem.com

Purchase:

To order an individual copy of this book , please visit
www.MrSystem.com

To obtain special discount for bulk purchase, purchase customized excerpts and cartoons, please contact:
marketing@MrSystem.com or call
1 (877) Win-Paper / 946-7273

Speaking Service

MrSystem.com also offers speaking services for keynotes, seminars, workshops, and trainings.

Topics such as motivation, management, techno-empowerment, will always be customized for your functions. For further details, please visit our website **www.MrSystem.com** or email to: **Speak@MrSystem.com**

Media Service

David Lam, Mr. System, is available for comments and discussion for various topics such as how to maximize low cost technology, home office and small office setup, marketing strategies, etc. For details, please contact:
Media@MrSystem.com or call
1 (877) Win-Paper / 946-7273

Free Membership

Visit us at **www.MrSystem.com** and signup as our member. It is absolutely free to join and no obligation. As a member, you will enjoy the following benefits:

- Enjoy member discounts for our products
- 6 Tier Affiliate Program
- Internet access to our exclusive eCommerce Training Center
- Many other member benefits …

Thank you for reading. We wish you all the success in your business and your personal life.

Notes

370
Notes